CRITICAL INSIGHTS

The American Dream

CRITICAL INSIGHTS

The American Dream

Editor
Keith Newlin
University of North Carolina, Wilmington

SALEM PRESS
A Division of EBSCO Publishing
Ipswich, Massachusetts

GREY HOUSE PUBLISHING

Critical Insights: The American Dream, 2013, published by Grey House Publishing, Inc., Amenia, NY, under exclusive license from EBSCO Publishing, Inc.

∞ The paper used in these volumes conforms to the American National Standard for Permanence of Paper for Printed Library Materials, Z39.48-1992 (R1997).

Library of Congress Cataloging-in-Publication Data

The American dream / editor, Keith Newlin, University of Arkansas.
    pages cm -- (Critical insights)
  Includes bibliographical references and index.
  ISBN 978-1-4298-3821-4 (hardcover)
  1. American literature--History and criticism. 2. American Dream in literature.
I. Newlin, Keith.
  PS169.A49A48 2013
  810.9'35873--dc23
                                                                    2012049036

ebook ISBN: 978-1-4298-3837-5

8 10. 9

A

PRINTED IN THE UNITED STATES OF AMERICA

Contents _____

Critical Contexts

Critical Essays

Resources

About This Volume _____

Keith Newlin

"The American Dream" is a phrase that has become such a part of our national identity that we find the phrase itself—or its chief components—underlying nearly every aspect of our lives. The founding document of our nation, the Declaration of Independence, identifies the assumptions that underpin the dream: "We hold these truths to be self-evident, that all men are created equal, that they are endowed by their Creator with certain unalienable Rights, that among these are Life, Liberty and the pursuit of Happiness." In the years since Thomas Jefferson penned these words, Americans have interpreted them to mean that it is "self-evident" that all Americans have a natural right to pursue happiness in whatever form it might take, from pursuing a meaningful occupation, to attaining a comfortable home, to enjoying the freedom to do as one pleases so long as that freedom does not infringe upon the rights of others, and especially to amassing enough wealth to buy the material objects that make a comfortable life.

We find these assumptions reflected in the phrases that all of us use to some extent: we admire the "self-made man (or woman)"; we believe in "equal opportunity" and "equal pay for equal work"; we see our country as "a land of opportunity"; we believe that "success comes to those that help themselves"; we venerate those who "raise themselves up by their bootstraps"; and we exalt those who rise "from rags to riches." When asked what they want from life, people often respond that they'd like to "get ahead," "seize the main chance," or "reach one's potential." Three values lie at the core of these phrases, which themselves are reflections of the key assumptions of the Declaration of Independence: One is a passionate belief in the value of work, of the right to profit from one's labor, and that one must earn what one gets (that is, in both meanings of the word: to work and to deserve). Another is a belief that education is a primary means of making a better life for ourselves; that with increased knowledge and/or professional or vocational training, we will better position ourselves to achieve the success that comes from hard work and, moreover, that if we do indeed work hard, anyone can achieve what he or she desires. Finally, at the core of the dream is a sense of hope and possibility integrally connected to the land itself. What impressed many of the Pilgrims and Puritans upon their arrival on what would become America's shores was a vista of space—land available to be claimed and settled, a place where people could realize their dreams. Of course they conveniently overlooked the prior claims of the Native American inhabitants, setting into motion what for years marked another key component of the American Dream—that it applied chiefly to the dominant (Anglo) culture—and which is in turn responsible for setting in motion an undercurrent of resistance and criticism of the American Dream that would increasingly come to preoccupy writers and others in the twentieth century.

Critical Insights: The American Dream offers thirteen original essays exploring the contexts and expressions of the dream as it is reflected in our imaginative literature. The first four essays provide a critical context for assessing the dream's scope and formulations. In "The Rise and Fall of the American Dream: From *The Autobiography of Benjamin Franklin* to *Death of a Salesman*," Donna Packer-Kinlaw surveys Americans' shifting response to the dream as represented by four key works: Benjamin Franklin's *Autobiography* (1793), Horatio Alger's *Ragged Dick* (1867), F. Scott Fitzgerald's *The Great Gatsby* (1925), and Arthur Miller's *Death of a Salesman* (1949). At the core of the dream, Packer-Kinlaw points out, is the notion of success, and what counts as success has evolved from an emphasis on morality and social standing in the eighteenth century to the pursuit of material goods and a comfortable middle-class job in the nineteenth century to the acquisition of wealth and social position and a subsequent questioning of the effects of wealth on the dream in the twentieth.

Linda Kornasky peers through the lens of gender criticism to explore how women fare in pursuing the dream in "'To Go into Partnership:' Gender, Class, Ethnicity, and the American Dream in Edith

Wharton's *The House of Mirth*." By examining what Lily Bart has been taught to value (being a beautiful ornament for a man) and the methods available to her to pursue her dream (marriage to a wealthy man), Kornasky concludes that "The novel reveals that the moral compromises demanded of . . . women and others excluded tacitly by the discriminatory practice of American Dream ideology" are antithetical to the value of freedom embodied in the dream itself.

Carol S. Loranger takes up the issue of women and the dream from the standpoint of working women in "Meaningful Work and Self-Determination: The American Woman's American Dream." Loranger compares four novels' depiction of women's work—Louisa May Alcott's *Work: A Story of Experience* (1874), Willa Cather's *O Pioneers!* (1913), Anzia Yezierska's *The Bread Givers* (1925), and Sandra Cisneros' *The House on Mango Street* (1984)—to argue that, unlike the male dream, freedom "was the goal, not the starting point of the American woman's Dream," and that the protagonists of these novels sought to discover "independence via meaningful work."

Finally, the Critical Contexts section concludes with Cara Elana Erdheim's "Why Speak of American Stories as Dreams?" an essay that explores how scholarship devoted to the American Dream has shifted to accommodate new works that enter the canon and new ideologies that shape literary interpretation. While early critical studies tended to define the dream in terms that tended to reinforce dominant white male cultural aspirations, later studies attempted to account for previously excluded minorities and minority literatures and, indeed, even question whether the dream, as initially defined, ever existed at all.

After this exploration of the context of the American Dream, the remaining essays offer amplification of the dream's central tenets and examination of how specific authors and works have responded to the dream. In "The American Dream, the Frontier, and Westward Expansion," Steven Frye traces the effect of the frontier on the imaginations of writers, beginning with the founding colonists who saw the continent as an opportunity to "establish a Christian civilization in a new

Promised Land on the far edges of the American wilderness." Enlightenment writers saw in the land "the possibility of new economic opportunities," while romantic writers were more ambivalent about the relationship of people to the land, for they observed people exploiting the land and being spiritually corrupted by that exploitation—a theme that is central to contemporary writers like Wallace Stegner, Larry McMurtry, and Cormac McCarthy.

The next two essays explore the corruption of the dream as exemplified by two major writers of the first part of the twentieth century. Roark Mulligan traces the effect of the rags-to-riches myth, best exemplified by the novels of Horatio Alger, on the work of a seminal American writer in "Dreiser and the Dream." In *Sister Carrie* (1900), *The Financier* (1912), and *An American Tragedy* (1925), Theodore Dreiser depicts characters "who seek versions of the American Dream, through marriage and hard work, but who find misery or disappointment in a world that does not offer permanent happiness." In so doing, Mulligan concludes, "Dreiser offers us both the dream and the nightmare, exposing our excesses and mistakes." In "*The Great Gatsby* and the American Dream," James Nagel argues that the version of the dream sought by Gatsby and Nick Carraway "is a degraded corruption of the idea, a formulation that reduces the objective to money and to social status based on surface riches, not on the more fulfilling aspects of the original conception."

The American Dream has long held a special attraction to immigrants, who came to America in search of a better life, and James R. Giles explores the effects of the implied promise of America in "Survival and Transcendence: The Jewish-American Immigrant and the American Dream." For both Anzia Yezierska (in *The Bread Givers*, 1925) and Michael Gold (in *Jews without Money*, 1940), education is the key to attaining the dream, but both encounter obstacles to realizing the dream, with Yezierska's protagonist finding that gender and religious assumptions impede her pursuit of happiness and Gold's protagonist discovering that poverty and the threat of violence inhibit ambition—a theme that reappears in Kevin Baker's *Dreamland* (1999). This theme of exclusion from realizing the dream is also the subject of Andrew Vogel's "Blurring the Color Line: Race and the American Dream in James Weldon Johnson's *The Autobiography of an Ex-Coloured Man*, Nella Larsen's *Passing*, and Jean Toomer's *Cane*." In tracing the effects of racism upon the aspirations of the novels' protagonists to attain the promises of the dream, Vogel concludes that each work suggests that "if the American dream cannot be enjoyed by every citizen, then it cannot be claimed, it cannot be respected, and it does not really exist for any citizen."

In "After Auschwitz, Connecticut? Dreams and Disappointments in Mid-twentieth Century American Literature," Tiffany Gilbert begins with a question: "what dreams could survive the nightmarish conflagration of the Holocaust and the atomic bomb?" Her answer, as revealed by a wide-ranging discussion of Sloan Wilson's *The Man in the Gray Flannel Suit* (1955), Richard Yates' *Revolutionary Road* (1961), Tennessee Williams' *Cat on a Hot Tin Roof* (1955), Lorraine Hansberry's *A Raisin in the Sun* (1959), Alan Ginsberg's *Howl* (1956), and Frank O'Hara's *Lunch Poems* (1964), is that the pursuit of the dream devolved into "mindless consumerism" and a "crushing banality" that led to dissatisfaction, isolation, despair, and angst. Quentin Martin similarly explores the failure of the dream in mid-twentieth century literature in "The Assimilated and Unassimilated in Bernard Malamud's *The Assistant*." Malamud's 1957 novel represents "an inversion of the usual immigrant saga of a foreign people . . . slowly assimilating and acculturating to their new American environment," Martin argues, for the novel's American protagonist, Frank Alpine, achieves success by "immersion in and embrace of the principles and behaviors of the unassimilated Jewish immigrant," but in the process he also fails socially and financially.

The theme of the failed promise of the dream is taken up by the final two essays in the volume. In "American Indians and the American Dream: 'a world in which we had no part,'" Lee Schweninger traces the ways in which native Americans have found it difficult to enjoy the basic rights and privileges promised by the Declaration of

Independence and the elements of the dream that other American take for granted, such as "the freedom to worship in accordance with tribal custom, the freedom to retain and use the land of one's ancestors and to move freely across that land, to have equal access to material goods, and to enjoy in the inalienable rights of life and liberty." Yet a contradiction also exists within Native American writings, for while Indians in general have experienced limitations, the writers themselves have enjoyed the successes promised by the dream. For Mexican Americans, Ramón J. Guerra suggests in "Mexican Americans Encounter the American Dream: *George Washington Gómez*," the struggle has been how to reconcile one's cultural identity with a dream that assumes, indeed requires, assimilation into the dominant culture. By examining Américo Paredes's novel *George Washington Gómez* (written during the 1930s, but published in 1990), Guerra traces the ways in which the dream meant the cultural death of Mexican American identity while also anticipating the Chicano Movement's rejection in the 1960s and 1970s of the dream as "a myth that was not fully available to all."

At the core of all of these essays is an expression of a resounding optimism, a dream, a hunger for better life for all, even if at times during our nation's history some people were excluded from full participation in the economic, political, social, and artistic life of our nation. When James Truslow Adams first coined the phrase "American Dream" in *The Epic of America* (1931) to refer to the promise that America as a country represented to its citizens and to others, the United States was in the midst of the Great Depression. After tracing the history of our country's development, Adams concluded with an epilogue expressing optimism for the future, an observation and a hope that the spirit that had led to the country's founding and settlement would prevail. Even critics of the dream share that optimism, for why point to inequities and exclusions if there were no hope that criticism would lead to improvement? Dreams by their nature are hopeful and optimistic, and what distinguishes the American dream is a belief, and a faith, that all Americans can improve their lives by embracing the principles that led to the nation's founding.

CRITICAL
CONTEXTS

The Rise and Fall of the American Dream: From *The Autobiography of Benjamin Franklin* to *Death of a Salesman*

Donna Packer-Kinlaw

In his 1931 *The Epic of America*, James Truslow Adams became the first to name and define the one desire that has united and characterized the American people since our beginnings. He called it the "American Dream" and identified it as the "hope of a better and richer life for all the masses of humble and ordinary folk" (363). This optimism about one's ability to have a better life and the "belief in the common man and the insistence upon his having, as far as possible, equal opportunity in every way with the rich one," according to Adams, is the "greatest contribution we have as yet made to the thought and welfare of the world" (viii). Although notions of success vary widely and interpretations of the dream have shifted over time, the notion of the American Dream can be traced back to the nation's beginnings, and it has remained a crucial aspect of the national ethos even into the twenty-first century.

In the seventeenth century, Americans dreamed about obtaining a better life through faith, hard work, and perseverance. For eighteenth-century Americans, success was inextricably tied to religion and morality; thus, success was measured, not only by the accumulation of material wealth, but also by one's moral code, one's standing in the community, and the contributions that an individual made to the community. By the nineteenth century, though religion and morality were still important, material success and work itself became the two most important aspects of the American Dream. Americans continued their practice of working hard, but they wanted money in the bank, large houses, and other symbols of wealth. It was important to be a respectable member of the community, but one's worth was measured, in large part, by one's profession and income. This emphasis on augmenting one's material wealth continued and, by the early twentieth century, many Americans dreamed about large bank accounts, even larger houses, and cars. By the mid-twentieth century, some began to question whether or not it was even possible to attain the American Dream, while others challenged notions of the dream itself. Yet, even in these moments, Americans in general remained optimistic and continued to believe that the United States was a place where if one worked hard, success would surely follow.

Since its beginnings, American literature has served as a chronicle of the American Dream, and some of the nation's most revered texts provide strikingly forthright portraits of individuals pursuing and living the dream. Perhaps no other text demonstrates the American Dream of the eighteenth century quite as accurately as Benjamin Franklin's *Autobiography*, as Franklin himself seems to embody the American Dream. Horatio Alger's *Ragged Dick* thoroughly exemplifies the hopes and aspirations of those living in the nineteenth century, and Alger's protagonist, Richard Hunter, or "Ragged Dick," demonstrates what can happen if one will only work hard and live honestly. In the twentieth century, F. Scott Fitzgerald highlighted the American Dream in his fiction, and he constructed a forceful image of the post–World War I dream in *The Great Gatsby*. Fitzgerald's characters, with their fine houses, clothes, and cars, seem to have reached the pinnacle of the "good life." Finally, Arthur Miller's *Death of a Salesman* demonstrates not only the enduring belief in the dream but also the dangers associated with having "the wrong" dream in mid-twentieth century America (Miller 138). Through Willy and Biff, Miller explores what the dream means at that particular moment and the reasons why it seems, for some, unobtainable and elusive. These four narratives provide an opportunity for us to survey the American Dream from the nation's beginnings through the twentieth century. Such a study exposes the relation between the dream and American literature, provides a better understanding of what the dream represented in different periods, and reveals the evolution of the dream from one era to another. Perhaps most importantly, it suggests the omnipresence of the American Dream in our national consciousness and demonstrates how tremendously significant it is to Americans, both individually and collectively.

Franklin's Autobiography

When the Pilgrims established Plymouth Plantation in 1620, they had a dream of practicing religion without the oppressive constraints placed upon them by the Church of England. Ten years later, in 1630, the Puritans arrived in Massachusetts Bay, bringing with them a similar desire to follow their own faith without the intervention of popes and bishops from other religions. Throughout seventeenth century, religious ideology guided American thought, and texts such as John Winthrop's "A Model of Christian Charity," the poetry of Anne Bradstreet, and *A Narrative of the Captivity and Restoration of Mrs. Mary Rowlandson* reflect the pervasiveness of religion in the American consciousness during this period. However, by the eighteenth century, dramatic changes in the social and philosophical environment, in the government, and in the sciences transformed how Americans perceived the world and their place in it. Although religion still played a central role in American life, many turned to science and philosophy to provide answers to their philosophical and moral queries. The American Dream, though it had not yet been named, was affected by these transformations.

In his *Autobiography*, Benjamin Franklin fashions a self-portrait that demonstrates this coalescing of religious and philosophical ideologies in the eighteenth century. Franklin's notions about religion and morality guide his life and actions, and they provide the foundation of his understanding of the American Dream. Even though he never used the phrase "American Dream," Franklin had a clear vision about how to be successful, and his ideas serve as the basis of the American Dream in the eighteenth century and beyond. For Franklin, the dream consisted of attaining moral perfection, earning the respect of one's fellow citizens, and becoming financially independent. In order to achieve such a position, one must live morally, work diligently, and practice frugality, and Franklin insists on the relation between success and moral fortitude. Thus, he confesses his faith and avows that he "never doubted, for instance, the Existence of the Deity" (89). Additionally, Franklin believes that "the most acceptable Service of God was the doing Good to Man," and he emphasizes work, rather than faith, as the key to realizing the dream (89).

By confessing his faith and linking one's work to God, Franklin attempts to establish morality and work as the path to success, and his narrative continually reaffirms that assertion. For example, he "conceiv'd the bold and arduous Project of arriving at moral Perfection" and confesses that he dreamed of living "without committing any Fault at any time" (90). In his effort to achieve moral excellence, Franklin banishes drunkenness, extravagance, indolence, dishonesty, and such vices, and thus positions himself as an honest, temperate, frugal, and industrious man. Such a man, it follows, should necessarily find success. Thus, Franklin concocts a plan wherein he attempts to gain control over thirteen different areas of his life, including "Temperance," "Silence," "Order," "Resolution," "Frugality," "Industry," "Sincerity," "Justice," "Moderation," "Cleanliness," "Tranquility," "Chastity," and "Humility" (91–92). By mastering each of these areas, or virtues, as he called them, Franklin believed that he would live a life of productivity, faultlessness, and rectitude. Although he confesses that he "fell short" of reaching the "Perfection" that he "had been so anxious of obtaining," he claims that he was "a better and a happier Man than I otherwise would have been" (99). What is more, he insists that his financial success and his outstanding position in the community stem from his dedication to living a life grounded in morality, industry, and frugality. In Franklin's view, these virtues lead directly to the attainment of his dream.

By the nineteenth century, perceptions of the dream shifted as Americans began to measure success by the amount of material wealth that they accumulated. The desire to obtain such wealth became so intense for some that Merle Curti, author of *The Growth of American Thought*, calls it a "quest" that Americans embark upon as they seek out "material fortunes as ends in themselves" (508). Whereas Franklin and his eighteenth-century contemporaries perceived work itself as a virtue, nineteenth-century Americans had a new interpretation of work, wealth, and success. Rather than a means of doing God's work and an opportunity to enhance the lives of one's fellow citizens, work now primarily served as a pathway to building individual fortunes. The goal, or dream, was to make more money than the competition, to see who could increase their capital the most. As Alan Trachtenberg explains in *The Incorporation of America*, work in the nineteenth century was perceived as "a field of personal competition, of heroic endeavor" (5). It is not surprising, then, that when Alexis de Tocqueville traveled to the United States during the 1830s and wrote about his journey in *Democracy in America*, he was struck by the American preoccupation with wealth. In Tocqueville's opinion, American men struggled with two fears: that they would not be as affluent as their fathers and that they would not amass a fortune large enough to ensure their sons' futures. Thus, despite their success, prosperous American men are "almost always disconnected with" their "fortune," and they are "constantly haunted by the desire of obtaining wealth, and they naturally turn their attention to trade and manufactures, which appear the readiest and most powerful means of success" (164).

Alger's *Ragged Dick*

In *Ragged Dick*, Horatio Alger makes this preoccupation with work and wealth a central part of his narrative about a young boot-black who manages to redirect his life and find the path to middle-class success through perseverance, frugality, and hard work. Written just before the rise of business titans John D. Rockefeller and J. P. Morgan, Alger idealizes the nineteenth-century dream of entering the business community, increasing one's wealth, and steadily improving one's position in society. Alger's protagonist, Richard "Ragged Dick" Hunter, dreams of moving beyond his lowly position as a bootblack. As he confesses to his new friend Frank Whitney, "I really wish I could get somethin' else to do. . . . I'd like to be a office boy, and learn business, and grow up 'spectable" (26). Yet Dick worries that his dream will remain unfulfilled. Anticipating a lifetime of deprivation and bootblacking, Dick expects nothing more than what he has been told, that he will likely "grow up to be a vagabone . . . and come to the gallows" (27). More, he acknowledges that his frivolous habits—"goin' to the theatre, and treatin' boys to oyster-stews, and bettin' money on cards"—hinder his ability to obtain a better situation (28).

However, nineteenth-century America was hopeful. It was a time, seemingly, when determination, a good work ethic, and strong morals were rewarded with success and upward mobility. It was a time when many believed, along with Henry David Thoreau, that "if one advances confidently in the direction of his dreams, and endeavors to live the life which he has imagined, he will meet with a success unexpected in common hours" (Thoreau 267). Such remarks all but promise the realization of the dream, if one will only try. In *Ragged Dick*, Frank Whitney, who serves as just one voice of morality and hope in the narrative, echoes Thoreau's sentiments. According to Frank, "If you'll try to be somebody, and grow up into a respectable member of society, you will. You may not become rich,—it isn't everybody that becomes rich, you know,—but you can obtain a good position, and be respected" (27–28). Frank's uncle, Mr. Whitney, also possesses this same hopefulness, and he instructs Dick to "save your money, my lad, buy books, and determine to be somebody" (49). By following these guidelines, Whitney claims, "you may yet fill an honorable position" (49). In each instance, the nineteenth-century dream of respectability, work, and increased wealth comes as a result of maintaining a good work ethic, practicing honesty and frugality, educating oneself, and having a strong moral compass.

Each man who assists Dick, from Whitney to Rockwell, is an honorable, Christian businessman. They have been successful in life, amassed significant wealth, and seemingly preserved their moral fortitude. And because Dick, our hero and a hopeful young lad, longs to emulate these men, it is unsurprising that he, too, possesses a similar work ethic. Like Benjamin Franklin before him, Dick works hard, lives within his means, and manages to save a bit of money. But perhaps most importantly, he "was above doing anything mean or dishonorable. He would not steal, or cheat, or impose upon younger boys, but was frank and straight-forward, manly and self-reliant. His nature was a noble one, and had saved him from all mean faults" (6). Such an emphasis on Dick's capacity for conforming to the morals and guidelines of nineteenth-century society reinforces the relation between the dream and virtue. That Alger stresses such character traits and links them to success is no accident. Intending his stories to teach boys that success and morality go hand in hand, Alger takes it as his duty as a writer to "exert a wholesome influence on his young readers" ("Writing" 126). Thus, he quite consciously emphasizes "honesty, industry, frugality, and a worthy ambition" in his narratives and attempts to create "heroes" who are "manly boys, bright, cheerful, hopeful, and plucky" (126).

Although attaining the American Dream seems a rightful reward for one's upstanding behavior during these early years in America, by the late nineteenth century, men like John D. Rockefeller and J. P. Morgan transformed the rules of business, and their questionable tactics created a chasm between morality and success. Not only did these giants of the railroad and oil industries redefine how businesses operated, but they also intimated the separation between ethics and business practices and the desire to accumulate wealth. As Adams explains, during these years and into the twentieth century, business "ceased to be a mere occupation which must be carried on in accordance with the moral code. It had itself become part of that code. Money-making having become a virtue, it was no longer controlled by the virtues, but ranked *with* them" (191). Because of this shift in the relation between business and ethics, the dreams of Franklin and Alger consequently drifted further from the nation's consciousness. Furthermore, because the acquisition of money was now perceived as a "virtue," to borrow Adams's word, Americans longed to display their wealth, and they exuberantly collected objects—homes, cars, art, and boats—that showed the world just how successful they had become.

The Great Gatsby

For Henry James, this obsession with wealth was one of the most important and anxiety-inducing aspects of American society in the early twentieth century. Returning to America after a twenty-two year absence, James was shocked by the transformation of his native country. In *The American Scene*, he gazes anxiously on skyscrapers built seemingly for no other purpose than "to bring in money" and wonders, "was not money the only thing a self-respecting structure could be thought of as bringing in?" (73). In this new America, there seems to be no room for architecture that represents aesthetic beauty, history, and culture. For James, the new commercial landscape suggests a troubling fixation on profitability and work, and a sublimation of leisure, art, and beauty. In addition, James believes that this obsession with affluence has even penetrated the nation's home life. Traveling through the nation's residential areas, he discovers "huge new houses, up and down" that "confessed to their extreme expensiveness" (10). From James's perspective, such homes serve as little more than testimonies of wealth and affirm that the "expensive" had become "a power by itself" in America (11).

The American Scene illustrates the extent to which wealth had become a force in American culture in the early twentieth century. This fixation deepened in the years leading up to World War I, and after the war the national enchantment with affluence intensified even more. By the end of the war, the nation had entered a period of tremendous prosperity: Industry was booming, new roads and technologies had emerged, there was greater wealth all around, and Americans had a fresh outlook on life. World War I had redefined America's sense of itself and its role in the world, and called into question notions of morality, convention, religion, and tradition. This is the backdrop that F.

Scott Fitzgerald's *The Great Gatsby* is set against, and the book provides one of our most vibrant and forthright portrayals of American life during this period. The book is also regarded as one of the most thorough assertions of the American Dream in the 1920s, and Fitzgerald depicts the effects of what happens when individuals pass their days in an attempt to live this new dream.

The Great Gatsby is populated by characters hoping to attain, or to at least touch, a life of great wealth. But unlike their predecessors, who dreamed of affluence as a consequence of hard work and dedication to a particular ethical standard, many in *The Great Gatsby* seek to circumvent the responsibilities and duties formerly associated with achieving material wealth and success. They seek a world where no one actually engages in meaningful work, but where money is inherited, is made through questionable or illicit dealings, or is discussed in books about "banking and credit and investment securities" and which promise to deliver the "shining secrets that only Midas and Morgan and Mæcenas knew" (5). In this world, work alone hardly earns respect, as Fitzgerald demonstrates with George Wilson, who owns his own garage and struggles to make it a success. Meanwhile, Wilson's wife, Myrtle, has an affair with Tom Buchanan, who, with his apartment in the city, new car, and no shortage of money, provides Myrtle with an opportunity, if only momentarily, to escape her lowly, ordinary life and assume the role of a more affluent woman.

As a man of tremendous wealth and leisure, Tom, who owns a "white Georgian Colonial mansion," a boat, horses, and a stable, appears to personify the American Dream (6). But it is Gatsby, more than anyone, who appears to have most fully recognized the dream. Born in a family of modest means and now the owner of a "mansion" described as a "colossal affair by any standard," Jay Gatsby appears to be a rags-to-riches type of man (5). As a boy, "Jimmy Gatz" wrote down a list of "resolves" in a notebook. The notes served the same purpose as Franklin's virtues, and to similar effect. According to the notebook, young Jimmy rose at six o'clock, exercised, read, studied "elocution, poise and how to attain it," and "electricity," among other subjects (110). He also resolved to avoid activities that wasted time, such as "smoking or chewing," and to save money and "Be better to parents" (110). Before he was twenty years old, he spent a year "beating his way along the south shore of Lake Superior as a clam-digger and a salmon-fisher or in any other capacity that brought him food and bed" (63). That Jimmy had presumably followed such a schedule ahd worked in such a capacity" suggests that, before he became "Jay Gatsby," Jimmy subscribed to a more conventional notion of the American Dream.

It is a dream that Gatsby's father, Henry C. Gatz, continues to believe in, and he is sure that his son has attained his riches through honest and meaningful work. Gatz claims that Jimmy "had a big future before him" and that he would have "helped build up the country" (107). But, as the narrative reveals, neither that dream nor that boy would survive. Gatsby associates with those who make their money by "fixing" sporting events and engaging in questionable, if not illegal, business practices. As a result of his "work," Gatsby now owns a home that is "a factual imitation of some Hôtel de Ville in Normandy, with a tower on one side, spanking new under a thin beard of raw ivy, and a marble swimming pool, and more than forty acres of lawn and garden"; he has a closet full of fine clothing; he employs numerous servants, and he owns a Rolls Royce, a hydroplane, and a number of boats (5). His outlandish parties provide others with a space where they can leave behind their inhibitions, dance to a live orchestra, and revel in a world where champagne flows freely. In such a life, as Fitzgerald suggests, the connection between work and a strong moral standard is shattered. Though there may be material wealth and financial independence, the price is too high.

But these dreams are not the only ones represented in *The Great Gatsby*. Fitzgerald also suggests that early twentieth-century Americans were nostalgic, that they longed for something that they had lost. Henry Gatz dreams that his son will use his work to make a contribution to the world and make it a better place. Such a dream reflects

Franklin's aspirations and reasserts the relation between work and morality. Yet Gatz is a part of the last generation, and that dream appears to have passed. For Gatsby and narrator Nick Carraway, too, the dream is steeped in nostalgia; it stems from something that happened long ago. Gatsby aspires to be rich—not necessarily because he longs for material wealth in and of itself, but because he wants to make an impression on Daisy, to win back her affections and to recapture their romance. For Nick, the dream is associated with something other than riches. He confesses that he "wanted the world to be in uniform and at a sort of moral attention for ever," a remark that suggests a desire to return to the type of order that existed before this moment of chaos and irresponsibility (3).

Death of a Salesman

After nearly a decade of such dreams, the year 1929 approached and brought with it the stock market crash and, after that, the Great Depression. In 1941, following the attack on Pearl Harbor, America entered World War II. Once again, our participation in a war caused a shift in the nation's manufacturing and financial sectors and transformed the workplace, and it altered the nation's cultural and social environment. In the aftermath of the war, while other nations struggled to regain their stability, America emerged as the supreme world power, both militarily and economically. Moreover, action by the federal government such as the passage of the G.I. Bill (the Servicemen's Readjustment Act of 1944), an increase in the minimum wage, and the National Housing Act 1949 helped to give birth to a large middle-class that dreamed of upward mobility, home ownership, and cars and appliances that would make Americans' lives more comfortable.

In literature, writers such as Zora Neale Hurston, Tennessee Williams, and John Steinbeck made these Americans and their dreams the focus of their narratives, and the wealthy elite faded into the background as more writers began to emphasize the middle and lower classes. In 1949, Arthur Miller's *Death of a Salesman* appeared, placing at the center of action Willy Loman, a man who can hardly be called a hero but who seems instead to be an everyman, an individual possessing a set of universal traits that nearly everyone can relate to (Fuller 243). The play opened to tremendous success. One reviewer, John Mason Brown, claimed that it "provides one of the modern theatre's most overpowering evenings" (207), while another correctly predicted that the play would be "performed over and over for many years" (Schneider 258). In addition to providing theatergoers with a memorable night out, the play speaks volumes about the American Dream in the twentieth century; it provides insight into our motivations and explores the reasons why Americans sometimes fail to achieve the dream. As critic William Hawkins put it, *Death of a Salesman* "is a fervent query into the great American competitive dream of success, as it strips to the core a castaway from the race for recognition and money" (202). By examining Willy's notion of the dream and then juxtaposing that with other assertions of the dream in the play, we begin to understand not only the dangers associated with having the wrong dream but also the timelessness of the relation between honest work and the attainment of the dream.

If having a home, a car, and a few modern comforts signify the realization of the dream, Willy, for all intents and purposes, has achieved it. Yet, even though he is one payment away from home ownership, Willy continues to pursue his version of the dream. Unlike those who overvalued material wealth, Willy's dream is not at all associated with possessions or the accumulation of capital. Rather, he yearns desperately to be someone important, to be seen as a mover and shaker, to be perceived as a man of consequence. According to Willy, "The man who makes an appearance in the business world, the man who creates personal interest, is the man who gets ahead" (33). He "always felt that if a man was impressive, and well liked, that nothing" could prevent his rise to the top (97). For Willy, then, success and likeability are inextricably linked. His dream is steeped in a desire to be liked, to be impressive and to have a presence. But this dream is problematic, for Miller clearly demonstrates that in Willy's line of work, or in any money-making business, success is measured by one's ability to produce sales and increase profitability. As a lackluster salesman with a delusional sense of self, Willy is destined to fail.

Following Willy's funeral, his son Biff asserts that Willy "had the wrong dreams" (138). In Biff's opinion, Willy's belief in the relation between success and one's reputation was misguided and perhaps even foolish. For Biff, the dream is associated with working with one's hands and being "outdoors, with your shirt off" (22). As one who values manual labor and who sees work as an opportunity to create something, Biff maintains that Willy was most successful, and happiest, when he worked with his hands: "making the stoop; finishing the cellar; putting on the new porch; when he built the extra bathroom; and put up the garage" (138). In Biff's opinion, there was "more of [Willy] in that front stoop than in all the sales he ever made" (138). Though Biff's dream hearkens back to those who looked westward and dreamed of building a nation, it seems out of sync with the rest of society, and by the end of the play, Biff seems no closer to realizing his dream than he was in the beginning. But, in his assertion that Willy's dream is misguided, Biff is not alone. Every truly successful male character in the play demonstrates the unsoundness of Willy's dream. Bernard, a neighbor, made the "best marks in school" (33), follows the rules, and eventually becomes a successful lawyer who is on his way to "argue a case in front of the Supreme Court" (95). Charley, Bernard's father, appears to be an honest, profitable businessman who understands how business really works. In Willy's opinion, neither man is "well liked," yet Miller portrays both Bernard and Charley in a way that suggests that they have found success and respectability. They have achieved the dream, while Willy and Biff spend their days chasing after dreams that seem entirely unattainable.

Conclusion

Although the American Dream has evolved and has, at times, seemed elusive, it nonetheless remains an important aspect of our national culture and ethos. In *Back to Work* (2011), former President Bill Clinton evokes the American Dream as he considers the relation between government and the economy. It is not necessary to recapitulate his arguments here; instead, what is relevant in the context of this study is Clinton's assertion of the dream. For Clinton and, indeed, for many Americans in the twenty-first century, the dream is understood in these terms: that "no matter who you are or where you're from, if you work hard and play by the rules, you'll have the freedom and opportunity to pursue your own dreams and leave your kids a country where they can chase theirs" (ix). Clinton's dream also reflects the most pressing concerns in our twenty-first-century world. He imagines an America that is once again prosperous, and he imagines a day when the nation experiences what he calls "American Dream growth," an economic and industrial boom characterized by "lots of new businesses, well-paying jobs, and American leadership in new industries, like clean energy and biotechnology" (x). Although Franklin, Alger, Fitzgerald, and Miller could not foresee a time when green energy would become a part of the American Dream, there is a clear connection between their assertions of the dream and Clinton's understanding of it as the promise of opportunity, not only for the individual in the present moment, but for the future as well. Although the dream has been transformed by changing business ethics, wars, and other events, its essence remains with us even in the twenty-first century, and it is to be hoped that it will live on, not only in our literature, but in our lives, for another two hundred years.

Works Cited

Adams, James Truslow. *The Epic of America*. Boston: Little, 1931. Print.

Alger, Horatio. *Ragged Dick or, Street Life in New York with Boot Blacks*. 1868. Ed. Hildegard Hoeller. New York: Norton, 2008. Print.

___. "Writing Stories for Boys." 1896. *Ragged Dick or, Street Life in New York with Boot Blacks*. 1868. Ed. Hildegard Hoeller. New York: Norton, 2008. 125–27. Print.

Brown, John Mason. "Even as You and I." Rev. of *Death of a Salesman*. *Death of a Salesman*. Ed. Gerald Weales. New York: Penguin, 1996. 205–11. Print.

Clinton, Bill. *Back to Work: Why We Need Smart Government for a Strong Economy*. New York: Knopf, 2011. Print.

Curti, Merle. *The Growth of American Thought*. 2nd ed. New York: Harper, 1951. Print.

Fitzgerald, F. Scott. *The Great Gatsby*. 1925. Hertfordshire: Wordsworth, 1993. Print.

Franklin, Benjamin. *The Autobiography of Benjamin Franklin and Other Writings*. Ed. Kenneth Silverman. New York: Penguin, 1986. Print.

Fuller, Howard, A. "A Salesman Is Everybody." Rev. of *Death of a Salesman*. *Death of a Salesman*. Ed. Gerald Weales. New York: Penguin, 1996. 240–43. Print.

Hawkins, William. "*Death of a Salesman*: Powerful Tragedy." *Death of a Salesman*. Ed. Gerald Weales. New York: Penguin, 1996. 202–4. Print.

James, Henry. *The American Scene*. 1907. Ed. John F. Sears. New York: Penguin, 1994. Print.

Miller, Arthur. *Death of a Salesman*. 1949. Ed. Gerald Weales. New York: Penguin, 1996. Print.

Schneider, Daniel E. "Play of Dreams." *Death of a Salesman*. 1949. Ed. Gerald Weales. New York: Penguin, 1996. 250–58. Print.

Tocqueville, Alexis de. *Democracy in America*. Vol. 2. Trans. Henry Reeve. Rev. ed. New York: Colonial, 1900. Print.

Thoreau, Henry David. *Walden and Other Writings*. New York: Barnes & Noble, 1993. Print.

Trachtenberg, Alan. *The Incorporation of America: Culture and Society in the Gilded Age*. New York: Hill and Wang, 1982. Print.

"To Go into Partnership": Gender, Class, Ethnicity, and the American Dream in Edith Wharton's *The House of Mirth*

Linda Kornasky

In the first chapter of *The House of Mirth* (1905), Edith Wharton depicts an amusing conversation between Lily Bart and Lawrence Selden that contains much more meaning than its playful tone might imply. Across a bachelor's stylish tea table, Lily, the novel's savvy, glamorous, and ambitious protagonist, chats with her tall, handsome, and young companion in terms that underscore the limits on individualism in the pursuit of the American Dream for anyone other than white, European American, upper-class men. Speaking to this would-be lover, Lily asks if he has ever considered marrying for money rather than for love. To his laughing, negative answer, Lily replies:

> Ah, there's the difference—a girl must, a man may if he chooses. . . . Your coat's a little shabby—but who cares? It doesn't keep people from asking you to dine. If I were shabby no one would have me. . . . Who wants a dingy woman? We are expected to be pretty and well-dressed till we drop—and if we can't keep it up alone, we have to go into partnership. (12)

In response, Selden merely brushes off the seriousness of Lily and her female peers' dilemma and returns to their drolly flirtatious banter.

As the following chapters unfold, Wharton repeatedly emphasizes that the unilateral imperative for partnership that women experience, discussed so casually by Lily and Selden, imbues each of the conflicts in the novel. Additionally, Wharton demonstrates that, although not as stringently as women, men from disfavored ethnic and class backgrounds are also limited when they attempt to gain the social status and material goods that commonly signify achievement of the American Dream. This limitation motivates women and such men to align themselves with those privileged men who have unimpeded access to opportunities and material resources.

According to Wharton, the need for partnership that motivates these characters reaffirms the value of the American Dream. However, Wharton also sharply criticizes the duplicity of the American Dream's premise of gender, class, racial, and ethnic equality, exposing the harm done specifically by the need for partnership among those women and disadvantaged men who seek to live the American Dream.

Using the "partnership" proposals forwarded by Lily and other characters, Wharton presciently explores the two more-or-less contradictory manifestations of the American Dream that the renowned historian James Truslow Adams delineated explicitly in his 1932 history of the United States, *The Epic of America*: First, the middle- and upper-middle-class American Dream ideal of freedom from both poverty and extreme materialism, allowing for one to live an aesthetically and intellectually "good life," and, second, the ideal of virtually unlimited wealth for a fortunate minority achieved either through great ingenuity and diligence or through a swift stroke of fantastic good luck.

Moreover, in the process of exploring these versions of the dream, Wharton insightfully addresses the four components of the American Dream that have been codified in American culture since the 1930s, and which historian Jim Cullen delineates in his 2003 study, *The American Dream: A Short History of an Idea That Shaped a Nation*: upward mobility; equality for everyone regardless of gender, ethnicity, race, or class; homeownership; and "effortless attainment" of great wealth and luxurious leisure, for which the rule is that "it's the rewards that are least strenuously earned that are the most savored." As Cullen elaborates, "Even those that *are* strenuously earned tend to be discussed in ways that suggest they aren't" (160).

Throughout the novel, Wharton aligns Lily's possible partnership with Selden—tacitly suggested in Lily's laments about her distaste for mercenary marriage in chapter 1 and in a later conversation directly imagined by Lily and Selden—with Adams's first model of the American Dream and with the middle two elements of Cullen's list. Their imagined future, Wharton implies, would exemplify an ideal democratic American philosophy, entailing justice and freedom for each individual, regardless of gender and class; they would embody, to quote Adams, "a dream of being able to grow to fullest development as man or woman, unhampered by the barriers which had slowly been erected in older civilizations, unrepressed by social orders which had developed for the benefit of classes rather than for the simple human being of any and every class" (405).

Using phrasing anticipating Adams's oft-quoted passage, Wharton expresses Selden's notion of ideal "success" in life: "personal freedom . . . . from everything—from money, from poverty, from ease and anxiety, from all the material accidents. To keep a kind of republic of the spirit" (70–71). In reply, Lily shares her own, less defined sense of this dream with Selden, and observes tellingly that as a woman taught only to pursue a rich man to marry, she had "no one" in her life "to tell me about the republic of the spirit." Unaware of the gendered means of access to this freedom, Selden chides, "There never is—it's a country one has to find the way to one's self," prompting her to credit him with providing her a clue about how to reach this republic, implying that for her, a marital partnership would be an expressway on which to get there: "Last evening at dinner—I suddenly saw a little way into your republic" (71).

However, the irony, unacknowledged by Selden, is that the necessity of entering a marital partnership to approach this ideal almost always holds for women but rarely for men. As Lily's subsequent casual remarks about her intentions to marry a rich man demonstrate, the hidden side of this ideal is that the financial stability and social autonomy underlying this dream are assumed to be, and in practice often are, primarily white-male entitlements granted to women generally through marriage.

Therefore, to live Adam's first model of the American Dream, Lily needs Selden (or someone like him) to make this model viable—to persuade her that the sacrifices it might entail are worthwhile and to overlook her gendered unawareness of it as an option. However, with sufficient income from his work as a lawyer, Selden does not need a compatible spouse to fulfill his version of the American Dream, an aesthetically informed life of the mind (although his romantic temperament leads him to desire such a spouse). Sadly, Selden knows a wife who would fit his ideal is not likely to be found, because the type of woman he would prefer to marry would likely pursue instead the second, materialistic American Dream model (and to seek the first and last of the elements on Cullen's list). Selden's conversation with Lily confirms his doubts about finding an attractive, smart wife.

In this conversation, Lily suggests her rationale for the three planned marital alliances, from one of which she expects to get rich quickly—a rationale that even Selden considers objectively valid. She finds herself with the options of marrying the extremely dull, but wealthy, Percy Gryce, a young, simple-minded, sheltered heir to a large, established New York fortune; George Dorset, an irritatingly self-centered, emotionally needy, middle-aged husband of a gold-digging wife; and Simon Rosedale, a clever, newly rich, Jewish American financier with ostentatious social ambitions, who is substantially older than Lily and who tries unsuccessfully to conceal his middle-aged plumpness in tightly tailored, expensive suits.

Lily's prospects show that the money-oriented model of the American Dream, with its emphasis on upward mobility and access to a steady cash flow, can be achieved by women only through a marital partnership built on a distasteful pretense of love for their rich husbands. Lily realizes uncomfortably that only steady, manipulative dissimulation can result in the money-oriented results she has been taught to expect. As Elizabeth Ammons contends, "Behind [Lily's marital] refusals lies a repugnance toward a relationship in which a woman is powerless" (35).

For most of Wharton's female characters, this emotional manipulation sits lightly on their consciences, and since it does not involve conventional labor, one can say that it is, in one sense, an easy proposition, providing an example of the ideal of "effortless attainment." Ironically, for these women, to let one's conscience interfere with such attainment constitutes a moral failing of intentional stupidity. Specifically, before her death, Lily's mother drilled into Lily a sense of the intellectual superiority of those who opt for the easily acquired wealth possible for young women with physical beauty and sufficient connections to upper-class society, no matter how poor they actually are:

> To be poor seemed to her such a confession of failure that it amounted to disgrace. . . . Only one thought consoled her, and that was the contemplation of Lily's beauty. She studied it with a kind of passion, as though it were some weapon she had slowly fashioned for her vengeance. It was the last asset in their fortunes, the nucleus around which their life was to be rebuilt. She watched it jealously, as though it were her own property and Lily its mere custodian; and she tried to instil [sic] into the latter a sense of the responsibility that such a charge involved. She followed in imagination the career of other beauties, pointing out to her daughter what might be achieved through such a gift, and dwelling on the awful warning of those who, in spite of it, had failed to get what they wanted: to Mrs. Bart, only stupidity could explain the lamentable denouement of some of her examples. (35–36)

Although Mrs. Bart appears shockingly mercenary by today's standards, her "moral confusion" makes sense historically in the context of the wider American attitude about economic ethics in 1905, as Adams suggests: "Chief among [the era's ideas] was the moral confusion caused by the expansion of the old conception of work as a moral virtue into the further conception of money making as both a personal virtue and a patriotic duty, with the resultant confusion as to its relation to the rest of the virtues and the whole scale of social and moral values" (194).

Even Carry Fisher, Lily's resourceful and refreshingly honest friend, relies primarily on marriage as a form of "effortless attainment" to maintain the inflow of financial resources sufficient to life in New York high society. Additionally, she uses two other methods of money making: giving sexual favors to her friends' husbands for cash payments, who allow her do so because they do not perceive her to be a serious threat to their own financial stability (she lacks the novelty and youth that might make a husband seek a divorce to remarry her), and her innovative paid work as a sort of a "life coach" for newly rich, upwardly mobile couples. Though this social coaching does involve considerable planning, it, like the first type of work, has to be conducted in such a way that it seems to be merely a part of her leisurely, luxurious existence.

Another example of the required appearance of effortlessness is Lily's part in the tableaux vivants scene, in which Lily chooses to recreate the famous Joshua Reynolds portrait *Mrs. Lloyd* (1776). The young women perform silently and motionlessly, highlighting the ideal of effortlessness they strive to embody. The only unmarried woman among the performers, Lily poses with studied leisurely body language to re-create Reynolds's playful depiction of a wealthy married woman enjoying a rustic outing, wearing an informal, loosely draping, light gown and spontaneously leaning over to carve her husband's surname into a tree. Selden notes that "the noble buoyancy of her attitude, its suggestion of soaring grace, revealed the touch of poetry in her beauty" (142). But, although Selden classifies Lily's ability to gracefully illustrate the ideal of upper-class leisure as poetry, one can just as accurately describe Lily's tableau more prosaically, using Thorstein Veblen's objectively sociological phrasing from *The Theory of the Leisure Class* (1899): "The greater the degree of proficiency and the more patent the evidence of a high degree of habituation to observances which serve no lucrative or other directly useful purpose, the greater the consumption of time and substance impliedly involved in their acquisition, and the greater the resultant good repute" (39).

Wharton similarly highlights the superficial effortlessness of Lily's three possible marriages for money: one to a man, Gryce, vain enough to be effortlessly fooled by a superficial show of wifelike affection; the second to a man, Dorset, motivated by a strong desire to exact revenge on his wife, the efficaciously "nasty" Bertha (46), who has made her show of false wifelike affection humiliatingly obvious to the couple's circle of friends; and the third to an intelligent and pragmatic man, Rosedale, who assures her directly he will not expect her to keep up such a pretense. Indeed, for the beautiful, socially well-placed Lily, the partnerships that would give her Adams's second version of the American Dream are readily forthcoming, but only if she plays by the rules of acquiring them. Her insightful awareness that money "may be used," as she points out to Selden, "either stupidly or intelligently, according to the capacity of the user" demonstrates that she does not want money for its own sake only (73). As Patrick Mullen points out, she might well be admirably "able to direct, to guide, to turn the force of [capital] flows to her own ends" if she chooses to do so (57).

However, despite her proven ability to use money to her advantage, she intuitively finds the rules for young women who seek to acquire wealth morally objectionable. The ethical trouble, Wharton suggests, is that for women such as Lily, the American Dream ideal is not what it purports to be; for women, individual initiative is not enough to make the American Dream possible, despite the efficacy of individualism in American Dream ideology for men. Worst of all for women, personal independence and the exercise of free will would generally lead not toward well-earned wealth but toward relative poverty and downward mobility.

Lily repeatedly chafes against the compromising and physically distasteful aspects of her plans to attain a permanent position of wealth and prestige through marriage to a man she would find unattractive, and her reluctance ultimately causes the failure of her available options to marry for money. One problem is that her independent streak precludes her from marrying any man she finds physically and/or emotionally unattractive. Furthermore, even the limited access to sudden wealth for women, via marital partnerships to rich men, is restricted to only those considered good-looking enough to be socially advantageous to the men in question. Lily's plain friend, Gerty Farish, for example, is entirely excluded from this model of the American Dream. Because of her plainness, Gerty does not have access to the middle-class woman's dream of either a home or love with a freely chosen husband. Giving up her unrealistic hope of attracting Selden, she ponders, "What right had she to dream the dream of loveliness? A dull face invited a dull fate" (171).

Of the two potential partnerships for Lily, Wharton suggests that a marriage to Rosedale is indisputably preferable Selden. Rosedale's sincerity and honesty about Lily's feelings for him are admirable in and of themselves, and Lily's alliance with him would undermine two injustices related to the model of the American Dream: that based on upward mobility effected through great wealth and that related to civil rights and equality in the early twentieth century—the exclusion of all women from capitalistic competition and of Jewish and other ethnically and/or racially stigmatized men (and women) from upward social mobility. Through marriage, Lily, because of her class and ethnic identity, which allow her to compete in the social arena, and Rosedale, because of his success in capitalistic enterprise, could transcend the ethnically biased, classist, and sexist barriers to Adams's second type of American Dream.

Nonetheless, despite the sympathy Wharton evinces for a marital partnership between Lily and Rosedale, she ultimately tips her hand toward Adams's first model of the American Dream and to the middle two elements on Cullen's list—home ownership and equality—rejecting the extremes of materialism often linked to the second model of the American Dream, by making a possible marriage to the upper-middle-class Selden her clearly preferred choice. While it may be objected that Selden's family was once financially upper class, Wharton specifies that during Selden's childhood, his family had become upper-middle class, and he works as a lawyer not just to have a nominal, respectable career but also for income on which to live. Nevertheless, his upper-class family connections in affluent New York society—and in no small measure, his looks—have permitted him, as a bachelor, to enjoy the luxurious pleasures of high society. However, if Selden were to marry Lily, a woman with limited inherited income, they would become a chiefly upper-middle-class couple, and both invitations to exclusive gatherings and opportunities to travel to Europe would be drastically reduced.

In part, Wharton's relatively sympathetic portrayal of Selden, and the upper-middle-class future he represents for Lily, suggests that, in spite of long-term relationships with Jewish friends, Wharton held anti-Semitic attitudes: She casts her European American suitor (Selden) as admirably free of crude materialism, but rich in aesthetic sensibility, and her Jewish American suitor (Rosedale) as thoroughly obsessed with, and defined by, money making, though not devoid of aesthetic sensibility.[1]

To be fair to Wharton, of the two men, the otherwise morally refined, Anglo-American Selden is more sexist than Rosedale, as seen in his inclination to give credence to the false accusations of Lily's sexual transgressions with her friends' husbands, Gus Trenor and George Dorset. Rosedale, in contrast, trusts that Lily is not morally capable of prostituting herself, and, unlike Selden, does not judge her for the pleasure-seeking commonality among young men and young women alike in their social set. Additionally, the vanity, triviality, and egotism of Dorset, Lily's third prospective marital/financial partner, appear far more unsympathetic than Rosedale. Dorset reveals the worst aspects of the fourth element of the American Dream—effortless attainment and luxurious leisure. His life is reduced to his digestive pains, and his petty sexual jealousies toward a woman who despises him, twin discomforts for which he spends lavishly to allay.

In the end, Lily does not act on either of her two remaining opportunities (Gryce has married someone else) to marry one of the two very rich men who express their conditional willingness, partly because of their older age and unattractiveness, and, more important, because the condition she must meet to effect a marriage would harm her two attractive young peers, Selden and Ned Silverton, who have been targeted as victims. To marry Dorset she would be expected to provide the evidence (letters and firsthand observations, respectively) she has acquired that proves Selden's and Silverton's romantic relationships with Dorset's wife. Lily knows that, capitalizing on these less affluent young men's desire for luxurious pleasures and drawn by their physical attractiveness, the pretty and bored Bertha Dorset has sexually exploited them in a manner that feminizes them, providing a parallel to Lily herself. Lily recognizes the same sort of vulnerabilities in them, because of their gendered situations, and her empathy for the two, bolstered in Selden's case by the deepening love between he and Lily, checks her determination to marry either Dorset or Rosedale.

There is reason to doubt whether Wharton intends readers to understand that the extremely attractive, narcissistic Bertha has actually shared the sexual affection that she seems to have promised to Selden and Silverton during each of their relationships. As Lily's friend Carry suggests, Bertha's infidelities are not directed toward her own or a lover's sexual pleasure but are part of a mind game she plays with her husband to prevent his divorcing her for her ill-concealed disaffection toward him. She realizes that divorce is a likely outcome, given his vanity and stupidity, if he should spend time with any equally beautiful, gold-digging woman who has better acting abilities than she.

In this psychosexual game, Bertha targets men younger and better looking than her husband (but who are too poor to consider as second husbands) for publically staged flirtations, threatening him with a sort of cuckoldry so humiliating that he fears to leave her side. To ensure success in holding on to her husband's money, she cleverly seeks out the company of gold-digging female rivals so that she can then pretend to be jealous of her husband's alleged attentions to them, providing herself with the legal means to countersue for a lucrative divorce settlement. For his part, Selden tires of this game before Bertha does, and she finds his resulting rejection painful to her ego, thus prompting the imploring letters she imprudently has sent to him; the less discerning Silverton is an easier mark for Bertha's scheme, gullibly believing Bertha's claims about Lily and George and foolishly expecting to benefit personally from Bertha's resulting divorce, which never materializes.

Rather than relying on such a scheme to marry for money, Lily opts for gambling, which she mistakenly sees as a short-term solution to her need for cash. The novel explores the problematic role played by gambling, a common element in American Dream narratives. Wharton demonstrates the degree to which, as Cullen articulates, in the United States, one of the most dominant versions of the "Dream of the Good Life," the money-oriented version, eschews "the idea of hard work, instead enshrining effortless attainment as the essence of its appeal" and recommends gambling in its many forms as the preferred means of money making (160).

Immersed in the pleasures of this materialistic version of the dream and in a social world that admires a winning gambler far more than a diligent worker, Lily not surprisingly succumbs to the gambler's irrational psychology when she plays high-stakes bridge: "Since she had played regularly the passion had grown on her. Once or twice of late she had won a large sum, and instead of keeping it against future losses, had spent it in dress or jewelry; and the desire to atone for this imprudence, combined with the increasing exhilaration of the game, drove her to risk higher stakes at each fresh venture" (28).

Later, Lily responds to her gains made in the speculations Gus Trenor wagers for her, which are actually sexual bribes, in the same manner. She senses the quid pro quo nature of these so-called stock speculations, of course, but she gambles (and later loses) on the small chance that she will be able to avoid being alone with him in sexually compromising situations.

She makes the same sort of gamble on the Dorsets' yacht trip to France and Italy, predicting incorrectly that she can prevent Bertha from maneuvering her and George into a falsely incriminating position, thus undermining her social standing with her friends, all of whom depend upon the material and social gifts the Dorsets provide. Even worse, when Bertha invents charges against Lily and George, to cover up her own adultery, and turns Lily off the yacht, Lily's aunt Julia Peniston reduces Lily's planned inheritance from $400,000 to $10,000, leaving the bulk of her estate to the dull Grace Stepney, Lily's cousin. Lily's wager that she can manage Bertha incurs a terrible outcome.

Nonetheless, the gambling culture in upper-class society is infused with a stubborn, generally illogical, optimism that disempowers anyone who, like Lily, employs it as a blindfold to avoid facing difficult decisions and necessary changes. For example, in reference to the risks of Bertha turning on her on the yacht, Wharton writes that Lily thinks, "If she was faintly aware of fresh difficulties ahead, she was sure of her ability to meet them: it was characteristic of her to feel that the only problems she could not solve were those with which she was familiar" (205). As her friend Carry Fisher advises, referring to the disastrous social ostracism that is the outcome of the yacht trip: "Half the trouble in life is caused by pretending there isn't any" (242).

Therefore, she tries Carry's social-life-coach occupation, attempting three times to become a live-in assistant to couples with ambitions for social upward mobility. Though Carry intends for her to manage these temporary situations carefully, to use them as a respectably leisurely means of support while waiting for conditions to move toward a marriage to either Dorset or Rosedale, Lily allows herself to be distracted by the false optimism she experiences in each new luxurious space in which she is allowed to spend her time.

Ironically, then, she is defeated mainly by her embrace of the pervasive "rampant optimism" emerging in America in the first half of the nineteenth century, as Adams describes, in which "unthinking optimism . . . [becomes] essential" for maximizing one's chances—one's potential to make the most of strokes of good fortune as they occur (184). Indeed, by the late nineteenth century, this optimism was formalized in the New Thought philosophy, which came to be known as "positive thinking" and which has retained a strong presence in American popular culture.

According to social critic Barbara Ehrenreich, the new "sin" of this philosophy is "negativity," to be avoided at all costs (90). Lily avoids it to her cost, ignoring Carry's advice to acknowledge her trouble, instead concentrating on the pleasurable sensations of any luxuries she can enjoy. For example, as she wakes on the first morning in the last place she takes for a social-coach position, her "sense of being once more lapped and folded in ease, as in some dense mild medium impenetrable to discomfort, effectually stilled the faintest note of criticism" (287).

Of course, Lily responds to these new luxurious spaces with such strong relief in part because she longs for a home in a distinctly American manner. As Cullen observes, homeownership, a bulwark of the American Dream, became "extraordinarily resilient and versatile" after the Homestead Act of 1862 and throughout the twentieth century (136). Most notably, the symbolic power of the dream of homeownership resonates in Lily's response to her unexpected meeting and cozy visit with Nettie Struther, a young, lower-middle-class woman whom Lily had helped in a brief philanthropic phase she initiated to quell her unconscious guilt over borrowing money from Trenor. Nettie has since married and had a baby. After visiting the couple's small flat, which Nettie proudly possesses (even if she and her husband are only renting), and after holding the infant in her arms, Lily becomes aware of a

feeling of being something rootless and ephemeral, mere spin-drift of the whirling surface of existence, without anything to which the poor little tentacles of self could cling before the awful flood submerged them. And as she looked back she saw that there had never been a time when she had had any real relation to life. Her parents too had been rootless, blown hither and thither on every wind of fashion, without any personal existence to shelter them from its shifting gusts. She herself had grown up without any one spot of earth being dearer to her than another: there was no centre of early pieties, of grave endearing traditions, to which her heart could revert and from which it could draw strength for itself and tenderness for others. (336)

Aligning with American Dream ideology, Wharton stipulates that a family home is the ground upon which the value of an individual human life is established:

In whatever form a slowly accumulated past lives in the blood—whether in the concrete image of the old house stored with visual memories, or in the conception of the house not built with hands, but made up of inherited passions and loyalties—it has the same power of broadening and deepening the individual existence, of attaching it by mysterious links of kinship to all the mighty sum of human striving. (336–37)

Logically, part of Lily's attraction to Selden stems from an intuitive sense that, as a child, he lived in such an "old house stored with visual memories" that represents his slightly economically precarious, middle-class status. As Wharton explains:

If [the Seldens'] house was shabby, it was exquisitely kept; if there were good books on the shelves there were also good dishes on the table. Selden senior had an eye for a picture, his wife an understanding of old lace; and both were so conscious of restraint and discrimination in buying that they never quite knew how it was that the bills mounted up. Though many of Selden's [rich] friends would have called his parents poor, he had grown up in an atmosphere where restricted means were felt only as a check on aimless profusion. (160–61)

With Lily, Selden imagines creating a similarly stable home, one intended not to build wealth but to build a lasting familial connection for parents and children.

Instead, Lily turns to paid labor at the millinery factory, in hopes of quickly establishing a lucrative business in designer hats that will allow her to straddle the American Dream ideals of, on one hand, upward mobility through creatively intelligent and sustained effort and, on the other hand, the "effortless attainment" of luxurious leisure. She imagines foolishly that after a short stint learning the trade as an entry-level seamstress at the millinery factory, she will move upward to leisurely business ownership:

> Here was, after all, something that her charming listless hands could really do; she had no doubt of their capacity for knotting a ribbon or placing a flower to advantage. And of course only these finishing touches would be expected of her: subordinate fingers, blunt, grey, needle-pricked fingers, would prepare the shapes and stitch the linings, while she presided over the charming little front shop—a shop all white panels, mirrors, and moss-green hangings—where her finished creations, hats, wreaths, aigrettes and the rest, perched on their stands like birds just poising for flight. (298)

Initially, she is, to employ June Howard's phrasing, "playing at proletarianization" at the factory (153), and she intends to play at management in the near future.

Eventually, after being fired from the millinery factory for incompetence in basic hat making, Lily must give up her ill-conceived plan. She realizes that she will not be able to borrow the funds needed to start a business unless she does so from Rosedale, which she is hesitant to do. In a scene that poignantly reveals the way that gender conventions interfere with economic freedom for women, Rosedale offers Lily a fair deal that would pay off Lily's socially compromising debt to Trenor and allow her to use the $10,000 legacy from her guardian, Aunt Julia for both her hat shop and collateral on loans to establish the operation. Thinking of the meaning that New York high society would give to such a loan from Rosedale, Lily refuses Rosedale's business proposition—his offer to "go into partnership" in her planned designer hat shop. Forced out of this valid business option by these problematic, gendered business ethics, Lily decides that, to move forward with her plan for "effortless attainment" of the wealth-oriented model of the American Dream, she will use Bertha's letters to Selden, those she acquired by a lucky chance.

Lily could use the letters to take Bertha's place, demoting Bertha in the pecking order of New York society (and to take Selden's presumed patriarchal place as the autonomous agent in his relationship with Bertha). Further, by blackmailing Bertha into accepting and fostering Lily's planned marriage to Rosedale, Lily could prevent Bertha from attempting to revive her relationship with Selden in the future. However, in the end, Lily does not desire to express her affection for Selden with an act of negation. In the impulsively loving act of burning the letters, during her last visit with Selden, Lily essentially chooses the antimaterialistic American Dream of an alternative upward mobility into the anticlassist, home-oriented "republic of the spirit." Her spontaneous choice to burn the letters without letting Selden know that she has done so, and to act without making any attempt to control his feelings for her or to embarrass him with the knowledge that she has had possession of the letters, ennoble her action.

Sadly, however, Lily experiences a final unlucky twist of fate when she uses sleeping medication, the unpredictable narcotic chloral, for the last time. Believing that the drug will not kill her and pessimistic about whether the love between she and Selden can be rekindled, she increases the dose of the drug by a few drops. Foolishly, she thinks she takes only "a slight risk in doing so" and inaccurately calculates that an accidental, deadly overdose would be "but one chance in a hundred" (340).

Falling into a drugged sleep and barely conscious:

> She said to herself that there was something she must tell Selden, some word she had found that should make life clear between them. She tried to repeat the word, which lingered vague and luminous on the far edge of

thought—she was afraid of not remembering it when she woke; and if she could only remember it and say it to him, she felt that everything would be well. (341)

She never wakes to learn that she is right, that the words of love that would have begun a sort of a life with Selden, one based on an American Dream very different from the one she had been taught by her mother to seek, would have been mutually spoken the next morning when Selden arrives with words of love.

Despite Lily's final failure to transcend her misguided all-or-nothing gambler's ideology and American-style false optimism, in *The House of Mirth*, Wharton ultimately reaffirms the worth of her protagonists' efforts to navigate the choices, limited though they may be by gender, class, race, and ethnicity. Wharton demonstrates that the materialistic excesses of one version of the American Dream prevent Lily, Selden, and Rosedale, specifically, from fully understanding that a more realistic and liberating American Dream is possible, one that is informed by both the values of the family home and individual freedom. The novel reveals that the moral compromises demanded of those who are taught to desire easy attainment of resources and social ascendency, especially women and others excluded tacitly by American discriminatory practices, are, in fact, contradictory to the "republic of the spirit" Wharton recommends to her readers.

Notes

1. For a thorough overview of critical analyses of the anti-Semitic aspects of Wharton's depiction of Simon Rosedale and a succinct reading of the novel along these lines, see Donald Pizer's *American Naturalism and the Jews* 50–58. On Lily's contrasting, Anglo-Saxon "personal specificity," so unlike Rosedale's typifying Jewish traits, see Jennie A. Kassanoff's *Edith Wharton and the Politics of Race* 51–52.

Works Cited

Adams, James Truslow. *The Epic of America*. Boston: Little, 1932. Print.

Ammons, Elizabeth. *Edith Wharton's Argument with America*. Athens: U of Georgia P, 1980. Print.

Cullen, Jim. *The American Dream: A Short History of an Idea That Shaped a Nation*. New York: Oxford UP, 2003. Print.

Ehrenreich, Barbara. *Bright-Sided: How the Relentless Promotion of Positive Thinking Has Undermined America*. New York: Metropolitan, 2009. Print.

Howard, June. *Form and History in American Literary Naturalism*. Chapel Hill: U of North Carolina P, 1985. Print.

Kassanoff, Jennie Ann. *Edith Wharton and the Politics of Race*. New York: Cambridge UP, 2004. Print.

Mullen, Patrick. "The Aesthetics of Self-Management: Intelligence, Capital, and *The House of Mirth*." *Novel: A Forum on Fiction* 42.1 (Spring 2009): 40–61. Print.

Pizer, Donald. *American Naturalism and the Jews*. Urbana: U of Illinois P, 2008. Print.

Wharton, Edith. *The House of Mirth*. 1905. *Edith Wharton: Novels*. Ed. R. W. B. Lewis. New York: Library of America, 1985. 1–347. Print.

Veblen, Thorstein. *The Theory of the Leisure Class: An Economic Study of Institutions*. 1899. New York: Modern Library, 1961. Print.

Meaningful Work and Self-Determination: The American Dream for Women_____

Carol Loranger

Well before the phrase "American Dream" entered the American national discourse in the early years of the twentieth century,[1] the promise that the country's freedoms granted every person the opportunity to gain economic success and improved social stature through hard work resonated with Americans. Striving for success is a central motif in Benjamin Franklin's autobiography, and the wide availability of work for the industrious in the colonies is a central element in Franklin's 1782 pamphlet "Information to Those Who Would Remove to America," in which he correlates useful employment with prosperity and social stature. Striving for success is also the fundamental plot trajectory in the wildly popular *Ragged Dick, Or Street Life in New York with the Boot-Blacks* (1868), as well as the subsequent series of books for boys by the prolific Horatio Alger, Jr. throughout the 1860s and 1870s.

Though the amount of time and effort required to achieve success and stature differed from group to group depending on social barriers, and many hardworking men were kept from success by circumstances outside their control, the promise of success for hard work was essentially kept for enough native-born and immigrant men of European ancestry that it has become an article of national faith: Work hard and success and stature must follow; work hard and achieve the American Dream.

However, for native-born and immigrant women of European ancestry, the formula was different. There was hard work aplenty for American women, but for many that meant the uncompensated labor of housekeeping for their families. Paid work frequently meant housekeeping for other families until one married and kept house without compensation for one's spouse. Among the more prosperous classes, women's work frequently meant supervising a housekeeping staff. While some women surely found some satisfaction in their domestic roles and knew their work to be both hard and necessary, many were aware that domestic labor was not only undervalued by their fellow Americans but also would never lead to success and stature. For American women, simply working hard was not enough to achieve prosperity and social status. Nor were prosperity and social status their only, or even chief, goals. The American Dream for women was to gain social and personal autonomy while performing meaningful work.

In the nineteenth and twentieth centuries, American women, while enjoying far more latitude than their European counterparts, did not possess the degree of political or social liberty enjoyed by their male counterparts. Work that occurred primarily outside the home and was compensated more or less adequately helped women gain freedoms they did not otherwise have: freedom from dependency and drudgery, freedom of movement and self-determination, and, possibly, financial success and social stature. However, within the typical native-born and immigrant household, domestic work was women's lot.

In agrarian cultures, domestic work is not easily separable from the striving of the whole family toward stature and success, and both in the early agrarian days of the American republic and on the expanding frontier, women's agricultural, craft, and domestic work visibly contributed to the well-being of the family. However, by the mid-nineteenth century, as the United States became an increasingly industrialized and mercantile nation, women's traditional work came to be deemed increasingly inconsequential and separated from family wealth and stature. Also, thanks to the patriarchal notion that men and women were ordained to separate spheres—a notion prevalent among different immigrant cultures as well as among the native born—it was difficult for women to freely leave the domestic sphere and seek their fame and fortune. Women who did so were literally set apart: They were spinsters, widows, actresses, or other social oddities.

Once outside the domestic sphere, women often lacked opportunity to pursue the sort of valued work that might result in financial success; even for those who might break free and succeed by virtue of their hard work, the right of self-determination in their personal lives was not a guaranteed outcome, as families and social communities exerted a continuing pressure to make them conform to their culturally determined roles. Thus, freedom—understood as autonomy or the right of self-determination—was the goal, not the starting point of American women's dreams, and it was a goal whose bar was frequently moved just out of their reach as they seemed to achieve it. The intimate connection between access to meaningful work and women's autonomy has been so central to American women's lived experience that it forms the explicit subject or the implicit subtext in writings by American women writers from the immediate post–Civil War period and throughout the twentieth century. Novels written by women during this period took up the question, and resoundingly located the possibility of self-determination and status in access to meaningful work.

Louisa May Alcott's *Work: A Story of Experience* (1873), Willa Cather's *O Pioneers!* (1913), Anzia Yezierska's *The Bread Givers* (1925), and Sandra Cisneros's *The House on Mango Street* (1984) each explore the American Dream for women. Each of these novels borrows elements of the coming-of-age story to spotlight its protagonist's development toward independence via meaningful work. With the exception of *O Pioneers!*, these are semiautobiographical novels, drawing deeply on their authors' pursuits of meaningful work and personal autonomy. In each, access to such work is frequently blocked by common social and familial expectations as well as by the women's own physiological and psychological needs, the expression of which may also be socially constrained: the need for sexual fulfillment, for simple companionship, or for the basic necessities of food and shelter. In order to achieve their version of the American Dream, these women are shown as being forced to give up on or defer other personal goals that are central signs of the achievement of the American Dream for males, including marriage and family, companionship, leisure, and status.

Alcott made explicit the equation between women's access to meaningful work and achieving freedom in a variety of novels and short stories at the same time Alger was penning his stories of financial success for boys. Daughter of utopian education theorist Amos Bronson Alcott and a harbinger of the Progressive generation, Alcott was an idealist and firm believer in the value of personal industry. She was nonetheless aware that women's industry was frequently unremunerative, tedious, and socially devalued in the United States. Her 1873 short story "Transcendental Wild Oats" deftly satirizes utopian communities like her father's unsuccessful experiment at Fruitlands by pointing out how much female labor underwrote the experiment and how little the women's labor was regarded by their masculine counterparts. While the familiar series of books *Little Women* (1868–69), *Little Men* (1871), and *Jo's Boys* (1886) explicitly make a claim for the value of women's domestic work, they primarily focus on Jo March's continuing search for self-realization through meaningful, nondomestic work, first as a writer, then as an educator. In the Jo March books and in *Work*, Alcott identifies "meaningful" work as that performed for the social and civic betterment of others, regardless of monetary compensation, a criterion adopted by both Yezierska and Cisneros.

Work centers its argument on the Declaration of Independence's defining phrase: "Life, Liberty and the pursuit of Happiness"—language that anticipates the formula of the American Dream. *Work* opens with "a new Declaration of Independence" (5), as the orphan Christie Devon announces her plan to leave her uncle's house and seek her fortune: "I'm willing to work," she declares to her aunt, "but I want work that I can put my heart into, and feel that it does me good, no matter how hard it is. I only ask for a chance to be a useful, happy woman, and I don't think that is a bad ambition" (11). It is significant that this conversation occurs in the kitchen, where Christie and her aunt are baking pies. Christie's first forays are into paid domestic work—housekeeper, seamstress, governess, companion, and housekeeper again. Eventually, however, the Civil War affords her meaningful work, first as a nurse, later as an activist for women's rights.

In *Work*, Alcott exhibits a relentlessly cheery idealism. Even so, she recognizes that seizing meaningful work may leave other parts of women's lives empty. Christie's energies become focused on progressive social change after her marriage to David Sterling. The marriage is brief, however. David's enlistment as a Union soldier precipitates the marriage; he departs within a day and is shortly killed in battle. Women characters, including a daughter born to Christie after David's death, come and go in the latter pages of the novel, but Christie spends the remainder of her life essentially alone. Alcott, herself unmarried, does not present this as a loss for Christie, and Christie does not seem to regret the loss of sexual intimacy with the loss of her husband, but the reader may see this as a tacit acknowledgement that marriage and domesticity are not compatible with Christie's expanding, and fulfilling, role as a speaker and a worker for Progressive causes.

By novel's end, while speaking at her first women's meeting, Christie explicitly identifies work as the prerequisite to woman's freedom: "No matter how hard or humble the task at the beginning," she tells the assembled women, "if faithfully and bravely performed, it would surely prove a stepping-stone to something better, and with each honest effort they were fitting themselves for the nobler labor, and larger liberty God meant them to enjoy" (332–33). Her practical and heartfelt impromptu speech is a success. Afterward, Christie muses upon her future—"'the task my life has been fitting me for. . . . A great and noble one'"—of working for women's freedom and opportunity. Christie pledges herself to "lay the foundation of a new emancipation whose happy success I may never see" (334). That happy success would be long in coming.

Unlike Alcott, Willa Cather did not explicitly concern herself with progressive social theory or "women's issues" in her novels. In her early work, Cather was far more concerned with exploiting the field she had staked out for herself: capturing in fiction the multicultural landscape of the immigrant communities of western Nebraska. Moreover, Cather was not one to use the novel to work out her social theories overtly. Her protomodernist preference for a stripped-down narrative that relied on suggestion rather than explanation left little room for the speech-making so characteristic of Alcott. However, Cather's second novel, *O Pioneers!*, by virtue of having a female protagonist and being set during the era in which the American breadbasket was carved out of the Great Plains, foregrounded women's difficulty in turning hard, meaningful work into the coin of personal freedom.

Alexandra Bergson is charged by her dying father to keep the family and their Nebraska farm together. Years of drought and farming techniques inappropriate to the dry plains have neighbors on the Divide (the high prairie region of Nebraska) selling off and moving to nearby cities to find employment. Alexandra's brothers want to do the same. However, though she has "not the least spark of cleverness" (31), Alexandra has an open mind and open eyes. She watches as banks snatch up nearby holdings and concludes that the land itself has a value that her brothers and neighbors do not grasp. She is willing to learn more sustainable and hygienic conditions for keeping pigs, from a hermit others dismiss as crazy, and the latest techniques for dryland farming, from university-trained farm agents. Also, she is willing to mortgage the property in order to buy land her less successful neighbors are selling off. By the end of the first part of the novel, Alexandra has increased her holdings, creating "one of the richest farms on the Divide" (43), leaving the rest of the novel for Cather to work out the implications of the personal sacrifices Alexandra has had to make and the weight of social pressure upon her to limit her autonomy.

Negative views of women's capabilities, some brought with her family from Sweden, some grown on western soil, surround her from the beginning. Her father, we learn, would have rather assigned to a son the task of keeping the family together, but he recognizes in his daughter essential qualities her brothers, Oscar and Lou, lack: "the strength of will, and the simple direct way of thinking things out, that had characterized his father in his better days. He would much rather, of course, have seen this likeness in one of his sons, but it was not a question of choice" (13). The brothers "did not mind hard work, but they hated experiments and could never see the use of taking pains" (23–24).

An advantage Alexandra possesses as a female striver is that the society of the Great Plains of Nebraska in the 1880s—the setting for part one of the novel—is primarily agrarian. On a farm, even women's traditional work has value, extending as it does to the keeping of chickens and milk cows, the tending of vegetable gardens, and the feeding of the men who perform the heavier labor in the fields. Alexandra extends to the outside world of the farm the same care as she does to the inside world of the farm house, and she is able to make the conceptual leap from domestic economy to financial and real estate transactions through which the Bergson family is able to thrive, capitalizing on all the siblings' labor and Alexandra's broader vision to achieve prosperity and positions of respect in the community.

Cather shows explicitly that Alexandra's broader vision arises from a special relationship with the landscape, which Cather presents as intimate and loving: "For the first time, perhaps, since that land emerged from the waters of geologic ages, a human face was set toward it with love and yearning. It seemed beautiful to her, rich and strong and glorious" (33). At this early point in the novel, Alexandra's human soul mate, Carl Linstrum, has departed with the other failed farmers. It is not certain she will ever see him again. The relationship with the land will sustain her in the absence of any other intimate relationship for the bulk of the novel.

More successful, ultimately, than her plodding brothers, Alexandra's eventual economic success and social stature emerge from her outward conveyance of domestic skills into the worlds of agriculture and commerce and sacrificing personal intimacy until she is well into her forties. The accumulating acreage is Alexandra's "house":

You feel again the order and fine arrangement manifest all over the great farm; in the fencing and hedging, in the windbreaks and sheds, in the symmetrical pasture ponds, planted with scrub willows to give shade to the cattle in fly tie. There is even a white row of beehives in the orchard, under the walnut trees. You feel that, properly, Alexandra's house is the big out-of-doors, and that it is in the soil that she expresses herself best. (43)

By contrast, the interior of the farm house is "curiously unfinished and uneven in comfort" (43).

Personal wealth enables Alexandra to hand over housework to a succession of Swedish girls, who perform domestic work in her kitchens until they meet and marry local farmers. Cather makes it clear that women's work in and of itself is no path to prosperity, nor are womanly pursuits and behaviors. In the first scene of the novel, Alexandra is dressed in handed-down men's clothing, in part because what she wears is representative of the reality of subsistence farm life in the late-nineteenth-century United States, but also to distinguish her from the more typically feminine characters Marie, Mrs. Lou, Mrs. Oscar, and the Swedish girls. We are more likely to see Alexandra outside with a hoe in her hands than indoors with a broom or rolling pin. Indoors she works with her account books. She neither embroiders nor sews. Like Christie, she prefers socializing with women; other than the hermit Ivar, her closest relationships are with the doomed, young Marie Shabata and the spry and toothless crone Mrs. Lee. Her affluence gives her the wherewithal to behave charitably toward her neighbors, protecting Ivar and extending emotional and financial support to the imprisoned murderer, Frank Shabata.

By becoming a successful farmer and a person of significance in her community among both the native-born and the immigrant populations of the Divide, Alexandra achieves prosperity and social status, but her personal autonomy continues to be under threat, and the value of her contribution to the Bergsons' success is not understood by her brothers. What she also lacks, for most of the novel, is an intimate relationship, marriage, and children. The arc of the novel takes Carl Linstrum away when the failed farmers leave the Divide in part one, returns him briefly in part two when Alexandra has achieved success, and returns him in part five when Alexandra has lost her beloved youngest brother and her best female friend.

Even in her positions as the community's primary landowner and the architect of her family's success, Alexandra finds her will actively opposed by her brothers. When Carl first returns to the Divide after an absence of sixteen years, Lou and Oscar are suspicious and resentful. Unmarried, Alexandra's wealth would go to them at her death; they fear a marriage to Carl. "The property of a family really belongs to the men of the family," says Oscar, "because they are held responsible, and because they do the work" (85). When Alexandra protests that she has worked as well, they scoff: "You liked to manage round, and we always humored you. There's no woman anywhere around that knows as much about business as you do, and we've always been proud of that, and thought you were pretty smart. But of course the real work always fell on us. Good advice is all right, but it don't get the weeds out of the corn" (85).

Alexandra is forty when Carl first returns—not necessarily too old to have children but old enough that her brothers believe marriage would make her look ridiculous. Carl also recognizes that he is too "little" to attach himself to a woman clearly more successful than he: "Poor Alexandra! It is your fate to be always surrounded by little men. And I am no better than the rest" (92). Alexandra's reply summarizes the predicament of the striving woman: "I don't need money. But I have needed you for a great many years. I wonder why I have been permitted to prosper, if it is only to take my friends away from me" (92).

Only her relationship with the land, which Cather figures throughout the novel as a lover, sustains Alexandra. At first, it is the passive recipient of her "love and yearning"; it "yields itself eagerly to the plow . . . with a soft, deep sigh of happiness" (39). Later, the reader learns that the land takes form in Alexandra's dreams as a masculine force: "He was like no man she knew; he was much larger and stronger and swifter, and he carried her as easily as if she were a sheaf of wheat. She never saw him, but, with eyes closed, she could feel that he was yellow like the sunlight, and there was the smell of ripe cornfields about him" (106). This sustaining and mildly erotic dream persists from girlhood and into Alexandra's adulthood, only disappearing when Carl returns for a second time, after much loss and sorrow. Though the novel ends with her reunited with Carl and about to embark upon a life with him, there is an element of loss, of melancholy, in the outcome. Alexandra exchanges her dream lover for Carl, for peace and companionship. She realizes that her dream "will never come true now, in the way I thought it might" (159).

The new emancipation for women was longer in coming than even Christie Devon might have imagined. Even as they gained more freedom of movement in the early years of the twentieth century, American women continued to lack routine access to meaningful work, as compared to American men. Solitude was still the price of meaningful work when found, and marriage and family relationships continued to compromise women's autonomy and lock them into cycles of drudgery. In 1910, looking back on her life at age fifty, before she founded Hull House, social-work pioneer Jane Addams recalled an anxious and socially perplexed, though economically privileged, younger self, uncertain how to be useful, "clinging only to the desire to live in a really living world and refusing to be content with a shadowy intellectual or aesthetic reflection of it" (64). As late as 1963, second-wave feminist Betty Friedan was classifying the problem faced by a generation of college-educated married women who had no meaningful work to put their hearts into as "The Problem That Has No Name":

> a strange stirring, a sense of dissatisfaction, a yearning that women suffered in the middle of the twentieth century in the United States. Each suburban wife struggled with it alone. As she made the beds, shopped for groceries, matched slipcover material, ate peanut butter sandwiches with her children, chauffeured Cub Scouts and Brownies, lay beside her husband at night—she was afraid to ask even of herself the silent question—"Is this all?" (15)

The need for meaningful work continued to haunt native-born and immigrant women in the twentieth century, and access to that work continued to be limited by their families, their own biological needs, and the culture at large.

Like Abraham Cahan before her, Anzia Yezierska produced novels and short stories examining the personal cost of assimilation for immigrant Jews. Because her protagonists were primarily female, those costs included sacrifices made in order to achieve and maintain autonomy. In *Bread Givers,* her most popular novel, Yezierska applies the same pattern of hard but meaningful work plus sacrifice of personal intimacy as the route to achieving independence for her character Sara Smolinsky. Like Cather, Yezierska emphasizes the great sadness that comes from the loss of intimacy. However, unlike *O Pioneers!*, in which the problem of woman's autonomy is peripheral to Cather's main project, *Bread Givers* takes the problem as its central question. Yezierska goes one step farther than Alcott or Cather in suggesting that the woman who embraces a relationship after achieving meaningful work and other personal successes risks losing her hard-won autonomy. For Yezierska, women are never entirely free from both the constraints imposed on them by family and by the cultural values they have internalized. Hanging over Sara from the beginning is a belief Yezierska ascribes to orthodox Jewry: "A woman's highest happiness is to be a man's wife, the mother of his children" (206). Finally, more than Alcott or Cather, Yezierska foregrounds her character's sexual needs as at odds with her drive toward independence.

For the four daughters of Reb Smolinsky, Sara, Bessie, Fania, and Mashah, living first in a tenement on New York City's Hester Street, then over a failing grocery in Elizabethtown, New Jersey, household drudgery and factory piecework are cloaked in a cultural wrapping that appears to make them meaningful. The women of the house must labor to support the family so that their old-world father may enjoy the leisure needed to study his holy books.

Because they are not male and, thus, cannot "say prayers after a father's death" (9), the women's statuses within the family are marginal, and, as eastern European Jewish immigrants, their poverty confirms their lesser status in the United States. As women, "they could be the servants of men who studied the Torah. Only if they cooked for that man and washed for the men, and didn't nag or curse the men out of their homes; only if they let the men study the Torah in peace, then, maybe, they could push themselves into Heaven with the men, to wait on them there" (10).

Within the family the mother, though frequently resentful of her husband's privileges and financial mismanagement, accepts her status, "lick[ing] up Father's every little word, like honey" (12) and enforces traditional gender status for herself and her daughters. The older daughters, Bessie and Mashah, struggle against their foreordained drudgery but both ultimately submit, leading the same limited lives as their mother and exhibiting the same intermittent resentment, but young Sara resists. Like Christie Devon, she makes a declaration of independence before leaving her parents for New York City, where she believes education and work performed for herself, and not for her father's benefit, will bring her her dream of self-determination:

Thank God, I'm living in America! You made the lives of the other children! I'm going to make my own life! . . . You think I'll slave for you till my braids grow gray—wait till you find me another fish-peddler to sell me out in marriage? You think I'm a fool like Bessie! . . . I'm going to live my own life. Nobody can stop me. I'm not from the old country. I'm American! (138)

"Drunk with dreams" (155), Sara enrolls in night school and gets a job in a laundry. Alone for the first time in her life, Sara feels "full of life and hope. . . . I, alone with myself, was enjoying myself for the first time as with grandest company" (157). Like Alexandra, as she strives to achieve her dream she must put aside other desires. Courted by the merchant Max Goldstein, "a talking roll of dollar bills" (19), Sara drops him when she learns he disdains her ambition to be educated: "To him a wife would only be another piece of property" (199). Though she feels "ripened for love" (200), Sara determines to be an old maid and pursue her dreams. This determination is not without a sense of loss: "I had made my choice. And now I had to pay the price. So this is what it cost, daring to follow the urge in me. No father. No lover. No Family. No friend. I must go on and on. And I must go on—alone" (208).

Sara moves to the Midwest—to a "new America of culture and education" (210)—to enroll in college and prepare to be a teacher. Healthily desirous of intimacy, and without a dream lover like Alexandra or a child to live for like Christie, Sara is drawn to other men as she pursues her dream, including a professor. However, not until she actually finds work as an English teacher to immigrant children in the Hester Street school of her childhood (essentially, once she has achieved her goals) does Sara enter into a permanent relationship with a man. First, though, she enjoys a "honeymoon" with herself: "Sara Smolinsky, from Hester Street, changed onto a person! . . . Once I had been elated at the thought that a man had wanted me. How much more thrilling to feel that I had made my work wanted! This was the honeymoon of my career" (237, 241).

Her elation is short-lived, however: "The goal was here. Why was I so silent, so empty? All labour now—and so far from the light. I longed for the close, human touch of life again." Sara remembers her father preaching that "a woman without a man is less than nothing" (270). Sara ultimately finds that human touch with her principal, Hugo Seelig, a striver like her, an immigrant Jew with the same beginnings in the same district in Poland. As the novel's pages thin, Sara seems to have achieved her dream of meaningful work and autonomy as well as sexual fulfillment, but Yezierska throws her a curveball. Learning that Sara's demanding and hitherto unsupportive father is impoverished, unwilling to be sent to the "Old Men's Home" and in need of home care, Hugo urges her to take him in with them even though Sara fears his "fanatical adherence to his traditions" (296) will cost them their happy home. The novel ends with Sara feeling "the shadow still there, over me. It wasn't just my father, but the generations who made my father whose weight was still upon me" (297).

Like *Work* and *Bread Givers*, Sandra Cisnero's *The House on Mango Street* employs autobiographical elements in the coming-of-age story of a young Latina, Esperanza Cordero, seeking a path toward self-determination and a life away from Chicago's impoverished Mango Street. The form of the novel—a collection of brief first-person vignettes recording Esperanza's observations of the people and events of Mango Street—combined with the limitations of placing the point of view in a character of thirteen or fourteen and a time frame of a single year during which Esperanza undergoes puberty, means that readers do not see whether the character achieves her independence or finds meaningful work as a writer. What the novel does allow is the recording of Esperanza's observation of the Latinas around her, mired in their domestic lives, tied by pregnancy, children, and marriage to lives of financial and emotional impoverishment. What she sees, as she comes to understand it, strengthens her resolve to leave Mango Street while she can.

Esperanza is named for her great-grandmother, "a wild horse of a woman, so wild she wouldn't marry. Until my great-grandfather threw a sack over her head and carried her off . . . as if she were a fancy chandelier" (11). Esperanza does not want to also inherit her great-grandmother's fate—trapped indoors looking sadly out the window. Even as she, like Sara Smolinsky, feels the pull of natural desire for sexual intimacy, the possibility of her great-grandmother's fate—one she sees worked out among the girls in her neighborhood (Rosa tied down by her brood of children; Alicia by her mother's brood, which she must care for after their mother's death; Minerva, Rafaela, and Sally trapped in abusive or controlling relationships with their husbands or fathers)—Esperanza resists.

Esperanza wants "to sit out bad at night, a boy around my neck and the wind under my skirt" (73). But her expression of this desire is followed immediately by the cautionary tales of Rafaela, Minerva, Sally, and Esperanza's own dissatisfied mother who "could have been somebody" (90). Toward the end of the year, Esperanza is assaulted by boys at the fair. This solidifies her ambition to step out on her own, away from Mango Street, to "pack my bags of books and paper. One day I will say goodbye to Mango. I am too strong for her to keep me here forever" (110). What Esperanza wants more than a boy is a house, "not a man's house. Not a daddy's. A house all my own. . . . Nobody's garbage to pick up after" (108). In that house, echoing Virginia Woolf, she wants a place to write her poems and stories. However, Esperanza's dream will not come to fruition with simply running away to write and direct her own life. Like Christie, Esperanza must work for the betterment of other women: "I have gone away to come back. For the ones I left behind. For the ones who cannot out" (110).

While Cisneros does not tell readers that Esperanza (whose name means "hope") achieves her dream, the "fact" of Esperanza's stories in readers' hands suggests she has. In her introduction to the twenty-fifth-anniversary edition of the novel, Cisneros writes of herself in the third person, clinching the identification of Esperanza with her author: "As a girl, she dreamed about having a silent home, just to herself, the way other women dreamed of weddings" (xii). Cisneros worries about whether her work, as a teacher and writer, is meaningful as well as re-munerative: "How can art make a difference in the world? . . . Should she give up writing and study something useful like medicine? How can she teach her students to take control of their own destiny? . . . What should she be doing to save their lives?" (xix).

Like Alcott, Cather, and Yezierska, Cisneros foregrounds personal autonomy and meaningful work as essential to women. All four writers recognize that intimate personal relationships threaten that autonomy. While Cather is less concerned with the political and social ramifications of this work, there is a sense among all four writers that work's

---

positive impact on self and others, rather than the prosperity arising from work, is what makes the achievement of the dream meaningful.

Notes

1. Historian James Truslow Adams is generally acknowledged to have introduced the complex concept of the American Dream in 1932 in *The Epic of America*; the phrase had earlier appeared in the 1911 novel *The Husband's Story*, by David Graham Phillips as, "the universal American dream of getting up in the world" (84).

Works Cited

Addams, Jane. *Twenty Years at Hull-House, with Autobiographical Notes*. 1910. New York: Macmillan, 1964. Print.

Alcott, Louisa May. "Transcendental Wild Oats." 1873. *The Portable Louisa May Alcott*. Ed. Elizabeth Lennox Keyser. New York: Penguin, 2000. 538–52. Print.

___. *Work: A Story of Experience*. 1873. New York: Penguin, 1994. Print.

Cather, Willa. *O Pioneers!* 1913. New York: Vintage, 1992. Print.

Cisneros, Sandra. *The House on Mango Street*. 1984. New York: Vintage, 2009. Print.

Friedan, Betty. *The Feminine Mystique*. 1963. New York: Norton, 1974. Print.

Phillips, David Graham. *The Husband's Story*. New York: Appleton, 1911. Google Books. Web. 5 Sept. 2012.

Yezierska, Anzia. *Bread Givers*. 1925. New York: Persea, 1999. Print.

Why Speak of American Stories as Dreams?_____

Cara Erdheim

The term "American Dream" conjures literary images of perseverance and promise on the one hand but disillusionment and defeat on the other: Ben Franklin pulling himself up by the bootstraps, Huck Finn "lighting out" for the territories, Gatsby insisting that he can "repeat the past," Willy Loman burying his face in his hands. Whether one accepts it as a reality, punctures it as a myth, or presents it as a nightmare, the American Dream has maintained its powerful presence in scholarly conversations throughout the decades. Traditionally, scholars have referred to classic American Dream texts such as Benjamin Franklin's *Autobiography* (1791–1790), Horatio Alger's *Ragged Dick* (1868), F. Scott Fitzgerald's *The Great Gatsby* (1925), and Arthur Miller's *Death of a Salesman* (1949). In their readings of these works, early critics tended to associate the dream with a pervasive American spirit, a belief in national innocence, and a vision of human perfectibility; while later scholars challenge these traditional mobility narratives, some contemporary critics deny that the dream ever existed in the first place.

The shifting trends in American Dream scholarship reflect an effort in American literary criticism to enlarge the borders of US literature to include formerly silenced voices. As attitudes toward the dream itself change, the literary canon expands to include formerly marginalized narratives related to race, gender, ethnicity, disability, and class. Since the growth of multiculturalism in the 1970s and 1980s, scholars have expanded what counts as American Dream narratives, others have rewritten the criteria, and some have even abandoned the canon established in 1941 by F. O. Matthiessen that centered on elite white men such as Ralph Waldo Emerson, Henry David Thoreau, Walt Whitman, Nathaniel Hawthorne, and Herman Melville. Scholars such as Jane P. Tompkins, Henry Louis Gates, and William L. Andrews have revised Matthiessen's master narrative to include long-neglected texts by African Americans, Native Americans, Asian Americans, Hispanics, and women; however, other critics claim that these works deserve their own place outside of the grand master narrative. As such, a similar dynamic occurs in scholarship devoted to the American Dream.

Defining the Dream

The birth, death, and rebirth of the American Dream show that the narrative has a life cycle of its own. One cannot really talk or write about American literature, which contains various voices and a multitude of perspectives, without referring to some element of the American Dream. The reverse is also true: Almost any discussion of upward mobility requires a reflection on the nation's literary traditions, which are dynamic and multifaceted. From its role as a British colony to its twentieth-century position as a "global superpower" (Newman 1), the United States has produced writings that both shape and are shaped by the dream.

Despite its omnipresence in American literature, the "American Dream" did not receive a formal definition until 1931; in the wake of the Great Depression, James Truslow Adams, in *The Epic of America*, defined the dream as one that would allow all men and women, regardless of their origin or social status, to prosper in a place of free and equal opportunity (416). While he did not deny the potential for financial mobility, Adams noted that his vision of the dream extended beyond dollars and cents. Specifically, he claimed that the American Dream, or the "great epic," transcended "mer[e] material plenty" (416) and did not, therefore, limit itself to "motor cars and high wages" (415).

However, nearly a decade before Adams, D. H. Lawrence's now-classic critique of American hero worship, *Studies in Classic American Literature* (1923), in many ways anticipated the major shifts in critical studies of the American Dream. In one of the first extended commentaries on Franklin, Lawrence takes pleasure in satirizing *The Autobiography*'s idealization of self-made success; rather than exalt Franklin as a sort of American hero, Lawrence identifies human "perfectibility" as a truly "dreary theme" (15). By mocking Franklin's concept of "the ideal man" (15), Lawrence demonstrates the flawed logic of American hero worship, which praises the ideal while celebrating the common.

Lawrence's *Studies in American Literature* exposes the national myths at play throughout the early narrative history of the United States. Though he does not have access to "American Dream" as a term, Lawrence takes aim at what he calls "the true myth of America" (60). Through his discussions of James Fenimore Cooper's Leather-stocking novels, Lawrence knocks off his pedestal Cooper's protagonist, Natty Bumppo, by identifying this white savage as "the stoic American killer of the old great life" (65). Rather than romanticize the hero and praise Bumppo as the personification of a nation's spirit, Lawrence claims that Cooper's characters capture "the essential American soul [as] hard, isolate, [and] stoic" (68). Just as he satirizes self-made success and mocks hero worship, Lawrence calls into question American claims to innocence.

Since these foundational studies, subsequent critics have incorporated their insights and revised them to accord with contemporary critical preoccupations. To map out the thematic shifts in thinking about the American Dream, it is helpful to cluster scholarship devoted to the dream as occurring in three "waves" that correspond to the eras 1950s–1960s, 1970s–1980s, and 1990s–present.

American Innocence and the Spirit of a New Nation, 1950s–1960s

Early commentators on the American Dream often looked back to the nation's earliest writings, ranging from Puritan narratives to Franklin's *Autobiography*, to understand the spiritual foundations for the concept. During the 1950s and into the 1960s, American scholars associated the dream with a new Eden, which early authors believed could fulfill biblical prophecies in ways that Europe and the Old World had not. Two decades after Adams popularized the term, the American Dream became central to critical conversations about the nation's literary traditions. *The Epic of America* generated a great deal of energy and enthusiasm among first-wave dream critics who used the phrase to develop a framework to discuss democracy, freedom, independence, Manifest Destiny, and upward mobility.

If James Truslow Adams inserted the term into popular discussions, then Frederick Carpenter gave literary life to the American Dream in *American Literature and the Dream* (1955), which provides a foundation for modern understanding of the dream, even if the study seems rather outdated. Carpenter begins by insisting upon defining the dream; like American literature itself, he says, the dream defies definition because of its vastness (3). Carpenter argues that American literature distinguishes itself from British writing because of the "constant and omnipresent influence of the American dream upon it" (3). Though he does not settle on one definition, Carpenter claims that the dream captures a distinct national spirit, which he calls a "new realization of the old religious ideals" (198). Readers can learn a great deal about early American beliefs by looking at how the dream has been shaped and reshaped by the literary imagination.

Carpenter's book opens with a comparative study of Puritan narratives and transcendentalist texts, which share the "dream of a new world" (14). Authors ranging from William Bradford and Jonathan Edwards to Emerson and Whitman look toward a new American Eden by rejecting the past, whether that history contains the Church of England, European culture, or British literary traditions. Indeed, much like the nation itself, the dreams expressed by these writings are future-oriented (28). Carpenter suggests that Edward Johnson's "A New Heaven and a New Earth" (1653) reflects the dream's connection to the earliest American settlers, by and large Puritans who believed a new biblical Eden would grow from American soil. Through his interpretation of the poem, Carpenter suggests that colonial Americans saw the new land as uncharted territory that granted its inhabitants spiritual and material rewards. "A New Heaven and a New Earth" thus establishes a narrative of American promise and hope that future writers such as Franklin and Thomas Jefferson would later explore in their own writings (5).

Considering his classic connection to self-made success, Franklin and his *Autobiography* receive surprisingly little attention in *American Literature and the Dream*. While he acknowledges Franklin's influence on the transcendentalists, Carpenter credits Emerson in particular with achieving a "realization" of the "ideal, democratic 'American' self" (17). Starting his study with the Puritans and Emerson, Carpenter then divides American literature into four categories, each of which distinctly present the nation and its dream: Emerson, Thoreau, and Whitman function as the dream's "philosophers," "Gentile Traditionalists" such as Amos Bronson Alcott oppose the dream, writers such as Hawthorne and Melville express romantic faith in the dream, and realists such as Sinclair Lewis critique the dream (5). Carpenter concludes with a question, which he seems to direct to future scholars: What, he asks, can the American Dream reveal about the nation's literary tradition, and vice versa?

In his 1968 essay "The Enlightenment and the American Dream," Theodore Hornberger probes the question posed by Carpenter; he takes on Carpenter's challenge of trying to define the dream by looking at shifts in American literature, history, and culture. Rather than start with the Calvinists, as Carpenter does, Hornberger begins in the American republic and focuses on Franklin, whose autobiographical writings he connects to the Age of Reason. Specifically, Hornberger identifies the original American Dream, as expressed by Franklin, with ideals such as "perfectibility, social progress, democratic government, and self-reliance" (17). The dream forms "an integral part of the Enlightenment" because it reflects the optimistic tone of the period; he defines it as the North American ability to reinvent the self, reconstruct one's identity, join new communities, and simply start over (17). Less focused on the spiritual aspect of the dream's national narrative, Hornberger stresses secular virtues, such as industry.

Like Hornberger, Lewis B. Wright, in "The Renaissance Tradition in America," argues that Enlightenment ideals, which celebrate the nation's newness on the one hand but its rich roots on the other (5), have shaped the dream since its inception. Furthermore, Wright associates the American Dream with unbridled mobility through the acquisition of land: "The New World offered undreamed-of possibilities for social advancement because land—the magical basis for gentility—could be had with relative ease" (7). What makes Wright's reading distinct from those of Carpenter and Hornberger is his study of the Greek influence on early America. Specifically, Wright traces the word "Renaissance" to the ancient world and argues that early narratives such as Franklin's *Autobiography* constitute a classical revival (8).

While Carpenter studies the Puritans, Hornberger focuses on Franklin, and Wright goes back to the Greeks, Walter Allen idealizes the democratic principles upon which the United States was founded. In *The Urgent West* (1969), Allen designates Jefferson's Declaration of Independence as the original dream document, and he claims that the American republic gave birth to a reality that did not exist for early North American settlers. Indeed, Allen's scholarship appears the most dated, especially when he insists that Americans, regardless of race and origin, share one universal experience and identity (5). To his credit, Allen does move on to modern illustrations of the failed dream, which he explores in relation to *The Great Gatsby* and Theodore Dreiser's naturalist novel *An American Tragedy,* both published in the same year, 1925.

Although published earlier than Allen's work, Malcolm Cowley's *The Dream of the Golden Mountains* (1964) further highlights the myth of unlimited American success. As a longtime journalist for *The New Republic*, Cowley takes a special interest in Upton Sinclair's muckraking novel *The Jungle* (1906), a naturalist narrative that exposed Chicago's unsanitary meatpacking industry, resulting in the 1906 legislation of the Pure Food and Drug Act under President Theodore Roosevelt. Moreover, *The Jungle*, Cowley argues, captures failed American aspirations through the urban experience of early twentieth-century immigrants such as Jurgis Rudkus, the novel's protagonist. Through his emphasis on "the working class [as] part of the dream" (118), Cowley anticipates second-generation criticism.

Manifest Destiny and the Myth of Upward Mobility, 1970s–1980s

While many first-generation dream scholars celebrated spiritual success and material wealth in narratives by Franklin and Alger, the next wave of criticism focused on twentieth-century texts in which prosperity fails in all forms. Plymouth, that Puritan "City on a Hill," had signaled rewards and pleasures for early American authors, but the biblically based Promised Land soon moved west with the ever-expanding frontier. In fact, some would argue that the 1849 California gold rush played the greatest role in creating a national myth that wealth would naturally flow. Second-generation dream critics exposed this western myth by looking in particular at the writings of John Steinbeck, whose novel *The Grapes of Wrath* (1939) "laid bare the bankruptcy of an ancient American dream about going westward to the Promised Land" (Athearn 90). Indeed, the frontier had failed those trekking west during the Depression years, and novelists such as Steinbeck poignantly capture this reality.

One year prior to the publication of *The Grapes of Wrath*, American poet Archibald MacLeish wondered whether the dream would continue to survive amid the nation's economic collapse in *Land of the Free*, a 1938 book of poetic verses and photographs. In a short poem within the book, MacLeish mused, "We wonder if the liberty is done: The dreaming is finished." MacLeish's work inspired historian Robert G. Athearn to explain that the statement both reflected a reality and created a national nostalgia for the "heartland of the old, romantic West" (88). However, at the same time that family farmers longed for an era gone by, the gospel of Manifest Destiny kept "nonfarming westerners" (91) hopeful that fortunes would follow on the frontier. Throughout his book *The Mythic West in Twentieth-Century America* (1986), Athearn acknowledges the power of 1930s fiction and film to show that the "American dream had become an illusion" (104). Part of this illusion involved the worship of white male heroes, from which second-wave criticism started to move away.

With the advent of multiculturalism in the 1970s and 1980s, literary scholars adjusted their definition of the American Dream to account for race, gender, ethnicity, and class. Kathryn Hume observed:

> With African Americans, the dream often refers to freedom in the North (an idealized Garden or Promised Land); for Native Americans, the "dream" often refers to desire for land ownership, freedom to practice native spirituality, the ability to achieve sovereignty, the want of protection against government or corporate practices that wreak environmental havoc on reservations and other lands. (iv)

Increasingly, scholars began to edit collections of writings by previously marginalized authors and called attention to the ways in which the writings engaged—or did not engage—with hallowed American traditions. William L. Andrews examined African American experience as revealed through autobiography and slave narratives, Duane Niatum turned attention to American Indian culture and traditions, James P. Gaffney shed light on the American Catholic dream, and Jane P. Tompkins located within women's writing and nineteenth-century sentimentalism another "American Renaissance," which had been overlooked by Matthiessen and others. While scholars reworked the canon, they also revised the original dream that had sustained the nation's literary tradition.

Second-wave American Dream scholars developed an interest in how African American works about slavery, segregation, and racism both expose the national myths surrounding upward mobility and show that the United States had never been a land free from sin. In *To Tell a Free Story: The First Generation of Afro-American Autobiography, 1760–1865* (1988), Andrews, one of the most influential scholars on African American autobiography, demonstrated the limitations of black upward mobility, both physical and financial. At the same time, Andrews highlighted the intellectual and spiritual triumphs of nineteenth-century slave autobiographers such as Frederick Douglass and Harriet Jacobs.

African American authors, ranging from Douglass and Jacobs to Lorraine Hansberry and Alice Walker, move the Garden of Eden from Plymouth or Concord to the northern industrial city. In Douglass's *Autobiographies*, the North represents freedom, both physical and spiritual, through his escape from slavery and the realization of his humanity through literacy. In Hansberry's 1959 drama, *A Raisin in the Sun*, African American characters such as Mama plant gardens in the northern housing projects where they live and thus create their own miniature Edens. However, in many of Walker's works, such as her 1970 novel *The Third Life of Grange Copeland*, African American dreams continue to fail in the new northern "Garden," which brings individuals, families, and communities new nightmares such as racism, segregation, poverty, and violence, a failed dream Walker addresses in her essay, "In Search of Our Mother's Gardens" (1974).

In his 1989 study *Race, Gender, and Desire*, Elliott Butler-Evans looks to the texts of twentieth-century African American female writers such as Toni Morrison to expose the crisis of subjectivity in literature written by and about black women (5). Calling attention to the "visibility of black culture" (7), Butler-Evans notes, Morrison uses nonlinear narrative structures, patterns, and forms to illustrate how whites have constructed African American identity through the American Dream, and vice versa.

Scholars in the 1970s and 1980s tended to reexamine the dream in three ways: by exposing the failures of the western frontier, exploring the multicultural dream and its realities, and examining the myth of upward mobility in classic narratives about failure rather than about success. In the 1970 essay "Gatsby: False Prophet of the American Dream," Roger L. Pearson insists that Fitzgerald's protagonist personifies "the Gospel of the corrupted American dream" (640). According to Pearson, the original dream contains a spiritual component, an aspect that has been polluted by Gatsby's delusions about his wealth. In order to demonstrate that the dream has changed over time, the article takes readers on a journey through American literary history. Beginning with the Puritan writer Jonathan Edwards, Pearson shows how "spiritual fulfillment" signified success in early national narratives (638). Pearson's essay works well to prepare readers for the third phase of literary dream criticism, which focuses on success and failure in an increasingly global literary marketplace.

The Post-Apocalyptic American Nightmare, 1990–Present

Little significant literary scholarship and cultural criticism on the American Dream emerged between 1990 and 1999. Perhaps because of the financial boom of the 1990s, there was less need for critical conversations about success and upward mobility. However, in an insightful commentary, Alex Pitofsky argues that Dreiser's naturalist novel *The Financier* (1912) is a twentieth-century Horatio Alger story in its depiction of the rise and fall of Frank Cowperwood, but also that through his story Dreiser exposes the "Horatio Alger myth" that underlies many conceptions of the American Dream. For many readers, Alger's heroes embody Americans' dreams of success, for in tale after tale, Alger traced the rise of his boy heroes from penury to middle-class respectability. Pitofsky notes that Dreiser's Cowperwood is the antithesis of Alger's heroes, because Cowperwood starts out his life with more privilege and aspires to far more wealth than does the typical Alger protagonist (281). Unlike Alger's heroes' ethical principles and intellectual curiosity, Cowperwood has little of both (282), says Pitofsky, who also claims that *Ragged Dick* is less about selfish individualism and more about assimilation into an upwardly mobile community (277).

The terrorist attacks of September 11, 2001, transformed literary criticism on the American Dream. In the first decade of the twenty-first century, scholarship became apocalyptic in tone; indeed, critics engage more with the nightmare than with the dream. In a postmodern world, scholars have perhaps the greatest challenge: to say something original about a dream that may never have existed, in literature or in culture. Interestingly, some contemporary critics have returned to the classic American Dream texts and have sought to imbue these narratives with new meaning. If scholars of the 1970s, 1980s, and 1990s spent time rethinking Franklin and Alger, then post–September 11 critics have produced new readings of Fitzgerald and Miller. Moreover, the Great Recession has sparked renewed interest in *The Great Gatsby* and *Death of a Salesman*. Willy Loman and James Gatz are among the most famous failed dreamers in American literature; critics never seem to grow tired of these tragic characters.

In "Success, Law, and the Law of Success" (2005), Galia Benziman focuses on the commercial context in which Miller created his drama. First produced in 1949, *Death of a Salesman* was composed by the playwright during the "consumer boom" that followed the Great Depression and the 1930s recession. Consumption had begun to supersede production in national importance (20). As much as the play critiques the nation's obsession at the time with "competition, materialism, and selfishness" (20), Benziman argues that Miller's drama seeks to reclaim the dream as originally intended; that is, a dream that exists beyond "self-centered ambition" and more in line with humble "upward social mobility" (21). *Death of a Salesman* shows readers and audiences that the American Dream does not have to be immoral or destructive so long as it does not involve "selfish greed." The play may even teach that the American Dream involves and even requires social and moral responsibility (21).

Throughout her study of Miller's drama, Benziman poses a number of complex questions, which she never fully answers, about the potential pitfalls of capitalism and consumerism: To what extent must the American Dream be associated exclusively with "commodity culture?" (22), and how much does Miller align "salesmanship" with "fraud?" (22). She argues that Miller's play works to achieve a balance between two aspects of the dream, selfishness and personal success (22). Benziman comes closest to addressing her inquiries about consumer culture when she makes the somewhat counterintuitive claim that *Death of a Salesman* tells a tragic tale about how "personal integrity" can still accompany capitalist success (25).

Benziman concludes her study of Miller's modern tragedy with a statement about how the most successful American Dream involves self-awareness, which Willy Loman does not have. Not only does Miller's tragic hero dream, but he also makes myths by denying reality, falsifying his success, and exaggerating his charisma; furthermore, he fails to read others, such as his sons Happy and Biff (28), and misreads himself. Like Gatsby, Loman has a certain degree of megalomania, and he often resorts to self-aggrandizement (30–31). Despite the belief that both men are well liked, almost nobody shows up for their funerals. The parallels between Gatsby and Loman are many, but modern scholars seem to engage less in comparative readings and more in individual studies of these two flawed characters.

In *The American Counterfeit: Authenticity and Identity in American Literature and Culture* (2006), Mary McAleer Balkun identifies Gatsby as the ultimate "American Counterfeit" who fabricates and falsifies his identity by collecting meaningless materials. Tracing the trajectory of American literary history from Whitman through Fitzgerald and beyond, Balkun claims that acquiring useless goods leads impulsive characters like Gatsby to falsify what they own and who they are; in essence, the acquisition of stuff brings about the formation of an imagined self, both personal and national. The Victorian or post-Victorian culture of commodities, then, reflects an evolving American fascination with commercialism and "consumerism" (129). Throughout *The Great Gatsby*, the act of collecting things also puts a new spin on the commonly juxtaposed ideas of old and new money (131).

Collecting in *The Great Gatsby* becomes a way to "restore the past to the present" and thus to expose the "interrelatedness" of both, according to Balkun (132). Collecting takes three forms, as one acquires "souvenirs" (Nick Carraway), "fetish objects" (Gatz/Gatsby), and "systematics" (Tom Buchanan through his acquisition of females) (132). Collecting functions throughout the novel, Balkun contends, as a means of molding the self and his or her worth for further "public consumption" (132). Daisy Buchanan, of course, becomes Gatsby's "object of desire," as well as a "curiosity" of sorts (134). Daisy, much like the idealized past itself, becomes increasingly inaccessible as the novel moves forward (135), so the search for authenticity proves impossible in the end (152).

Benziman and Balkun express interest in the material side of the American Dream, but modern critics still debate the degree to which wealth figures into the original concept. While Betty Sue Flowers, in *The American Dream and the Economic Myth* (2007), claims that the grand "economic myth" remains embedded in the dream, Norton Garfinkle takes a slightly different approach by distinguishing the dream from its rivaling "Gospel of Wealth." Modern scholars have perhaps the greatest challenge, as they seek something original to say about a concept that has for so long been recycled, re-created, and re-envisioned.

Hume offers one of the most innovative commentaries on the twenty-first century American Dream, as reflected in American literature and culture. Although published one year prior to the terrorist attacks of September 11, *American Dream, American Nightmare: Fiction since 1960* (2000) captures the apocalyptic tone of the era. Hume's book is perhaps the only one to examine post-1960 fiction written by and about marginalized peoples that expressed a growing "disillusionment" with the American Dream (i). One of the few dream critics to focus on late twentieth-century ethnic American Dreams, Hume examines writings focused on Jewish Americans by Abraham Cahan, as well as Chinese and Native American narratives composed by women. While she does acknowledge some success stories, such as Bharati Mukherjee's *Jasmine*, a 1999 novel about the experience of an Indian immigrant in the United States, Hume argues that the culturally, ethnically, and racially marginalized women in post-1960s fiction share a feeling of estrangement from the dominant white male culture that promises success (viii).

Hume connects ideas about failure to environmental narratives, which she comes to understand as toxic national nightmares. Through her study of *Ecotopia* (1975) and *Ecotopia Emerging* (1981), both by Ernest Callenbach, Hume claims that green texts critique the American Dream by envisioning a sort of environmental or ecological revolution (160–61).

Ecological interdependence also replaces a "rugged individualism," associated with the classic western narrative (163), which moves from innocence to experience. The more environmental critics discuss nature, the harder it becomes to define; similarly, conversations about the American Dream seem to exhaust the term of all meaning. At the same time, though, dream-driven discussions are significant because they reveal something about how national narratives have been constructed by writers and readers alike over time.

As the foregoing suggests, the critical literature devoted to the American Dream is vast and varied. The large scope of literary criticism on the dream itself is overwhelming enough, but there also exists a wealth of material on classic texts such as *The Great Gatsby* and *Death of a Salesman*. It is just as difficult to speak about literary representations of the dream without mentioning Willy Loman as it is to reflect on Miller's tragic hero without invoking the American Dream. As the American Dream continues to permeate American political and social discourse, it is significant that cultural critics and literary scholars continue to generate new perspectives on a formative American theme.

Works Cited

Adams, James Truslow. *The Epic of America*. 1931. London: Routledge, 1945. Print.

Alger, Horatio. *Ragged Dick and Struggling Upward*. 1867. New York: Penguin, 1986. Print.

Allen, Walter. *The Urgent West: The American Dream and Modern Man*. New York: Dutton, 1969. Print.

Andrews, William L. *To Tell a Free Story: The First Century of Afro-American Autobiography, 1760–1865*. Champaign: U of Illinois P, 1988. Print.

___, ed. *Six Women's Slave Narratives*. New York: Oxford UP, 1988. Print.

Athearn, Robert G. *The Mythic West in Twentieth-Century America.* Lawrence: UP of Kansas, 1986. Print.

Balkun, Mary McAleer. *The American Counterfeit: Authenticity and Identity in American Literature and Culture.* Tuscaloosa: UP of Alabama, 2006. Print.

Benziman, Galia. "Success, Law, and the Law of Success: Reevaluating *Death of a Salesman*'s Treatment of the American Dream." *South Atlantic Review* 70.2 (2005): 20–40. Print.

Butler-Evans, Elliott. *Race, Gender, and Desire: Narrative Strategies in the Fiction of Toni Cade Bambara, Toni Morrison, and Alice Walker.* Philadelphia: Temple UP, 1989. Print.

Carpenter, Frederick. *American Literature and the Dream.* New York: Philosophical Library, 1955. Print.

Cowley, Malcolm. *The Dream of the Golden Mountains: Remembering the 1930s.* New York: Viking, 1964. Print.

Fitzgerald, F. Scott. *The Great Gatsby.* 1925. New York: Penguin, 2008. Print.

Flowers, Betty Sue. *The American Dream and the Economic Myth.* Kalamazoo, MI: Fetzer, 2007. Print.

Franklin, Benjamin. *Benjamin Franklin's Autobiography.* Ed. Joyce E. Chaplin. New York: Norton, 2012. Print.

Gaffey, James P. *Francis Clement Kelly and the American Catholic Dream.* Bensenville, IL: Heritage, 1980. Print.

Garfinkle, Norton. *The American Dream vs. the Gospel of Wealth: The Fight for a Productive Middle-Class Economy.* New Haven: Yale UP, 2006. Print.

Gates, Henry Louis, and William L. Andrews, eds. *Slave Narratives.* New York: Lib. of America, 2000. Print.

Hornberger, Theodore. "The Enlightenment and the American Dream." *The American Writer and the European Tradition.* Eds. Margaret Denny and William H. Gilman. New York: Haskell, 1968. 16–28. Print.

Hume, Kathryn. *American Dream, American Nightmare: Fiction since 1960.* Champaign: U of Illinois P, 2000. Print.

Lawrence, D. H. *Studies in Classic American Literature.* 1923. New York: Penguin,1990. Print.

MacLeish, Archibald. *Land of the Free.* New York: Harcourt, 1938. Print.

Matthiessen, F. O. *American Renaissance: Art and Expression in the Age of Emerson and Whitman.* New York: Oxford UP, 1941. Print.

Miller, Arthur. *Death of a Salesman.* 1949. New York: Penguin, 1998. Print.

Newman, Otto, and Richard de Zoysa. *The American Dream in the Information Age.* New York: St. Martin's, 1999. Print.

Niatum, Duane, ed. *Carriers of the Dream Wheel: Contemporary Native American Poetry.* New York: Harper, 1975. Print.

Pearson, Roger L. "Gatsby: False Prophet of the American Dream." *English Journal* 59 (1970): 638–45. Print.

Pitofsky, Alex. "Dreiser's *The Financier* and the Horatio Alger Myth." *Twentieth-Century Literature* 44 (1998): 276–90. Print.

Tompkins, Jane P. "The Other American Renaissance." *The American Renaissance Reconsidered*. Ed. Walter Benn Michaels and Donald E. Pease. Baltimore: Johns Hopkins UP, 1989. 34–57. Print.

Walker, Alice. "In Search of Our Mother's Gardens." 1974. *In Search of Our Mother's Gardens: Womanist Prose*. Orlando: Harcourt, 1983. 231–43. Print.

Wright, Louis B. "The Renaissance Tradition in America." *The American Writer and the European Tradition*. Ed. Margaret Denny and William H. Gilman. New York: Haskell, 1968. 3–15. Print.

CRITICAL
ESSAYS

The American Dream, the Western Frontier, and the Literature of Expansion_____

Steven Frye

"America" began as a concept in the European mind, as an irrepressible impulse to imagine possibilities beyond the oppression that defined daily experience in the Old World. Powerful economic interests, together with the imperial ambitions of the Western European monarchies, motivated the initial exploration and settling of the Americas, but after the first expeditions, massive numbers of colonists braved the Atlantic Ocean in the hope of a new life.

The initial dream, the first stage of the "American Dream," was deeply rooted in the relationship of individuals and communities with the land. The identification with landscape had much to do with the primarily agrarian preindustrial economies, but it had even more to do with the narratives, stories, and myths people disseminated. Europeans had their own myths, which they carried forward into their concept of the future. Many of these narratives were linked to the wilderness, the frontier, and the journey west. Wild places have always been the substance of Western dreams. Generations of children had grown up on the myth of the Garden of Eden, a natural paradise that was humanity's origin, the prelapsarian ideal that they had long since lost.

Later in the same biblical epic, the ancient Israelites were delivered into the wilderness of the Arabian Desert, where they were tested by God before being lead to the Promised Land. For the explorers and the colonists, most of them Christians, America held the possibility of recovery, the chance to rediscover a new Garden of Eden and a new Promised Land. These ideas were at the heart of the settlers' ambitions; they formed the dream that gave them the courage to take risks most people today cannot imagine. F. Scott Fitzgerald remembers this dream at the conclusion of *The Great Gatsby* (1925), as he describes the island of Manhattan as it must have appeared to the first Dutch colonists. It was "the fresh, green breast of the new world," and it "flowered" before them, a rare moment in time that was "commensurate to [their] capacity for wonder" (182). These sailors were moving into a wilderness, into a frontier, into what was then the West. The western frontier—in all its raw power, danger, beauty, and sublimity—is at the heart of the American Dream.

The colonization of the Americas is a complicated process with many dimensions, sources, and motivations. Traditionally, history books have tended to focus on the British movement onto the eastern seaboard. This focus is based on the fact that the nation and culture that became the United States was initially populated by northern Europeans, mainly British, in four major migrations: the Puritans, who came to New England in the early sixteenth century; the tidewater explorers who settled the Virginia territory at roughly the same time; the Quakers, who migrated to the region around Pennsylvania in the late sixteenth century; and the Scotch-Irish and British border people who came through the Delaware Valley and settled in the Appalachian mountains in the early eighteenth century, becoming the rough, violent, and unlettered toughs that were the first storied American frontier heroes. These groups established the British colonies that later rebelled against the mother country. However, the rebellion was based in European natural-rights theory and a notion of British liberty that stems from the Magna Carta, written in the thirteenth century.

The United States began as a primarily British nation, and in many ways it remains so. However, from its earliest stages the country drew from other nations and cultural traditions. The initial explorations and explorer narratives of Christopher Columbus, Hernan Cortés, Álvar Núñez Cabeza de Vaca, Bartolomé de Las Casas, and Samuel de Champlain demonstrate the influence of the Spanish and French, and elements of their cultures remain in the American West, the Caribbean, and in the Midwestern portions of North America that were French territories before the Louisiana Purchase in 1803. All these narratives focus on the frontier. They more than describe it: They elevate it to the level of symbol and myth. There was something transformative and powerful about the first European experiences of American lands that captivated the human imagination. Explorers and settlers could do no less than invest what they saw with the substance of all their hopes.

The evolution of the American Dream and its relationship to the frontier can be traced to the early writings of the American Puritans. As radical religious believers who emerged out of the Protestant Reformation, the Puritans had become a recognizable subculture on the European continent and in Great Britain. Founding their theology on the work of the French reformer John Calvin, they thought the Reformation in England, which led to the formation of the Anglican Church, had not gone far enough. The English church maintained many of the ritualistic practices of Catholicism, and Calvinists hoped to institute what they thought was a more devout and intensely pious religious observance centered on the notion that human beings were utterly subjected to the will of God. Calvinists believed in predestination, the notion that all events and the details of each individual life are written by God in the book of history. This idea motivated how they organized communities and families and how they worshipped. These radical reformers were recognizable and their communities prevalent, but they were outsiders, and in the early seventeenth century, many of them took the opportunity to travel to the New World. The "Puritans," as these Calvinists were often called by their detractors, took with them the notion of "special mission," the idea that they were ordained by God to live a unique life, to establish a Christian civilization in a new Promised Land on the far edges of the American wilderness.

The notion of "special mission" was informed by the way the Puritans saw the world, and they read the world not on its own material terms but through the optic of the most important book in their history—the Holy Bible. Later in the nineteenth century, Ralph Waldo Emerson encouraged Americans to read the "book of nature," to treat the natural world as a divine text, to interact with it in order to apprehend the divinity within it. The Puritans had anticipated him, but they looked for nature in the Bible, sought mythic patterns of symbol in the scriptures themselves, patterns they could use to interpret their own lives and experiences. They thought in terms of typology. They did not read the Bible as history alone, but as story, myth, and art. They looked to the literary motifs, forms, and symbols of the Bible and tried to uncover their complex meaning and to observe a pattern in history.

For Puritans (and other Christians as well) the movement of the Israelites in Exodus into a wilderness where they would be tested spiritually was a story "type." In the New Testament, Christ's movement into the wilderness, where he is tested before undergoing his mission, was an "antitype." The Israelites were tested for forty years, Christ for forty days. These types and antitypes were written into the Bible over many centuries to give it a sense of order, to link the Old Testament with the New Testament, and to portray history as a patterned and meaningful process. The Puritans read the Bible to find types and antitypes of this sort, and when they came to America, they brought this understanding with them as the key to the interpretation of their own experience. They saw themselves in precisely these typological terms—they were a chosen people with a special mission, sent into the wilderness to be tested; eventually they would be delivered into a Promised Land. Thus, the American Dream begins in an encounter with the wilderness, not the wilderness of scripture alone, but a wilderness imagined, with the conception that the raw and untamed land of North America was a thing to be conquered, nurtured, worshipped, and made into a new Eden.

These ideas can be observed in the writings of the first Puritan settlers. These colonists did not possess a modern conception of art; they did not see it as a form of human expression predicated on the celebration of the imagination. In fact, they often saw the imagination as a realm of evil, the irrational mind being the place where Satan might enter and corrupt. They viewed writing as a handmaiden to religion, as a way of clarifying and interpreting the Bible. Nevertheless, they produced a remarkable body of literature. There were a number of notable Puritan poets, specifically Anne Bradstreet, Michael Wigglesworth, and Edward Taylor. However, much of the literature of the early American colonies took the form of sermons, journals, and histories, and the richness and beauty of these works serves to challenge the modern notion that literature can only fit the restricted categories of fiction, poetry, and drama. The Puritan writings clarify their preoccupation with typology and special mission.

The first colony began in Plymouth in 1620 with the "separatists" who traveled on board the *Mayflower* and established Plymouth Colony. Their governor was William Bradford, and their purpose was to separate themselves entirely from the English church. Ten years later and a few miles to the north in what became Boston, a larger group of Puritans established Massachusetts Bay Colony. They were dissenting but nonseparating, believing it was their purpose to come to the New World and establish themselves as an example of righteousness that the rest of Europe might follow. It is in the earliest writings of their first governor, John Winthrop, that readers can observe the idea of "special mission," one of the first expressions of American exceptionalism and the American Dream. As the Puritans traveled the Atlantic on board the *Arabella*, Winthrop delivered his sermon "A Model of Christian Charity." Echoing Saint Augustine, Winthrop articulated their purpose in the New World:

> We shall find that the God of Israel is among us, when ten of us shall be able to resist a thousand of our enemies; when He shall make us a praise and glory that men shall say of succeeding plantations, "the Lord make it like that of NEW ENGLAND." For we must consider that we shall be as a city upon a hill. The eyes of all people are upon us. (176–77)

Drawing upon Augustine's notion of the "City of God," Winthrop argued that the Puritan's journey was divinely ordained, an essential part of God's plan for the development of history. They were chosen to be a beacon that would lead the corrupt and decaying Old World into the light of the New. The Americas were a promise in the deepest and most reverential sense, but they were a promise that came with an obligation and a command for absolute devotion. Winthrop and every-one aboard the *Arabella* knew they were traveling into a wilderness. Nothing awaited them but the raw land out of which they would build a colony. However, as devout readers of biblical typology, they would necessarily understand that wilderness as more than wild land. It was a landscape of mind and spirit, a sublime realm through which God would affect their transformation and the transformation of the world.

The wilderness, the frontier, and what was then the West was an ambiguous place. It was a typological wilderness in which transformation was predicated upon a spiritual test. Before it could become a "New Garden," the landscape would confront them as a foreboding realm, a wilderness where evil waited. This first encounter was ordained by God and was an essential part of what would make them ready to do God's work. Like the ancient Israelites, it was an important stage in the journey to the Promised Land.

Two Puritan writers capture this symbolic figuration of the wilderness as a dark element in the early embodiment of the American Dream: Bradford and Mary Rowlandson. Bradford was the first governor of Plymouth Colony. In his history *Of Plymouth Plantation* (published in 1856, but written between 1630 and 1650), he recounts the experiences of the Plymouth settlers, the Puritan separatists that came to New England ten years before the larger group of nonseparating Puritans who migrated with Winthrop to Massachusetts Bay Colony. In his account, Bradford does much more than portray their experiences, he interprets them, and in doing so, he provides a clear articulation of "special mission" as it relates to the American wilderness. He explicitly identifies his followers as a chosen people who are entering a new wilderness. They are all players in a grand drama and the playwright is God himself. God will write the story, and they all must take direction from his guiding hand.

The first act in this grand drama is an encounter with a land full of danger. Bradford begins by establishing a justification for the Calvinist cause, considering the idea of reforming the English church. As a separatist, he believes the endeavor is a lost hope, and he recounts the process by which his people come to this realization. He then moves on to a discussion of "The Reasons and Causes of Their Removal," recounting persecutions in both England and Holland. He uses biblical typology by identifying his people directly with the Hebrews, recounting their voyage to New England and demonstrating the belief that God is actively involved in the lives of his chosen people. In recalling the treatment of the separatists in Europe, he establishes a typological link between them and the ancient Israelites and their persecution by the Egyptians in the book of Exodus before they were delivered by God through Moses. Initially, the separatists fear the wilderness, apprehending the danger:

> The miseries of the land which they should be exposed to, would be too hard to be borne; and likely, some or all of them together, to consume and utterly to ruinate them. For there they should be liable to famine, and nakedness, and the want, in the manner, of all things. (126)

The apprehensions of the Puritan separatists were quite real, but they could only be understood in light of their reading of the wilderness in Exodus. Their motives were religious, their mission divinely ordained. They would confront physical hardship and even the direct confrontation with evil in the form of "savages" who might harm and destroy them. Bradford's history becomes a fairly continuous story of the events in Plymouth Colony during the first thirty years of its existence, as it records their dealings with the Native Americans, and their disputes, during and after the voyage, among themselves and with other colonists. Nonetheless, in all of these historical details, Bradford's interpretation of events is typological and providential. A particularly notable passage occurs in chapter 10, when a loud and obnoxious seaman, who persecutes the Puritans (not everyone who traveled on the *Mayflower* were Puritans), is taken ill and dies. Bradford sees this as God's retribution on an unjust man, stating, "Thus his curses light on his own head, and it was an astonishment to all his fellows for they noted it to be the just hand of God upon him" (131). For Bradford and his Puritan comrades, all events large and small were a part of the tapestry of God's history; their persecution in Europe, their movement into the wilderness, and the moments of persecution and divine intervention they observed along the way were all a part of a plan that could be interpreted typologically. The wilderness that would first confront them as a spiritual and physical ordeal would eventually become the place they would transform into a beautiful new land of righteousness, plenty, and divine ordination. The American Dream, initially an explicitly religious vision, was intimately bound to the idea of a "New Frontier."

Among the Puritans there was one story that most fully embodies the idea of the wilderness as typological: *The Narrative of the Captivity and Restoration of Mrs. Mary Rowlandson* (1682). The actual story is quite simple. On February 20, 1676, Rowlandson was taken captive during an Indian attack on the frontier town of Lancaster, Massachusetts. She was wounded but spared from death, though many others were killed. After she was finally delivered from captivity through a negotiation, she was returned to her family. Later, she tells the story in detailed terms, but in doing so, like Bradford, she sees her experience in providential and typological terms. The historical reality is complicated and, like all wars, morally vexing. The American Indians who captured her were brutal, killing many of their captives, including some of Rowlandson's children. In describing this brutality, Rowlandson tells the truth, but she portrays the Indians as more than combatants in a war; she sees them as the demonic embodiment of evil in a typological wilderness that will test her fortitude and faith. The body of her narrative is structured around the twenty different "Removes," or forced marches, through the wilderness, as the Indians maintain a distance from the Puritan forces in pursuit.

Rowlandson's language reflects her dislike and distrust toward her captors. She refers to them as "black creatures" and "merciless enemies." Undercutting this is a spiritual question: How can the Indians be both the tools of Satan and the tools of God? Given the notion of the wilderness as a realm of transformation, both can be true and there is nothing contradictory. Rowlandson's narrative is one of religious experience. She reads her trial in the same terms as all her Puritan brethren were encouraged to interpret it, as an experience akin to that of the Israelites in Exodus and Christ in the wilderness of temptation. It is an opportunity for redemptive suffering and the embodiment of divine providence. For Rowlandson and most other American Puritans, the wilderness was both a historical experience and a dream in the making. It was not always a pleasant dream, but it was deeply symbolic and central to how they conceived of their future. The frontier was a place that held both danger and promise, a thing to be confronted and transformed into something new, beautiful, and, in the end, redemptive, both for individuals and the new social order they would form.

Over time, the Puritan control of the New England colonies waned. There were always settlers among them who were not Calvinists, people who came for secular or commercial purposes. Nonetheless, throughout the seventeenth century the Puritans controlled the civil body politic. Their control faded over the last half of the century. However, the religious and social values of the Puritans remain influential: in American utilitarian ideals, in the near religious zeal that often attends American nationalism (which is still imbued with a sense of special mission), and in the idea of the Puritan work ethic. However, what is called the "declension," the decline of the political dominance of the Puritans, has much to do with broader intellectual currents that had been present since the European Renaissance but accelerated in the seventeenth century and became a part of the social texture of Europe and America in the eighteenth century. These ideas led to what is called the Enlightenment or the Age of Reason.

The Renaissance of the sixteenth century brought a new emphasis on humanism, a renewed belief in the power of the human mind drawn from the classical age of Greece and Rome. In the ensuing age of Enlightenment, advances in scientific methodology and practice led to a new understanding of the natural world, coupled with the sense that humans were capable of understanding the world more fully than was previously thought possible. The new liberal mindedness did not reject religious belief. Major thinkers of the seventeenth and eighteenth centuries, such as Isaac Newton, René Descartes, and John Locke, were all religious believers in different ways. However, there was a new embrace of human freedom, free will, autonomy, and a sense that human beings could direct the course of history through intellect. It was, in fact, the birth of the modern era and the scientific age.

In the political sphere, the Enlightenment was informed by seventeenth- and eighteenth-century natural-rights theory, the ideas upon which the US Constitution and most modern democracies are based. The notion of natural rights suggests that, as rational creatures, all human beings possess inherent rights that no other human can take away. The "Creator" has made human beings an intelligent species capable of exercising free will through reason, and collectively, humans might expect that they will exercise those capacities to create just societies based upon rational principals. These are the ideas upon which the American Revolution was founded, and in the eighteenth century, the American Dream was layered with secular and democratic ideals. Nonetheless, the American Dream never lost its connection with the frontier and the hope of a physical transformation of American lands, initially on the eastern seaboard and later in the West.

Thomas Jefferson and J. Hector St. John de Crèvecoeur, two writers of the American Enlightenment, most fully conceptualize the American Dream in the eighteenth century as it relates to landscape. Jefferson is best known as the author of the Declaration of Independence and as the third president of the United States, but his ideal for the new nation was built upon an agrarian concept: America was to be an egalitarian democratic society populated mainly by farmers working small plots of land. In fact, he believed that the land itself was a source of human identity, that a close association with the land developed human character and moral sense. He expresses his ideas about the relationship of the individual to the landscape in *Notes on the State of Virginia* (1785). In "Query XIX: Manufactures," he makes a direct claim for the moral superiority of the farmer: "Those who labour in the earth are the chosen people of God, if he ever had a chosen people, whose breasts he has made his peculiar deposit for substantial and genuine virtue" (677). For Jefferson, American lands and the open frontier in the West offered not only the possibility of new economic opportunities for the many settlers migrating to America but also an open space of moral transformation and a new American identity. It would be an identity in which virtue itself, a uniquely American virtue, would emerge from an interaction with pastoral agrarianism, a newly civilized land created out of the wilderness.

Jefferson never lost his sense of American lands as transcendent and distinctive, imbued with a sense of quasireligious significance. In "Query V: Cascades," he describes a setting in Virginia: "The Natural Bridge, the most sublime of Nature's works . . . is on the ascent of a hill, which seems to have cloven through its length by some convulsion. . . . It is impossible for the emotions, arising from the sublime, to be felt beyond what they are here: so beautiful an arch, so elevated, so light, and springing, as it were, up to heaven, the rapture of the spectator is really indescribable" (668). While his most dominant idea of nature is pastoral, his sense of American identity is predicated on the dream of a nation born of the sublime reality of the landscape itself.

In *Letters from an American Farmer* (1782), Crèvecoeur develops similar ideas, indicating that they were not exclusive to Jefferson but were widely held notions. In "Letter III, What Is an American?" he divides America into three regions: the mercantile coasts, the agrarian middle space, and the Western frontier in the mountains. The farmers of the middle space are morally superior; they are conditioned by their working relationship to a pastoral landscape. It is this ethical center that will become essential to the development of American democracy. Like the Puritans, the major writers of the American Enlightenment made the landscape more than literal. It was a region of mind, of dreams, future possibility, and the vision out of which the American Dream would be achieved.

Enlightenment ideals were immeasurably influential and remain so in modern political philosophies, concepts of human rights, and the emphasis on scientific inquiry. In the nineteenth century, they were equally important, and with respect to the response of Americans to the land, they are reflected in a theory of historical process called "stadialism." At the core of Enlightenment notions of reality, all things—the universe, nature, human behavior, and history—proceed according to predictable rules or natural laws. For Enlightenment stadialists (many of them influenced by Scottish Common Sense philosophy), history proceeds through a series of stages or cycles. Historians and philosophers of the period looked into the past and observed certain modes of economic and social arrangement, all related to economics and the relationship of human beings to the land. One common stadialist pattern was the movement from a hunter-gatherer phase to primitive agrarian, advanced agrarian, and mercantile modes of social and economic arrangement.

What might be called the highest form of civilization, and what many Enlightenment thinkers believed Europe and America were progressing toward, was an advanced agrarian civilization with a strong mercantile element. These notions certainly influenced Jefferson and Crèvecoeur, but they also found their way into some of first and most popular American fictions: historical romances. Writers of these novels included William Gilmore Simms, James Kirke Paulding, and Robert Montgomery Bird, but the most popular American historical-romance novelist was James Fenimore Cooper, who wrote the famous Leatherstocking Tales. The series consists of five lengthy novels or "romances" (called romances because they are re-creations in the novel form of ancient, mythic, and heroic epics). The Leatherstocking series consists of *The Pioneers* (1823), *The Last of the Mohicans* (1826), *The Prairie* (1827), *The Pathfinder* (1840), and *The Deerslayer* (1841).

Not unlike the Greek heroes from Homer's *Iliad* (ca. 750 BCE; English translation, 1611) and *Odyssey* (ca. 725 BCE; English translation,

1614), Cooper's characters are larger than life, often defined by valor and military skill, mythic insofar as they represent the virtues of the nation as the population would like to see itself. As mythic characters, they offer a genuine picture of evolving American values and the American Dream. In the Leatherstocking Tales, through the character of Natty Bumppo (often also called Leatherstocking, Hawkeye, Pathfinder, or Deerslayer), readers can see that the basic characteristics of the American hero are initially bound to the country's complex relationship to the frontier and the West.

Bumppo is a white man raised by American Indians. His allegiance is always to the whites, and he refers regularly to his "white gifts," but he also respects his American Indian friends and compatriots, and many of his greatest virtues emerge from his "red gifts," the skills he has acquired because of his intimate relationship with the frontier. It is because he lives on the frontier, has learned of its beauty and its secrets, that he is able to lead settlers into the wilderness and help them reshape it into a new civilization. In the most famous of these romances, *The Last of the Mohicans*, Cooper's inquiry into the role of the frontier in the formation of the American Dream is explored through his portrayal of American Indians, and in that complex rendering of the natives, many contradictions and ambivalent attitudes about the wilderness become apparent.

The Last of the Mohicans is set during the French and Indian War (1754–63) in the prerevolutionary era when the British were at war with the French. Certain American Indians of the Iroquois Confederacy allied with the British, others with the French. Natty is a frontiersman and a British subject. His compatriots are Chingachgook and his son Uncas, members of the Mohican tribe. Their primary enemy among the Americans Indians is Magua, a member of the Huron tribe. Chingachgook, Uncas, and Magua demonstrate a conflicting attitude toward American Indians and, indeed, the shaping influence of the frontier. The villain Magua is avaricious, brutal, and deceptive, reflecting the "savagery" people often associated with the natives. On the other hand, Chingachgook and Uncas are foundational examples of a pattern of characterization as "noble savages"— courageous, virtuous, selfless, and imbued with a mysterious wisdom and ability that can only be achieved through an intimate relationship with the untrammeled wilderness—that continues in most popular literary and cinematic renderings of American Indians.

In creating Natty Bumppo, who becomes the first archetypal American hero, Cooper firmly establishes an American mythology of the frontier. Natty is independent of institutional authority, physically able, hardworking, utilitarian, and skilled in fighting. These basic patterns have formed the substance of most American heroes. In American history, the Founding Fathers—George Washington, Benjamin Franklin, John Adams, and Jefferson, among others—are admired but not often thought of as "heroic" (with the possible exception of Washington). In the most refined sense, American heroes are the characters in American stories or mythology. From the beginning, these heroes have been men of the wilderness such as Natty Bumppo. The basic virtues defined by Cooper find their way into fictional renderings of Western heroes of the nineteenth century such as Davey Crockett, "Buffalo Bill" Cody, James "Wild Bill" Hickok, and later in the novel and film genre of the Western, with cowboys, lawmen, and sometimes even virtuous outlaws. These figures are later translated into characters that are not directly linked to the wilderness or the West but retain their influence; these include the heroes of police dramas and science fiction, men who display the same independence and resistance to authority. What distinguishes them is what distinguishes their prototype in Natty: They at once represent and protect American civilization, but they stand apart as outsiders, fiercely self-defined, unwilling to be bound by any rules they do not participate in creating.

Noting that the roots of American concepts of heroism are derived largely from the romances of Cooper and other writers of his generation, one can see how important the experience of the wilderness and the frontier became in shaping American identity. The American concept of heroic virtue owes much to the historical and imagined relationship to the wilderness, and heroism is certainly at the core of any notion of the American Dream. "Manifest Destiny," an idea popularized during the mid-nineteenth century and one that remains popular, first appeared as a term in the July/August 1845 issue of *United States Magazine and Democratic Review*, in an article entitled "Annexation" by John L. O'Sullivan. Clearly a mid-nineteenth century conception of the American Dream, Manifest Destiny asserted that the United States was destined by God to settle the frontier and expand the reach of democracy. Cooper certainly anticipates this idea in the Leatherstocking Tales.

While Cooper creates the prototype for many affirmative American heroes, his historical romances reflected a genuine moral ambiguity with respect to America's relationship to the land. In *The Prairie*, the third novel written in the series, Natty Bumppo is an old man on the Western plains. Though he has spent his life as a frontiersman advancing the development of white civilization in its move westward, he questions the motives and the effects of that process, as the land is corrupted by the very presence of "civilized" people of various kinds, such as scientists who murder to dissect and businessmen who destroy the beauty of the land for its resources. Even as he celebrates the virtues of civilization, Cooper expresses concern for how Americans relate to the land, how they are sowing the corruption of their own American Dream through greed.

Cooper anticipates a tradition in American nature writing that has exerted a monumental influence on world culture, that is, the writing of American transcendentalists Emerson and Henry David Thoreau. In *Nature* (1836), Emerson firmly links the landscape to an imagined concept of national identity. He argues first that Americans must establish an original relation to the universe and then claims that this relationship should be founded on an understanding that nature itself is an embodiment of the divine. In *Walden; or, Life in the Woods* (1854), his friend and student Thoreau recounts his two years living in relative seclusion on Walden Pond near Concord, Massachusetts. Thoreau writes of the ways in which he has been spiritually and personally enriched by his close connection to nature and the spirit that gives the land its sublime beauty and power. However, in the first chapter, "Economy," he expresses his concern with what is actually happening during his time. People are exploiting nature as the industrial age begins, and they are becoming enslaved by the material possessions they have produced because they are degrading and destroying the natural world. He argues for an ethic of simplicity, asserting that we should moderate our materialist expectations, and learn that nature provides a spiritual and emotional sustenance beyond the physical. Thus, the notion of American "special mission" and the American Dream evolved over time in unpredictable ways. The wilderness, the West, and the frontier are at the heart of America's evolving identity and self-conception.

In the mid- and late twentieth century, a new group of writers took the West as their primary interest. These writers founded what is termed "the literature of the American West." They were—and still are—interested in the ways the American Dream and its relationship to westward expansion has been conceptualized, realized, and, in certain identifiable ways, corrupted, insofar as westward expansion was oftentimes a rapacious and brutal process that decimated the land through economic exploitation that benefited the few.

There are many writers in this evolving tradition, but three of the most notable are Wallace Stegner, Larry McMurtry, and Cormac McCarthy. In *The Big Rock Candy Mountain* (1943), Stegner writes an unflinching and intensely autobiographical account of the early twentieth-century West. He tells the story of Bo Mason, an ill-fated dreamer who takes his family all over the West in the hope of striking it rich. In the process, his wife, Elsa, is broken and never achieves the family stability she desires, and their son Bruce's resentments build to the point of fierce if not violent anger. The American Dream as it relates to westward expansion is seen in all its dark and personally destructive manifestations, as Stegner explores how greed, exploitation, and the desire for wealth had, in part, become the engine of that dream.

Stegner's *Angle of Repose* (1971) won the Pulitzer Prize for Fiction. This novel also considers the consequences of American expansionism and, indeed, the common outcome of the American Dream as it relates to the land. Based on the actual nineteenth-century letters of Mary Hallock Foote, it is the story of retired history professor Lyman Ward, who is an amputee suffering from a debilitating illness. Largely abandoned by his wife and children, he lives alone in his grandmother's home. In an attempt to find meaning and purpose, and to sort out his own troubled circumstances, he reads and studies the letters of his grandmother, Susan Burling Ward, a New York socialite who traveled with her husband, following his oddly misbegotten dream of a new life in the West during late nineteenth century. As Lyman Ward writes her history based on the letters, he explores her experiences and her response to events and circumstances, and a complex history of the West emerges.

The American Dream, shared by both Susan and her husband, is seen as both corrupt and noble. It is corrupt because it is essentially a materialist dream, predicated on the desire for wealth and the willingness to destroy the land to attain it; it is noble in that the dream is never about money alone but the beauty and possibility wealth seems to imply. Susan is an artist and a refined socialite. She appreciates beauty in all its forms. However, to re-create her eastern world in the West requires that it be civilized and exploited. It is in this context that the novel's title comes into play: "Angle of repose" is a geological term to describe the point at which moving soil rests as it rolls down an incline. Through this geological metaphor, Stegner explicitly links the notion of the American Dream to the land. The dream in its original context implied a destination and a goal. In *Angle of Repose*, Susan Burling Ward possesses all the hope, energy, and capacity to achieve that dream. However, as she and her husband pursue their materialist ambitions, her intentions are compromised by the corporate forces present in the West before she arrived; her intentions are equally compromised by her own sometimes selfish desires and actions. She becomes a personification of a dream both beautiful and destructive. In all this, she emerges as an individual of extraordinary strength and resilience, characteristics often associated, appropriately, with those who settled the West. Thus, in Stegner's work, the American Dream is a deeply complex and morally ambiguous ideal.

The same ambiguity and ambivalence appears in the work of McMurtry. Though prolific, he is perhaps best known for two series: the Thalia Trilogy—including *The Last Picture Show* (1966), *Texasville* (1987), and *Duane's Depressed* (1999)—and the *Lonesome Dove* saga, which includes *Lonesome Dove* (1985), *Streets of Laredo* (1993), *Dead Man's Walk* (1995), and *Comanche Moon* (1997). The first two novels of the Thalia Trilogy were adapted into film, the first by Peter Bogdanovich to great critical acclaim. *Lonesome Dove* won the Pulitzer Prize in 1985. For some, this popularity calls into question McMurtry's seriousness as a writer. His writing is at once highly readable and unadorned. However, he sets his stories in his native Texas, taking the region and its unique history as a grand metaphor for the West and, perhaps, the United States. In the Thalia Trilogy, his richly drawn characters contend with the twentieth-century shift from ranching culture to oil culture, and while they are the beneficiaries of the wealth that emerges from these complex economic forces, they are also displaced, reduced, and confused by the ubiquitous influence of corporate America.

Like Stegner, in the context of modern history, McMurtry explores how an American Dream centered on the western frontier is corrupted by economic motives that are often more destructive than productive. Ranching involved a brutal transformation of the land clearly inconsistent with the Puritan ideal of the "New Garden," and oil culture extended that process. These same themes are explored in the *Lonesome Dove* saga. Written in much the same vein as the historical romances of Cooper, these novels involve mythic Western heroes, Texas Rangers, in the nineteenth-century West. What gives the novels their interest, however, is that characters Augustus McCrae and Woodrow Call, though traditional frontier heroes in many ways, are confronted with historical forces they cannot control, and their American Dream, which involves an embrace of personal freedom, autonomy, and an intimate relationship with the land, is challenged and ultimately reduced as they confront the brutality of the land itself, reflected in the historically accurate representation of Comanche and Comancheros. McCrae and Call's idealistic vision is equally compromised as they come to understand that their way of life is giving way to the advance of eastern economic interests. Thus, in McMurtry as well as Stegner, the American Dream is bound to Western landscape, but it is an ideal that is as elusive as it is evocative.

Perhaps one of the most complex, experimental, and philosophically engaged novelists of the contemporary period is Cormac McCarthy. Though his first four novels were set in the South, his later works, *Blood Meridian: Or the Evening Redness in the West* (1985) and the Border Trilogy, which includes *All the Pretty Horses* (1992), *The Crossing* (1994), and *Cities of the Plain* (1998), are set in the Southwest. Though McCarthy was renowned in artistic circles for decades, winning many awards and the coveted MacArthur Fellowship, he became generally known to the public and, indeed, to the academic community, only after the publication of *All the Pretty Horses*, which won the National Book Award in 1992. He has come to be considered one of the greatest American novelists of the later twentieth century, and a 2006 *New York Times* poll of academics and intellectuals judged *Blood Meridian* as one of the best American novels of the previous twenty-five years. Interestingly, upon publication, the novel received mixed reviews from critics, primarily because of its unflinching portrayal of the violence that attended westward expansion.

Loosely based on a historical account by Samuel Chamberlain entitled *My Confession: The Recollections of a Rogue*, *Blood Meridian* recounts the experiences of a fourteen-year-old boy who has unwittingly joined a band of scalp hunters who kill Indians for money and often murder Mexicans in the process. At the center of the narrative is the demonic Judge Holden, who professes a philosophy of violence, proclaiming that "war is God" (249). Through the judge, McCarthy explores the source and nature of violence in the universe, and the novel transcends region in its deep philosophical and religious concerns. However, in its identifiable location in the West, on the American frontier, *Blood Meridian* becomes one of the most vivid and unsettling portrayals of westward expansion, reflecting both the beauty, brutality, and sublimity of the land and the human cost of its destruction. In McCarthy's novel, the concepts of a "New Garden" and a "pastoral middle-space," both early notions of the American Dream that centered on the positive transformation of the landscape and the frontier, are replaced with a historically accurate rendering of murder and exploitation. Like Stegner and McMurtry, as a late twentieth-century novelist who takes the American Dream and the West as a primary focus, McCarthy crystallizes the complex and morally ambiguous relationship of American ideals and American landscape.

From the Puritans to the moderns, the American Dream is a tangible force in the development of national identity, and it is frequently bound to nature. Puritans read into the lands they encountered the meaning derived from their most sacred texts. The land was the embodiment of hope and possibility that transcended economics. It was a landscape of interiors and exteriors, a place to live and an ultimate and indescribably beautiful destination of the spirit. Enlightenment thinkers were more grounded in the desire to transform human society for the greater good, predicated on the notion of an agrarian utopia. Later authors began to reveal underlying motives predicated on human avarice and greed, motives that tend to compromise any human aspiration, though in doing so these writers never reject the dream entirely. Beautiful and destructive, the American Dream commands respect, a certain reverence, and an equal measure of critical scrutiny, since it seems to form much of the essential substance of the nation's dynamic history and, presumably, its future.

Works Cited

Bradford, William. *"Of Plymouth Plantation." The Norton Anthology of American Literature.* Ed Nina Baym, et al. Vol. A. 8th ed. New York: Norton, 2012. 122–56. Print.

Cooper, James Fenimore. *The Last of the Mohicans.* 1826. New York: Scribner's, 1986. Print.

Fitzgerald, F. Scott. *The Great Gatsby.* New York: Scribner's, 1925. Print.

Jefferson, Thomas. "Notes on the State of Virginia." *The Norton Anthology of American Literature.* Vol. A. 8th ed. New York: Norton, 2012. 668–77. Print.

McCarthy, Cormac. *Blood Meridian: Or the Evening Redness in the West.* New York: Random, 1985. Print.

McMurtry, Larry. *Lonesome Dove.* New York: Simon, 1985. Print.

Stegner, Wallace. *Angle of Repose.* Garden City, NY: Doubleday, 1971. Print.

___. *The Big Rock Candy Mountain.* 1943. New York: Penguin, 1991. Print.

Winthrop, John. "A Model of Christian Charity." *The Norton Anthology of American Literature.* Vol. A. 8th ed. New York: Norton, 2012. 166–77. Print.

Dreiser and the Dream _____

Roark Mulligan

As a young man, Theodore Dreiser (1871–1945) read rags-to-riches stories in which young boys worked hard, behaved morally, and achieved one version of the American Dream—wealth. As young women, his sisters read sentimental romances in which young women valiantly maintained their virtue, so they could eventually marry honorable men who could provide them with another version of the dream—a home and children. These popular fictions contrasted dramatically with Dreiser's and his family's experiences. His father (a German immigrant, a skilled weaver, and a religious man) married, had thirteen children, worked hard, and eventually became the manager and part owner of a woolen mill; however, two years before Theodore's birth, a fire at the mill bankrupted the family and a falling beam disabled the elder Dreiser, and the family never fully recovered from the setback. Eventually, Dreiser's parents separated, and the older children left home.

Growing up in poverty, Dreiser suffered a sense of shame and betrayal that shaped all of his writing. In his first two novels, *Sister Carrie* (1900) and *Jennie Gerhardt* (1911), Dreiser drew on his sisters' experiences, realistically exploring the struggles of young women to achieve dreams that were out of their reach. In his *Trilogy of Desire*—consisting of *The Financier* (1912), *The Titan* (1914), and *The Stoic* (1947)—Dreiser narrates the life of Frank Algernon Cowperwood, a robber baron who, like F. Scott Fitzgerald's Jay Gatsby, achieves some version of the American Dream but is never fully satisfied. And in his masterpiece, *An American Tragedy* (1925), Dreiser traces the brief life of Clyde Griffiths, a young man not unlike himself, whose desperate chase of the American Dream (wealth, social success, and marriage) destroys him and his pregnant girlfriend. In all eight of his novels and in his often-anthologized short stories "Free" (1918), "The Second Choice" (1918), and "Typhoon" (1927), Dreiser portrays characters who seek versions of the American Dream through marriage and hard work, but who find misery or disappointment in a world that does not offer permanent happiness.

In his fiction, Dreiser invokes then reverses the melodramatic narratives of this youth, showing that those who blindly pursue idealistic dreams experience brutal nightmares. The influence of these early romances is detailed in his autobiography *Dawn* (1931), where Dreiser describes himself as a child devouring the serialized stories that appeared weekly in popular magazines:

> I began to read with interest *The Family Story Paper*, *The Fireside Companion* and *The New York Weekly*, all romantic periodicals which flourished at that time and sample copies of which were thrown over our fence almost weekly. Finding one lying on our front lawn one day, I picked it up and began reading one of those dramatic introductions by which the reader is lured to "continue in our next." Forthwith I was lost. . . . Having from either my mother or Paul extracted the required nickels, I proceeded every Friday or Saturday to the nearest news-stand to purchase, as might a drug addict, this latest delight. (125)

With the boys of the neighborhood, he also read Horatio Alger's serialized adventures, *Brave and Bold*, *Luck and Pluck*, *Work and Win*, stories in which heroic young men travelled the globe on righteous quests, achieving their dreams through good deeds. These narratives caused Dreiser to dream, to wish for a new life away from the poverty and shame of his home, but "practical considerations arose and interfered—money for one thing; parting from mother, Ed and others of the family" (*Dawn* 126). The contrast between his own life and the lives of his fictional heroes caused Dreiser to realize that the American Dream described in romantic narratives as a reward for good behavior did not exist, at least not for himself and his siblings. He read of successful individuals in the newspapers, but he came to realize that they triumphed because they had natural talent or luck, because they bribed or blackmailed others, or because of a thousand other factors that favored them, and they failed because they lacked these same advantages. Growing up in the late 1800s, Dreiser witnessed dramatic social, spiritual, scientific, and economic shifts, changes that intensified his desire for the American Dream, but he also came to realize that the dream, as presented in popular fiction, was based on two conditions that assumed free will: Individuals can improve their lives if they work hard and remain moral; and individuals can control their destinies if they virtuously persevere. In *Mechanism and Mysticism: The Influence of Science on the Thought and Work of Theodore Dreiser*, Louis Zanine describes Dreiser's complicated view of free will: "Although Dreiser asserts that the development of free will is progressing at the present stage of evolution, his description of human behavior in the future is very deterministic" (43). Realizing that some work hard and fail, that some cheat and succeed, and that all who succeed or fail can only partially, if at all, control their own destiny, he wrote fiction that empathetically depicts characters from all walks life (the rich and the poor, the strong and the weak, the gifted and the unfortunate) who struggle but ultimately fail to gain a lasting happiness.

As early as 1932, literary critic Clifton Fadiman recognized the American Dream as a central theme or motif running through Dreiser's fiction. In his essay "Dreiser and the American Dream," Fadiman argues that a personal fear of poverty, a desire for wealth and success, a wish for respectability, and a dread of humiliation drive and inform Dreiser's writing—the difficult conditions into which Dreiser was born caused him to focus on the American Dream, as both a desired goal and an unattainable and possibly harmful fantasy. In all his fiction, Dreiser empathetically depicts characters who, like himself, seek the American Dream, but he also reveals the extent to which these individuals are part of what he often called an "equation inevitable," a universe with forces that prevent them, or anyone, from achieving a permanent dream state.

Sister Carrie

Based on the life of his sister Emma, Dreiser's novel *Sister Carrie* (1900) was a revolutionary work that received little attention until it was republished in 1907. A brutally realistic narrative that broke from the popular formulas of romantic and sentimental literature, the novel presents and questions traditional values as depicted in popular fiction, ultimately undermining the premises on which the American Dream depends. In the opening scene, Caroline "Carrie" Meeber, a young woman of eighteen years, leaves her family and her rural hometown of Columbia City, Wisconsin, for opportunities in the big city of Chicago. Living at first with her sister Minnie and her brother-in-law Sven Hanson, Carrie, after a difficult search, gains employment in a shoe factory for $4.50 a week. The inhumane factory conditions and the drudgery of her sister's life cause Carrie to question both marriage and hard work, the two means by which young men and women in sentimental romances were supposed to gain the American Dream. With her meager weekly salary, Carrie can pay room and board to her sister, but no money remains for other expenses: winter clothes, streetcar fare, or entertainment. On the streets of Chicago, when she encounters Charles Drouet, a gregarious salesman she had met on the train from Wisconsin, Carrie abandons traditional values by accepting a twenty-dollar loan: "Carrie left him, feeling as though a great arm had slipped out before her to draw off trouble. The money she had accepted was two soft, green, handsome ten-dollar bills" (45).

This pivotal scene appears early in the novel and signals a new literary realism that honestly explores the forces that buffeted young women as they adjusted to city life. With twenty dollars, Carrie can pay her rent, purchase clothing, buy food, and ride the streetcar, but this simple monetary exchange violates the morals promulgated by sentimental novels. Given ostensibly as a loan, this money obligates Carrie to Drouet, an obligation that Drouet wishes to develop into a sexual relationship. In essence, Carrie, not by working hard or living virtuously, secures a small portion of the American Dream (wealth, clothing, luxuries) from a male admirer who is not considering marriage. In rejecting her sister's life of toil, Carrie abandons not the American Dream but the means to that dream that sentimental novels expounded.

Besides new clothes, fine dinners, and entertainment, Drouet eventually offers Carrie a comfortable apartment—a dream that she could not achieve through virtue or hard work. Because Carrie turns to Drouet, not as a wife but as a mistress, the novel shocked early readers. If Dreiser had based *Sister Carrie* on the sentimental novel formula, then a young woman such as Carrie who abandons her virtue and the Puritan work ethic, a young woman who chooses luxury and comfort, not morality, should die before the narrative ends, as occurs in other realistic works of the period, such as Stephen Crane's *Maggie: A Girl of the Streets* (1893) and Kate Chopin's *The Awakening* (1899). This moralistic formula and its reversal have been analyzed frequently by critics such as Leslie Fiedler, whose work *Love and Death in the American Novel* details Dreiser's embrace and subsequent rejection of sentimental ideals. Carrie's youth and goods looks, not her virtue and hard work, are her means to the dream. As the narrative develops, Carrie exchanges Drouet for George Hurstwood, a married man who is the successful manager of a popular saloon. Obsessed with Carrie's youth and beauty, Hurstwood steals money from his employer, leaves his family, and tricks Carrie into boarding an eastbound train. Eventually, the couple settles in New York City, where Hurstwood slowly fails, eventually committing suicide. But in New York, Carrie succeeds as an actress, attaining wealth and fame and independence.

By the end of the novel, Dreiser introduces and dismisses almost every imaginable version of the American Dream: rural village life, a career, marriage, success, wealth, and fame. Though living in a luxurious hotel, though possessing all the money she will every need, though loved by fans, Carrie remains alone and unfulfilled, as the narrator emphasizes in the final sentence of the novel: "In your rocking-chair, by your window, shall you dream such happiness as you may never feel" (355). After reading *Sister Carrie*, we should wonder if the

American Dream is possible. Does Carrie represent the human condition? Are we all doomed to dream but never to be satisfied? Dreiser presents the American Dream as a mirage that takes many forms but vanishes as Carrie approaches each one. In the final chapters, Dreiser introduces one more version of the dream, one personified by Robert Ames, a handsome and intelligent inventor from Indianapolis, Indiana, Dreiser's home state. Ames helps Carrie to imagine a new life, one that allows her to use her talents altruistically, but Carrie fails to comprehend his vision. For Ames, happiness, a part of the American Dream, can be achieved if one dedicates one's life and one's work to others, and he tries to convince Carrie that this might be possible for an actress, but the novel ends with Carrie longing for an unknown dream that she will never realize.

Since it republication in 1907, *Sister Carrie* has been widely read and analyzed, because the novel was the first to represent and honestly question so many versions of the American Dream, versions that had appeared as moral absolutes in previous fiction. On the first page of the novel, when Carrie leaves small-town America, she is leaving behind a life that for much of our history had represented the American ideal, an ideal represented by the citizen farmer and described by Thomas Jefferson as the moral and economic backbone of the country, an ideal that Dreiser himself grew up admiring. Living in small Indiana towns, Dreiser viewed successful village inhabitants as possessing the social standing that his family lacked. His first wife, Sara White, represented this ideal—her home and family in rural Missouri illustrated this version of the dream well, and in his autobiography, *Newspaper Days*, Dreiser describes how this home affected him and his concept of marriage. In Dreiser's mind, the White's family farm signified the traditions described in the song "My Old Kentucky Home" (551), and this romantic ideal offered security and happiness that his family lacked: "To be married, to have your beloved with you, to have a charming home to return to of an evening or at any hour, sick or well" (400).

In *Virgin Land: The American West as Symbol and Myth*, Henry Nash Smith describes the extent to which our concepts of rural life have symbolized the American Dream: "The image of this vast and constantly growing agricultural society in the interior of the continent became one of the dominant symbols of nineteenth-century American society—a collective representation, a poetic idea . . . that defined the promise of American life" (123). But in the first chapter of Dreiser's novel, Carrie, leaving the village for the big city, turns her back on these ideals, as did Dreiser, never to return, not even to visit her family. In this early scene, Dreiser briefly depicts a revolt from American village life, a revolt that writers who followed Dreiser, such as Sherwood Anderson and Sinclair Lewis, would develop into a modern literary theme.

As a resident of large American cities like Chicago and New York, Carrie accepts her role as a mistress and her later career as an actress, dismissing marriage as a woman's only means to the American Dream. Like Edith Wharton, who was also writing during this period, Dreiser exposes marriage, for men and women, as only one possible means to the dream, one that usually fails and that should often be avoided. In *Psychological Politics of the American Dream: The Commodification of Subjectivity in Twentieth-Century American Literature*, Lois Tyson analyzes the extent to which authors such as Wharton and Dreiser deconstruct the sentimental linkage of marriage and the American Dream: "Women are represented as marriage commodities who sell themselves to the highest bidder in their attempt to move up the American dream's socioeconomic ladder" (17). In Dreiser's fiction, this sale of the self in marriage or in other, less traditional relationships promises wealth or comfort but rarely delivers the dream that was promised. For example, in *Jennie Gerhardt*, Dreiser's second novel, the author again draws on the experiences of his sisters and his family, exploring the financial pressures that force women, such as Jennie and Carrie, to abandon both marriage and conventional morals. Like Carrie, Jennie becomes a wealthy, independent woman, achieving material success, but neither character does this through marriage and neither is presented as happy, nor as achieving the American Dream; both remain perplexed by life and longing for something more.

In the last thirty years, *Sister Carrie* has been analyzed as a novel that represents and embraces a developing consumer economy in which individuals seek happiness or define their worth through possessions and luxuries. In his influential work *The Gold Standard and the Logic of Naturalism: American Literature at the Turn of the Century*, critic Walter Benn Michaels argues that the novel reveals the materialist aspects of the American Dream: "The power of *Sister Carrie*, then, arguably the greatest American realist novel, derives not from its scathing 'picture' of capitalist 'conditions' but from its unabashed and extraordinarily literal acceptance of the economy that produced those conditions" (35). In his depiction of a modern urban economy, Dreiser accepts and realistically depicts the material and economic conditions that confront his characters, but in Carrie's unhappiness, despite her fame and wealth, Dreiser portrays her as a character who wins the game, who achieves success, but who has not found her dream; thus Dreiser questions modern consumerism as a means to happiness. Like Carrie at the end of the novel, we are left without a clear sense of what the American Dream might be or how we might achieve it, for Dreiser questions both the means by which individuals pursue their dreams and the dreams themselves.

Trilogy of Desire

In three of his eight novels, *The Financier* (1912), *The Titan* (1914), and *The Stoic* (1947), Dreiser, in minute detail, explores the dreams of a single financier, Frank Algernon Cowperwood, a character based on an American robber baron named Charles Tyson Yerkes. In explaining why Dreiser, a naturalist who empathetically portrayed the struggling poor, turned his literary gaze to a wealthy capitalist, Donald Goodfellow, in his critical essay "Theodore Dreiser and the American

Dream," looks to Dreiser's youth, when the author was reading rag-to-riches stories: "From childhood Dreiser had longed for better things for himself; but at the same time that he envied and admired the wealthy and the strong, he sympathized with the poor and the weak" (55). Throughout the three Cowperwood novels that Dreiser referred to as his *Trilogy of Desire*, he represents and questions versions of the American Dream and the means by which one achieves these dreams, focusing on the financial successes that he found in Horatio Alger's stories. In this trilogy, he traces Cowperwood's life from his youth and early financial adventures in Philadelphia, to his development and consolidation of the Chicago streetcar system, to his expansion of the London Underground, and finally to his death in New York City. Alternating between Cowperwood's business and romantic adventures, the novels explore the connection between the financier's private and public life. He marries twice, leaving his first wife and children for the teenage daughter of a business partner, then leaving her for an even younger woman, pursuing women as boldly as he pursues money and art.

Cowperwood's motto is "I satisfy myself," which he does, and with his wealth he enjoys every luxurious and hedonistic activity that he can imagine. So we might say that he achieves the American Dream by amassing the riches necessary to supply every good and service desired, and that he achieves all this through hard work, one means to the dream, but not through virtuous behavior, the second means that appears in all rags-to-riches narratives. Cowperwood is born a child of fortune in an environment where his skills serve him well—life favors him: "He was a financier by instinct, and all the knowledge that pertained to that great art was as natural to him as the emotions and subtleties of life are to a poet" (12). In these novels, Dreiser realistically depicts the unconventional means (bribery, fraud, betrayal) by which Cowperwood amasses the money to "satisfy himself." Even criminal activity does not retard his pursuit of the dream: At one point in the narrative, Cowperwood is arrested for fraud and spends over three years in jail, only to emerge more powerful and more successful than before.

In American society during the Gilded Age, Dreiser witnessed the conflation of wealth and success with virtue and happiness. He saw the American Dream personified by robber barons such as J. P. Morgan, Andrew Carnegie, and Charles T. Yerkes, and in his financial fiction Dreiser realistically represents their success, but he also truthfully questions and reveals the means by which their success was achieved and the unhappiness that even the most successful experienced. For the business magazine *Success*, Dreiser regularly conducted interviews with wealthy men, including Andrew Carnegie, who espoused Horatio Alger's morality and who insisted that hard work and virtuous behavior brought them wealth, but Dreiser felt that these men achieved their success by other means. In *The Financier*, as a young man, Cowperwood gains wealth and happiness through marriage and financial dealings, but his business schemes require bribery, collusion, and fraud if they are to succeed. Involving his father and his father's bank in his financial manipulations, Cowperwood eventually destroys their reputation—his father is forced to resign his position as bank president and live in shame. In his business relationships with others, Cowperwood, as a financier, is always competing, always looking for an advantage, always betraying or being betrayed. To achieve his dreams, he must sacrifice traditional values, the virtues that sentimental stories posited as the only means to success.

In the end, despite all his success, Cowperwood dies without having accomplished his goals and, after his death, his fortune, which was intended to build a hospital for the poor and a museum for his great art collection, is lost, devoured by a market crash, legal fees, and court settlements. Like Carrie, Cowperwood realizes early that the means to achieve the American Dream are not those that one encounters in sentimental novels, and Cowperwood, despite achieving great material success, understands that he will not ultimately gain what he desires—true happiness seems ever out of his reach. During his life, there are moments when he is truly happy, but during these moments, Cowperwood is chasing the dream, not possessing it, and the chase must eventually end. In the final chapter of *The Financier*, the first novel of the trilogy, when Cowperwood is still young and wealthy, Dreiser summons the three witches from Shakespeare's *Macbeth*, and they foretell Cowperwood's future: "'Hail to thee, Frank Cowperwood, master and no master, prince of a world of dreams whose reality was sorrow!'" (555). The great financier will gain what many imagine to be the American Dream, but he will remain unhappy, and he will die without securing his legacy. As the historical commentary for the Dreiser Edition of *The Financier* notes, the trilogy is not a success story: "*The Financier* is an epic tragedy that ends with witches falsely promising an immortality that Cowperwood and other robber barons could achieve by unscrupulously amassing unprecedented fortunes" (573). Dreiser shows that the American Dream of wealth can be achieved, but that this does not secure lasting happiness or a meaningful legacy. For Dreiser, the dream is in some sense based on a false premise, on the idea that any state of existence might last forever. The America Dream presumes agency, opportunity, and free will, but Dreiser assumed that change is inevitable, that unknown forces govern our actions, and that an "equation inevitable" brings the high low and the low high, as he explained in an essay of the same name published in his 1920 collection *Hey-Rub-a-Dub-Dub*.

In his essay "The American Financier," collected in the same volume, Dreiser describes the traits of an American robber baron, a figure fully developed only in the United States. Calling this individual the "genus financier," as though the robber baron is a separate species, he describes him in detail as both a negative and positive force:

Often humorless, shark-like, avid, yet among the greatest constructive forces imaginable; absolutely opposed to democracy in practice, yet as useful an implement for its accomplishment as for autocracy; either ignorant or contemptuous of ethical niceties as related to thine and mine, yet a stickler for all that concerns mine; moral and immoral sexually— both types abound; narrow to all but an infinitesimal line in nearly all that relates to the humanities as applied to individuals; wise and generous in the matter of large, even universal benefactions, yet guilty of the meanest subterfuge where their own interests are concerned; and seeking always to perpetuate their own fame. (74)

Dreiser's Cowperwood is a perfect example of the "genus financier," a man who unapologetically seeks his version of the American Dream with an intensity that few could emulate or imagine; and in the end, one might question his methods and whether he achieved what he wanted, but one cannot deny that he was driven by a dream. For Dreiser, Cowperwood is not necessarily corrupt or immoral, because his actions helped to develop great cities. Without individuals who pursue dreams, whether they accomplish them or not, civilization would not exist. In his analysis of Dreiser's financial fiction, critic David Zimmerman recognizes this drive to dream and create, a drive that financiers exemplify so well: "In Dreiser's naturalist panic novel *The Financier* (1912), financial behavior, no matter how self-serving, corrupt, or predatory, does not morally incriminate individuals; it merely expresses individuals' natural drive to satisfy their wants and accumulate power and profit" (35).

Like Charles Foster Kane in the iconic film *Citizen Kane* (1941), Cowperwood personifies the American Dream and the idea that one can better oneself, a theme that authors employ throughout our literature, from Benjamin Franklin to James Fenimore Cooper, Dreiser, Willa Cather, F. Scott Fitzgerald, and beyond. We might even argue that this ability to work hard and rise is identified as a particularly American trait and that this trait is represented and admired in our cultural works. But these authors, especially Dreiser, depict the reverse, the process that strips one of everything that one has achieved.

An American Tragedy and the Short Stories

Often considered Dreiser's masterpiece, *An American Tragedy* (1925) explores the dreams and nightmares of Clyde Griffiths, a young man from a poor religious family, not unlike Dreiser. In his analysis of the novel, literary critic Richard Lehan praises the work as a "supreme narrative achievement," in that Dreiser "reveal[s] the innocent dreamer caught in a web of antithetical forces" (169). In fact we might think of Clyde as an insect trapped within a web of desires, seeking various aspects of the American Dream: wealth, romance, fame, social standing, and happiness. Despite repeatedly pursuing that which his society values, Clyde, again and again, finds himself lost and excluded. The novel opens with Clyde, a boy of twelve, and his family proselytizing on the streets of Kansas City, attempting to attract lost souls to their storefront mission. Repelled by his parents' poverty and religion, Clyde quits school and begins a series of jobs, first as an assistant in a drug store and then as a bellboy at the magnificent Green-Davidson Hotel, where the red bellhop uniform with its brass buttons impresses him as a sign of social and economic advancement. The salary at this job allows him to purchase a new suit of clothes and other incidentals, so on his days off he can socialize with coworkers, enjoying restaurants and occasional dates. As a bellhop at this fine hotel, he observes the wealthy and their habits, learning the social skills that will allow him to pursue his dreams of money, romance, and social advancement; however, during an automobile outing with a group of friends, he is involved in an accident that kills a child, forcing Clyde to flee Kansas City. Settling in Chicago and working at the prestigious Union League Club, again as a bellhop, he encounters his wealthy eastern uncle, Samuel Griffiths, who offers Clyde employment at his shirt and collar factory in upstate New York. After moving to the small manufacturing town of Lycurgus, Clyde works first on the manufacturing line and then as a foreman, slowly realizing that his relationship to the wealthy Griffiths grants him an improved social stature and the opportunity for professional advancement. As the head of a small department, Clyde, lonely and isolated, develops a clandestine relationship with one of his workers, Roberta Alden, the daughter of a poor farmer, but their relationship violates a company rule that prohibits fraternization.

Because he is polite, young, and handsome, and because he looks like his wealthy cousin Gilbert, Clyde is eventually invited to social events where he meets Sondra Finchley, the daughter of a wealthy Lycurgus manufacturer. As their relationship develops, offering Clyde the prospect of acquiring the ultimate American Dream (marriage, social standing, and wealth), he learns that Roberta is pregnant and expecting marriage. Reading of an accidental drowning in the newspaper, Clyde devises a plan that involves the promise of marriage, an elopement, and Roberta's drowning. At a local lake resort, Clyde rents a boat and rows Roberta to a secluded spot where the couple struggles—Roberta then falls overboard and drowns. Although Clyde is clearly responsible for her death, the degree of his responsibility is never fully known, and not even Clyde completely understands his culpability. Eventually, he is arrested, tried, and executed.

For years before writing the novel, Dreiser collected news accounts of young men who killed their pregnant lovers to advance socially, including the case on which the novel is based, the murder of Grace Brown by Chester Gillette. For Dreiser, this case and others like it represent a uniquely American tragedy, one that occurred because young men desperately attempt to gain some form of the American Dream through an advantageous marriage. Dreiser believed that these tragedies concretely revealed the dangers of sentimental novels and Horatio Alger's adventures, stories that encouraged young, virtuous men to chase unrealistic goals and to expect spectacular rewards. If Clyde had a fault, it was that he strove too hard to be successful according to the metrics set by his society. His murder of Roberta and his unborn child is not solely an antisocial act. In an essay that Dreiser wrote to explain and analyze his own novel, titled "I Find the Real American Tragedy," he explicates the extent to which Clyde embraces the dreams and values of his society: "This was really not an *anti-social* dream as Americans should see it, but rather a *pro-social* dream. *He was really doing the kind of thing which Americans should and would have said was the wise and moral thing for him to do had he not committed a murder*"

(297). Clyde dreams of wealth, success, and social acceptance, cultural values that Dreiser desired, and the easiest, fastest way to achieve these social prizes was through marriage.

As a young man in the 1890s, long before he wrote *An American Tragedy*, Dreiser lamented the fact that wealthy American women were not interested in marrying poor but promising young geniuses such as himself. In one editorial for *Ev'ry Month*, a music magazine that Dreiser edited for his brother, he laments the fact that young American heiresses marry European royalty and, in another column, he bluntly concludes that young, talented American men such as himself, will "suffer, repine, and die" without the aid of a "beautiful, sympathetic girl" (94). For Clyde, Sondra is that sympathetic girl, who can deliver his American Dream through marriage, and he imagines that Roberta, his pregnant girlfriend, is the only obstacle to happiness. If required to marry Roberta, Clyde imagines a life of poverty, drudgery, and pain— this marriage would "force him to do something which would be little less than social, artistic, passional or emotional assassination" (*American Tragedy* II: 9). On the other hand, he imagines marriage to Sondra as a guarantee of the American Dream.

Several years before writing *An American Tragedy*, in a 1919 interview titled "Dreiser Favors Federal Control; Hits Financiers," published in the *Huntington Press* newspaper in Indiana, Dreiser argued that America is represented in fiction as a land of promise where anyone can achieve the dream, where anyone can be a millionaire or president of the United States, but that this dream, for most, is a false promise, a dangerous delusion: "That idea is a myth. . . . Why the rank and file of the people of this nation have no chance under the sun of ever becoming a Rockefeller, unless one of them is a heaven-born genius or a brilliant crook" (64). In *An American Tragedy*, whether running from an accident or from a pregnant fiancée, Clyde's problems develop because he believes that he can achieve the American Dream, even if this entails covering up the death of a child or murdering a girlfriend. By the end of *An American Tragedy*, before his execution, Clyde begins

Cullen, Jim. *The American Dream: A Short History of an Idea That Shaped a Nation.* Oxford: Oxford UP, 2003. Print.

Delbanco, Andrew. The Real American Dream: A Meditation on Hope. Cambridge: Harvard UP, 1999. Print.

Dreiser, Theodore. *An American Tragedy.* 2 vols. New York: Boni & Liveright, 1925. Print.

___. "Dreiser Favors Federal Control; Hits Financiers." *Huntington Press* [Indiana] 18 June 1919: 1. Rpt. in *Theodore Dreiser: Interviews.* Eds. Frederic E. Rusch and Donald Pizer. Urbana: U of Illinois P, 2004. 63–64. Print.

___. *The Financier.* Ed. Roark Mulligan. Urbana: U of Illinois P, 2010. Print.

___. *Hey Rub-a-Dub-Dub: A Book of the Mystery and Wonder and Terror of Life.* New York: Boni & Liveright, 1920. Print.

___. "I Find the Real American Tragedy." *Mystery Magazine* 11 (1935): 9–11, 88–90. Rpt. in *Theodore Dreiser: A Selection of Uncollected Prose.* Detroit: Wayne State UP, 1977. Print.

___. "Free." *Free and Other Stories.* New York: Boni & Liveright, 1918. Print.

___. *Jennie Gerhardt.* Ed. James L. W. West III. Philadelphia: U of Pennsylvania P, 1992. Print.

___. *Newspaper Days.* Ed. T. D. Nostwich. Philadelphia: U of Pennsylvania P, 1991. Print.

___. "Reflections." *Ev'ry Month* (May 1896). Rpt. in *Theodore Dreiser's Ev'ry Month.* Ed. Nancy Warner Barrineau. Athens: U of Georgia P, 1996. 41–44. Print.

___. "The Second Choice." *Free and Other Stories.* New York: Boni & Liveright, 1918. Print.

___. *Sister Carrie.* Ed. Donald Pizer. New York: Norton, 2006. Print.

___. "Typhoon." *Chains: Lesser Novels and Stories by Theodore Dreiser.* New York: Boni & Liveright, 1927. Print.

Fadiman, Clifton. "Dreiser and the American Dream." *Nation* 135.3511 (1932): 135–351. Print.

Fiedler, Leslie. *Love and Death in the American Novel.* New York: Criterion, 1960. Print.

Goodfellow, Donald M. "Theodore Dreiser and the American Dream." *Six Novelists.* Ed. Norman Knox. Pittsburgh: Carnegies Inst. of Technology, 1959. Print.

Lehan, Richard. *Theodore Dreiser: His World and His Novels.* Carbondale: Southern Illinois UP, 1969. Print.

Michaels, Walter Benn. *The Gold Standard and the Logic of Naturalism: American Literature at the Turn of the Century.* Berkeley: U of California P, 1987. Print.

Parrington, Vernon L. *American Dreams: A Study of American Utopias.* Providence: Brown UP, 1947. Print.

Pizer, Donald. *The Novels of Theodore Dreiser: A Critical Study.* Minneapolis: U of Minneapolis P, 1976. Print.

Ringer, Robert J. *Restoring the American Dream: The Defining Voice in the Movement for Liberty.* New York: Wiley, 2010. Print.

Shestakov, Vyacheslav P. "American Dream and American Culture." *The Origins and Originality of American Culture*. Ed. Tibor Frank. Budapest: Akademiai Kiado, 1984. 583–590. Print.

Smith, Henry Nash. *Virgin Land: The American West as Symbol and Myth*. Cambridge: Harvard UP, 1950. Print.

Trilling, Lionel. *The Liberal Imagination*. New York: New York Review of Books Classics, 2008. Print.

Tyson, Lois. *Psychological Politics of the American Dream: The Commodification of Subjectivity in Twentieth-Century American Literature*. Columbus: Ohio State U, 1994. Print.

Zanine, Louis J. *Mechanism and Mysticism: The Influence of Science on the Thought and Work of Theodore Dreiser*. Philadelphia: U of Pennsylvania P, 1993. Print.

Zimmerman, David A. *Panic! Markets, Crises, and Crowds in American Fiction*. Chapel Hill: U of North Carolina P, 2006. Print.

The Great Gatsby and the American Dream _____

James Nagel

After a rather inauspicious early reception, F. Scott Fitzgerald's *The Great Gatsby* (1925) has come to enjoy a position as one of the most widely read American novels of the twentieth century. In a sense, this august position is remarkable, in that the book does not involve heroism in war, remarkable achievement in humanistic enterprise, or the fulfillment of romance, standard fare for highly popular fiction. Rather, it is a story about failure and death, an idealistic quest for unworthy goals, and the almost total collapse of the aspirations of nearly all of the principal characters. Jay Gatsby lies dead at the end, mourned by his father, his neighbor Nick Carraway, and almost no one else. The narrator and, in an important sense, the protagonist, Nick has returned to the Midwest at the time of the narration, and he speaks with a tone of ironic detachment and bitter disillusionment about the events of two years before, when he left his home in Minnesota to head east to make his fortune in the bond market. He thought he was chasing the American Dream, the central mythological structure at the heart of life in the New World the Puritans established. His objective proved not only elusive but destructive, a depraved goal certain to yield an outwardly successful appearance concealing an empty core of superficial values.

The central problem in this plot is not that the quest for the American Dream is in some way fundamentally destructive, but rather that the version of it sought by Gatsby and Nick is a degraded corruption of the idea, a formulation that reduces the objective to money and to social status based on surface riches, not on the more fulfilling aspects of the original conception. When John Winthrop spelled out the basic principles of what became known as the American Dream in his 1630 sermon "A Model of Christian Charity," it presented his vision of a perfect society bound together by love and mutual respect, by religious devotion, and by the establishment of a deeply meaningful sense of community. In this model society, individuals would strive for economic advancement because their well-being was a tacit manifestation of the approval of the Deity, but the model also involved a concern for the welfare of others and a willingness to subordinate personal ambition to the common good. The acquisition of wealth was not the sole objective; also essential was the internal growth of the individual, the acquisition of knowledge, compassion, insight, and a human understanding that allowed for the harmonious progress of society. This model of the new social order, Winthrop maintained, would amaze the world and inspire other countries to imitate New England.

Benjamin Franklin seems to have understood this substantial view of the American Dream, for in his autobiography he outlined a plan for personal development in terms of internal personal growth in addition to the discipline and determination required to achieve financial success. Well beyond simple avarice, he outlined the need to develop modesty and humility, intellectual achievement, high moral principles, and a devotion to the welfare of the community at large. Given what his father reveals about him, Jay Gatsby apparently read Franklin's commentary and gleaned from it only the most simplistic portrait of its economic surface. As Kirk Curnutt has indicated:

> Whereas Franklin endorses values tied to character (temperance, humility, chastity), Gatsby is exclusively concerned with external surfaces of personality (elocution, physical fitness, appearance). . . . His ultimate goal is to have his existence validated by the recognition of others. What he fails to comprehend is that the attention that the mystique personality generates is transitory. . . . His real desire—to be accepted by the wealthy world that Daisy represents—cannot be achieved through personality. (42–43)

Thus, the central themes of the novel rest not on the American Dream itself but on a corrupted view of it that limits personal growth to the acquisition of money. The social structure that Winthrop envisioned in 1630 in establishing the Massachusetts Bay Colony encouraged economic opportunity, to be sure, but he also called upon his flock to live humbly, to contribute to the welfare of the community, and to emphasize justice and mercy. As he made clear in "A Model of Christian Charity," those were to be the central elements of his "city upon a hill," the new society they were about to establish (Winthrop). Gatsby is not a learned man, and in an attempt to win Daisy, he grasps at the most superficial aspects of this idea, gaining wealth without acquiring knowledge or wisdom. He has a large library, but the pages in his books are uncut. He has an extremely limited frame of reference, unlike Nick, and his thinking is limited almost exclusively to current events, the bond market, and his romance with Daisy.

Fundamentally, the novel is the story of two men who pursue the national dream, the one who became known as Jay Gatsby and who was really James Gatz and another midwesterner who narrates, Nick Carraway. He tells the story roughly two years after the events have concluded, when he has returned home to the Midwest and a simpler life. This fact establishes the important realization that Gatsby is presented entirely in Carraway's memory and never intrudes directly into the novel even for a moment. The order in which Nick reveals his subject is significant because it is out of chronology, proceeding incrementally from their first meeting. Nick presents his information not in the progression of Gatsby's life experiences but in the sequence in which he learned about him.

The major scenes in which Gatsby is a key figure begin with the party in chapter 3, in which Nick finds himself discussing war experiences with a handsome gentleman he does not know. Nick remarks that he has not seen the host of this lavish affair and is startled when his companion suddenly says, "I'm Gatsby" (53). Always perceptive, Nick senses something false about his new friend, something slightly absurd in the formality of his speech, for example, and this realization continues to be reinforced. In their next meeting, Gatsby lies to Nick about his background, saying he comes from wealthy midwesterners and was educated at Oxford. When Nick inquires about where the family lived in the Midwest, Gatsby replies, "San Francisco," a comment often misinterpreted in criticism. Its significance is not that Gatsby does not know that the city is in California, as some people have assumed (Lehan 60). Rather, it is a wiseacre response that means something akin to "none of your business," a point Nick clearly understands. Nonetheless, he is astonished when Gatsby produces a photograph from Oxford and medals from the war, which lead him to the false conclusion that "it was all true" (67).

The next plot revelation concerns Gatsby's early romance with Daisy, a moment in his life that determines all the rest. This account comes to Nick from Jordan Baker, Daisy's close friend, and Nick reproduces it in Jordan's voice as he heard it. Jordan knew Daisy in Louisville when Gatsby was a young lieutenant at Camp Taylor in 1917. Despite his relative poverty, Gatsby fell in love with the wealthy Daisy, but she rejected him the following year to marry Tom Buchanan, the wealthy heir to a family fortune. The driving force in this alliance is clearly riches, not romance, for Daisy seems to have loved Gatsby all along but felt that he was unworthy of her socioeconomic standing. This experience drives Gatsby to commit his life to the acquisition of wealth for the sole purpose of winning back Daisy. It is this expression of Gatsby's idealization that impresses Nick to say to his friend, "They're a rotten crowd. . . . You're worth the whole damn bunch put together" (134). As Jonathan N. Barron has commented, "That Gatsby was never in it for the money is to Nick proof that his is a story of the West after all" (66). It would seem to be realizations of this kind that eventually lead Nick to abandon his quest for wealth in the New York bond market.

Jordan Baker's flashback scene from 1917 is juxtaposed to the "present" in 1922 when, after an arranged meeting at Nick's house, Gatsby has an opportunity to give Daisy a tour of his opulent home, and his display of wealth causes her to weep. At this instant in the novel, the American Dream for Gatsby seems to have been an astonishing success: He became fabulously prosperous, and his money has brought his beloved back into his life just as he had hoped. For him, the money was a tool, not an end. Even a mansion means nothing to him without the love of Daisy. The song someone plays on the piano, "The Love Nest," from the George M. Cohan musical *Mary* of 1920, expands the theme. One line of it maintains that a simple love nest for two is "better than a palace with a gilded dome." A business person rather than a humanist, Nick is forced into a poignant realization of the depth of Gatsby's affection for Daisy.

It is at this juncture, two years after Gatsby's death, when Nick could have revealed everything in chronological order as best he knew it, that he reaches back to explain Gatsby's childhood and early life. One key part of it was Dan Cody, who employed the young James Gatz on his yacht in Lake Superior. He taught Gatsby about wealth, about the accoutrements of money and how to enjoy them. Under Cody's tutelage, Gatsby learned how to acquire prosperity and what to do with it. At first, he is mentioned only in the conversation between Gatsby and Daisy on her tour of the house (88), but soon, the full meaning of Cody's example becomes clear. Gatsby had a brief stint at St. Olaf College in Minnesota, a Lutheran institution in the Norwegian tradition, but he soon left to seek his fortune at Lake Superior. He spent five years under the wing of Dan Cody, and he inherited knowledge, but not money, from him. At some point in their friendship, Gatsby confided this information to Nick, who now incorporates it into his narrative, helping to explain the motivation for the events.

One other dimension of Gatsby's early striving is revealed to Nick at the funeral by the grieving father, who lauds his son's generosity to him. He also shows Nick a copy of a Hopalong Cassidy novel on which the young Gatsby had written his schedule for self-improvement, emulating Franklin's similar scheme. This is the plan for the achievement of the American Dream, a poignant objective for a poor boy who strives to better himself. (Unfortunately, it is dated September 12, 1906, four years before Clarence E. Mulford published the first of his Western novels about his celebrated hero. Fitzgerald was never much of a scholar.)

Gatsby's profound idealization of Daisy is what made him deeply meaningful to Nick, who is in the party coming back from New York City when Myrtle, thinking that Tom is driving, runs out onto the road and is killed by the car Daisy is driving. As Peter L. Hays has argued, "The circumstances of Myrtle's death point out the immorality: Daisy is responsible for the hit-and-run, but she never tells Tom how Myrtle was killed (letting Gatsby take the blame), and Catherine commits perjury at the inquest into her sister's death" (170). Gatsby immediately offers to take responsibility for the accident, and Daisy allows him to do so. Even worse than that, she flees with her husband, leaving Gatsby to face the punishment. Ironically, he never realizes that Daisy has betrayed him, because Myrtle's husband, George, shoots Gatsby in the swimming pool. It is Nick who carries the full realization of the empty shell of Daisy's love in contrast to Gatsby's deep emotional commitment, inspired five years earlier in Louisville.

The protagonist of a novel is generally taken to be the character who experiences the most significant internal conflicts and who is changed in an important way by the struggle. Thus, the lead character is dynamic in a way the supporting cast is not, secondary figures being essentially static. Although Nick's portrait of Gatsby clearly shows that Gatsby changed enormously from his early childhood through World War I, other than acquiring a fortune as an adult, he is basically the same throughout the period from the war to his death in 1922.

As Richard Lehan has observed, "In creating himself, Gatsby had no social or moral context to give his intensity direction," so he never gives depth to the invention of himself (3). Although he attended Oxford after the war, he dropped out upon learning that Daisy had married Tom. In essence, Gatsby is not educated, and in an attempt to win Daisy, he grasps at the most superficial aspects of the American Dream, gaining wealth without acquiring knowledge, insight, or wisdom. Nick is disappointed that he is a reluctant conversationalist with little to say (65). What is painfully clear is that he has an extremely limited frame of reference, unlike Nick, and his thinking is restricted almost exclusively to his economic concerns and his romance with Daisy.

Nick, on the other hand, is a much more interesting and dynamic character than Gatsby. For one thing, he has a sly sense of humor, an ironic perspective on life that demonstrates he understands the psychological dramas that unfold before him, and he constantly studies human interactions. As is clear from the beginning, he has come to New York in pursuit of his own American Dream, one that relies on making money in the bond market, but he engages that objective in the context of human interaction. In fact, he says almost nothing about his work, and he leaves it after Gatsby's funeral. He came east in pursuit of money; what he found on Long Island was something much richer, an exposure to Gatsby's intense romantic longing, the mystery of his fortune, his reunion with Daisy, and his death as a result of a profound misunderstanding. It is enough to cause one to ponder the meaning of life, and Nick does his fair share of this.

Nick's humor is evident from the opening and runs throughout the novel. Irony implies sufficient distance to assess disparities, and Nick is at once sympathetic to the people around him and yet removed enough to sense the contradictions in their lives. In the first chapter, for example, he visits Tom, whom he had known in college, and Daisy, a "remote second cousin once removed." He has keen insights into Tom, who had been a football star at Yale, and Nick senses that given that early stature "everything afterwards savours of anti-climax" (22). The reflections that Nick offers about him are consistently those of someone who is physically and psychologically cruel. Tom is unfaithful to Daisy, for example, and his affairs involve the most tawdry of women, foremost of whom is Myrtle Wilson. His social views are profoundly racist, and he is impressed by a recent book he cites as *The Rise of the Colored Empires* by Goddard. Historically, the book would have been *The Rising Tide of Color Against the White World-Supremacy* by Lothrop Stoddard, published by Fitzgerald's own publisher, Scribner's, in 1920. Henry H. Goddard was a scientist, not a social commentator.

Tom thus displays a false sophistication based on pretense, just as virtually everything about him is charade. He has little genuine affection for Myrtle: He breaks her nose in their small apartment in the city, and it is her husband who mourns her death. Tom did not achieve the American Dream; he was born to wealth, and he proves unworthy of it.

Daisy married for money, secretly still loving Gatsby. In the opening scene in her house, Nick perceives the current status of her life: "Daisy took her face in her hands, as if feeling its lovely shape, and her eyes moved gradually out into the velvet dusk. I saw that turbulent emotions possessed her" (30). He understands both Tom and Daisy, just as he grasps the essence of Gatsby, insight drawn from the depth of his own humanity. Nick's pursuit of the American Dream is based on a code of improvement not dramatically different from Gatsby's own early plan. Still, as Scott Donaldson perceptively argues, "Nick Carraway and Jimmy Gatz come from the same part of the country, but they belong to vastly different worlds. . . . Nick is a not farmer from the country. He graduated from Yale, and so did his father. He knows about El Greco and Kant and Petronius" (138). As Nick reveals in a self-reflexive passage, in the early months of his arrival in New York, he was preoccupied with his work at Probity Trust, where he seems to be a bond salesman. As he explains, "I took dinner usually at the Yale club . . . and then I went upstairs to the library and studied investments and securities for a conscientious hour" (59).

Nick is on his own program of self-improvement which includes the adoption of abstract codes of conduct that he has internalized. When he begins a relationship with Jordan Baker, he has a troubled conscience about an emotional entanglement still unsettled in the Midwest. He confesses that "I am slow thinking and full of interior rules that act as brakes on my desires, and I knew that first I had to get myself definitely out of that tangle back home" (61). Nick's feelings are in direct contrast to Tom's narcissistic rush for gratification and Gatsby's later involvement with the married Daisy. Nick might tell about such things, but his actions and personal moral standards are another matter. He is disappointed in Jordan when he learns that she lied about having left a convertible out in the rain with the top down and that she had cheated in golf, moving her ball from a bad lie (60). When Gatsby suggests that Nick invite Daisy over for lunch, setting the stage for their reunification, Gatsby begins describing a business opportunity that would make a good deal of money. Nick cuts him short, avoiding any suggestion that he was performing a service for Gatsby in return for remuneration, an idea that offends Nick's sense of honor.

At the time of the telling of the novel, Nick is removed both temporally and geographically from the scenes he relates. He is in the Midwest after Gatsby's death, looking back on what happened, what it meant, and how it changed his life. After roughly two years of reflection, Nick comes to realizations he did not have at the time of the action. For example, he now offers the assessment that "Jay Gatsby, of West Egg, Long Island, sprang from his Platonic conception of himself" (92). All of the terms of this observation are meaningful. The man Nick knew was Jay Gatsby, not James Gatz, the poor young man who transformed himself into Nick's wealthy neighbor. That he did so as a result of his "Platonic conception of himself" probably reflects something of Nick's education at Yale.

Plato proposed that reality was an abstract, spiritual realm in which the perfect essence of everything on earth resided. Human beings could grasp only an impression of this ideal state and create flawed copies in physical form. From Nick's perspective, therefore, he sees his friend as having envisioned the ideal of the man he intended to become, and he reconstituted himself toward that objective, affecting a well-dressed persona with perfect elocution, for example. The problem is that Gatsby's vision covered only the surface elements of a human being, and his relentless striving to win Daisy by fulfilling his initial conception of himself is doomed from the beginning. He never realizes that she is unworthy of his transcendent vision of her, even when the evidence is directly in front of him. He dies with his dreams intact, his illusions unsullied, his quest ongoing.

Thus, the American Dream is a powerful concept animating the lives of many of the characters, even some secondary ones. Meyer Wolfsheim, for example, pursues wealth but without even a glimpse of the inner enrichment at the center of Winthrop's original idea. Similarly, George and Myrtle Wilson seek economic advancement but have little to offer the world in their quest. George's chief objective seems to be to sell Tom's expensive car and somehow get rich himself. Myrtle mistakes the sordid trappings of her love nest in the city for elegance, and she misinterprets Tom's sexual dalliance with her as some kind of emotional commitment, which is why she runs out to his passing car when she is killed. She is desperately seeking a better life with him as her means.

Jordan Baker seems to live comfortably in the wealthy circles of East Egg, but she cheats and lies habitually, a clear violation of the moral standards of her social set. Tom has wealth but an impoverishment of character, cheating on his wife during their honeymoon and engaging in countless affairs. His social attitudes and racist proclivities reveal the dark interior of his mind. Daisy, too, has already achieved the financial objectives of economic advancement, but she is cynical and emotionally unfulfilled, and she lives with a philandering husband. When she is reunited with Gatsby, she quickly begins an affair with him, mirroring Tom's behavior.

Jay Gatsby is most visibly engaged in the financial pursuit of the American Dream, but he does so to achieve the social and economic status Daisy requires of him. When he shows her his house, she is profoundly moved not by the depth of his devotion to her, but by the extent of his wealth. The shallowness of her emotion is revealed when she allows him to take responsibility for her driving accident, which costs him his life. On his journey to wealth, he has affected the style, dialect, and appearance of the upper crust, but he has not grown internally, still arrested in his infatuation of 1917. That is the tragedy of his life.

Gatsby's triumph, as Nick regards it, is his steadfast, unflinching devotion to his dream of Daisy as the transcendent fulfillment of romantic love. In his assessment of her, Barron has maintained that "if one reads Daisy as a Southern belle, one must also read her as too invested in her cultural heritage to welcome Gatsby into her arms as a husband. What Daisy requires is certitude and security, and, no matter how racist and philandering Tom may be, he will always provide her with the lifestyle to which she has grown accustomed" (66). She is grossly unworthy of Gatsby's intense commitment to her, but he is oblivious to the facts, impervious to experience.

Nick serves as the true protagonist in the novel, because he experiences emotional conflict and moral turmoil, and he grows and changes in response to it. Behind him is his time at Yale and his service in the war, but he nevertheless sustains his illusions about finding fortune in New York. Instead of wealth, he encounters the internally enriching world of Jay Gatsby and Daisy, and he learns much from it. He is progressively more empathetic to his neighbor's romantic quest, and he shares his insights into the key players in the drama with the readers of the novel he narrates.

As John B. Chambers points out, even from the beginning, Nick comments on the inner values of the people around him: "Varieties of conduct are presented not as indicators of gradations on a social scale but as expressions of an inner moral code" (111). He reflects on the moral dimensions of his own brief romances, cutting off one relationship back home and drifting away from Jordan when he is uncomfortable with what he discovers about her. The strongest evidence of his growth, however, is that at the time he narrates he is home in the Midwest, having rejected the superficial trimmings of life in the East in favor of a simpler but more substantial future in the region he knows best. He is a sympathetic and perceptive viewer of life who observes more than he acts. His wry perceptions into the inner resources of those around him, and his playful manipulations of language, provide ironic humor to an otherwise darkly tragic chain of events. The sweep of the story he tells covers much of what was modern America at the time. As Lehan has suggested:

The loss of an ideal, the disillusionment that comes with the failure to compromise, the effects of runaway prosperity and wild parties, the fear of the intangibility of that moment, the built-in resentment against the new immigration, the fear of a new radical element, the latent racism behind half-baked historical theories, the effect of Prohibition, the rise of a powerful underworld, the effect of the automobile and professional sports on postwar America—these and a dozen equally important events became the subject of *The Great Gatsby*. (2)

It is Nick's mind, his experience, and his rejection of the corrupted surface of the American Dream, however, that make *The Great Gatsby* one of the finest modern novels in American literature.

Works Cited

Barron, Jonathan N. "Teaching Regionalism and Class in *The Great Gatsby*." *Approaches to Teaching Fitzgerald's* The Great Gatsby. Ed. Jackson R. Bryer and Nancy P. VanArsdale. New York: MLA, 2009. 59–67. Print.

Chambers, John B. *The Novels of F. Scott Fitzgerald*. New York: St. Martin's, 1989. Print.

Curnutt, Kirk. "All That Jazz: Defining Modernity and Milieu in *The Great Gatsby*." *Approaches to Teaching Fitzgerald's* The Great Gatsby. Ed. Jackson R. Bryer and Nancy P. VanArsdale. New York: MLA, 2009. 41–49. Print.

Donaldson, Scott. "The Trouble with Nick." *Critical Essays on Fitzgerald's* The Great Gatsby. Boston: Hall, 1984. 131–39. Print.

Eble, Kenneth. *F. Scott Fitzgerald*. Boston: Twayne, 1977. Print.

Fitzgerald, F. Scott. *The Great Gatsby*. New York: Scribner's, 1925. Print.

Hays, Peter L. "Enough Guilt to Go Around: Teaching Fitzgerald's Lesson in Morality." *Approaches to Teaching Fitzgerald's The Great Gatsby*. Ed. Jackson R. Bryer and Nancy P. VanArsdale. New York: MLA, 2009. 169–74. Print.

Lehan, Richard. The Great Gatsby*: The Limits of Wonder*. Boston: Twayne, 1990. Print.

Winthrop, John. "A Model of Christian Charity." *Old South Leaflet No. 207*. Ed. Samuel Eliot Morison. Boston: Old South Meetinghouse, 1916. Print.

Survival and Transcendence: The Jewish American Immigrant and the American Dream_____

James R. Giles

In a vignette from John Dos Passos's 1925 novel *Manhattan Transfer*, two men in a rowboat observing the yellow quarantine flag on a steamer carrying immigrants into New York engage in the following conversation:

> "I'd give a million dollars," said the old man . . . "to know what they come for."
>
> "Just for that pop," said the young man . . . "Aint it the land of opportoonity?"
>
> "One thing I do know," said the old man. "When I was a boy it was wild Irish came in the spring with the first run of shad. . . . Now there aint no more shad, an them folks, Lord knows where they come from."
>
> "It's the land of opportoonity." (49)

Between 1880 and 1925, approximately two million of "them folks" were Jewish immigrants fleeing poverty and political and religious oppression, particularly the bloody pogroms in Russia and Poland. They did indeed hope to find in America the opportunity to establish a new life, to live the American Dream of prosperity, security, and freedom to practice their faith without fear.

But for these people, realizing the American Dream was not an easy matter. In fact, its relevance to them was not universally assumed in their new home. In the late nineteenth century, nativist sentiment was not receptive to Eastern Europeans of Jewish descent, just as earlier it had not been to Irish Americans. The ambiguous relationship of Jewish immigrants, and indeed of all nineteenth- and early twentieth-century Eastern European immigrants, to the American Dream is apparent in James Truslow Adams's *The Epic of America* (1931), the text that popularized the concept.[1] Adams sees the American Dream

---

as originating in America's frontier history, with its promise of numerous opportunities for the improvement of an individual's economic and social position, and indeed of the re-creation of the self. However, the phenomenon of the frontier was obviously irrelevant to immigrants after its closure in the last decades of the nineteenth century.

Adams devotes little text to these new "alien" arrivals to American shores, mentioning Jews only once (312). He is clear in his implication that the Eastern European immigrants were alien to the history and traditions of the United States. Nevertheless, Adams ends *The Epic of America* with a long quotation from Mary Antin's *The Promised Land* (1912), a highly idealistic account of the immigration of Antin and her Jewish family to Boston from a Russian community:

> Sitting on the steps of the Boston Public Library, where the treasures of the whole of human thought had been opened to her, she wrote, "This is my latest home, and it invites me to a glad new life. . . . My spirit is not tied to the monumental past, any more than my feet were bound to my grandfather's house below the hill. . . . No! It is not I that belong to the past, but the past that belongs to me. America is the youngest of the nations, and inherits all that went before in history. And I am the youngest of America's children, and into my hands is given all her priceless heritage, to the last white star espied through the telescope, to the last great thought of the philosopher. Mine is the whole majestic past, and mine is the shining future." (416–17)

For Antin and her family, the promise of America does not lie in material success, the proverbial immigrant dream of America as the land with streets of gold, but in intellectual and social advancement through education: In America, "education was free. . . . the treasure that no thief could touch, not even misfortune or poverty" (148). Antin's attainment of the treasure is realized, especially in her acquaintance with the "Grand Old Man of Boston," Edward Everett Hale (269).

In two novels dramatizing the Jewish immigration experience during roughly the same time period and utilizing a comparable narrative structure as Antin's memoir, the quest for the dream does not go so smoothly. In both Anzia Yezierska's *Bread Givers* (1925) and Michael Gold's *Jews without Money* (1930), education is again seen as the key to attainment of the dream, but the obstacles to that attainment are considerable. In fact, while the female protagonist of *Bread Givers* is ultimately liberated by education, Gold's male protagonist is denied higher education and must turn for salvation to a European socialist ideology reshaped by the American Dream of equal opportunity.

A novel published almost seventy years after Gold's, Kevin Baker's *Dreamland* (1999), offers a grimly naturalistic look back at the experiences of Jewish immigrants in 1910 New York. Baker's novel contains three central protagonists, two men and one woman; and only the latter even attempts to realize a dream of idealistic self-creation.

Much of the action in these novels takes place in the Lower East Side tenements of New York City, depicted at least initially in all three narratives as a claustrophobic space degraded by poverty and haunted by a repressive past. All three novels contain protagonists struggling to transcend tenement existence and create a new self, capable of realizing the American Dream. In Yezierska's and Baker's novels, the women's future is additionally threatened by the patriarchal Old World values of their fathers. Like Gold's *Jews without Money*, Yezierska's *Bread Givers* is a semiautobiographical novel, and her life has some important parallels to that of Mary Antin, with the crucial exception of the absence of a supportive father figure, as noted in Alice Kessler-Harris's 1975 foreword to the novel:

> Yezierska's old world was like that of many turn-of-the-century immigrants. She was born in a small town—probably a shtetl called Plinsk—in Russian Poland about 1885. The exact date of her birth went unrecorded, for her family was large—there were nine children—and her parents poor. Her father, a Talmudic scholar, had chosen, Yezierska later wrote, "to have his portion in the next world." The family lived off the neighbors'

contributions of food and clothing and the mother's occasional earnings from selling small items in the local market. (Kessler-Harris, v–vi)

Yezierska's fictional counterpart in *Bread Givers* is Sara Smolinsky, one of four daughters of a Talmudic scholar who largely leaves remunerative work to his wife and four daughters. The novel opens in New York, and the reader learns through a speech by the wife that the family fled the Pale of Settlement (that part of the western Russian Empire where Jews were allowed to reside) to escape both an attempt by the czar's soldiers to recruit the father to participate in a pogrom, and their subsequent impoverishment. Physical safety, economic security provided by his family, and the opportunity to study the Talmud in peace were the father's reasons for immigration to America.

Otherwise, he has no idealistic belief in the American Dream of personal re-creation. Indeed, just as he had in Europe, he hopes to attain economic security through marrying one of his four daughters to a successful Jewish man. At one point, he mocks the mythic vision of America that lured Jewish and other immigrants away from their homelands: "Don't you know it's always summer in America? And in the new golden country, where milk and honey flows free in the streets, you'll have new golden dishes to cook in, and not weigh yourself down with your old pots and pans" (9).

A strong feminist subtext runs through *Bread Givers*. It is worth noting that historian Jim Cullen argues that the American Dream "has largely been a male dream" (119). The father's selfish otherworldliness forces his wife and ultimately three of his daughters, Bessie, Mashah, and Fania, to focus exclusively on their economic survival, destroying any possibility of their constructing a new, distinctly American identity. Of the three, Mashah, the beauty, holds out the longest before surrendering to her father. In contrast to her three sisters, Sara vows as a child to defy her father and resist his attempt to force her into a marriage that she does not want. The novel's subtitle is "A Struggle between a Father of the Old World and a Daughter of the New." At one point, Sara succinctly summarizes her father's view of proper gender relationships:

> The prayers of his daughters didn't count because God didn't listen to women. Heaven and the next world were only for men. Women could get into Heaven because they were wives and daughters of men. Women had no brains for the study of God's Torah, but they could be the servants of men who studied the Torah. (9–10)

Very early, Sara determines that the world she cares about is this one, and she is determined to succeed in it on her own terms. The first step in her construction of an independent, Americanized self comes early in the novel. A visit of the landlord's rent collector results in a violent confrontation between this woman and father Smolinsky and the subsequent arrest of the father. While Sara's mother is momentarily reduced to hysteria over the arrest and the absence of any food or virtually any money in the house, Sara takes things into her own hands by peddling some old, crushed herring that a peddler sells her for a quarter. In part because of her youth and the neighborhood awareness of the family's desperate economic condition, she proves to be a quite successful salesperson. Afterward, she is overjoyed: "Twenty-five cents profit. Richer than Rockefeller, I felt" (22).

The scene is a crucial one. Sara refuses to accept the passive, survivalist role that her father has forced on the other women in his family. There are symbolic overtones to the scene as well. She is given the herring by a Jewish vendor whose family is almost as destitute as her own, demonstrating that, even as she constructs an American identity, she is not abandoning her Jewish heritage. Still, she describes her jubilation through reference to an American millionaire. Unlike her father, she will adapt her Jewish heritage to the new reality of America and redefine it in the context of the American Dream. An irony of the scene is made manifest later in the novel when the father fails completely as a storekeeper. Even though her focus is not materialistic, the reader knows that, if Sara wanted to, she could be a more successful business-person than her father.

Sara quickly realizes that she must fight to escape the dual trap of the tenement world and her father's domination, that she must tran-scend the repressive traditions of the past and the poverty of her pres-ent existence: "More and more I began to think inside myself, I don't want to sell herring for the rest of my days. I want to learn something. I want to do something. I want some day to make myself for a person and come among people" (66). The phrase "come among people" has an almost biblical resonance; and, indeed, Sara is vowing to be born anew in this American world.

Her realization of her need "to learn something" foreshadows her later focus upon education as her avenue to self-renewal and the Amer-ican Dream. In this way, she recalls Mary Antin. Having witnessed her father's interference in and destruction of her sisters' romances, and his forcing them into loveless marriages to cruel and duplicitous hus-bands, she vows to choose her own husband: "I'd want an American-born man who was his own boss. And would let me be my own boss. And no fathers, and no mothers, and no sweatshops, and no herring!" (66).

At this point, Sara's liberation from the past is not complete. She is still thinking a man is central to her construction of a new self. Inadver-tently, Moe Mirshy, the abusive husband of her sister Mashah, points Sara to the path of her ultimate salvation when he drives her out of the house in which he lives with Mashah and their children.

Seething with anger over the brutal treatment she has just received from Moe and which Mashah and her children receive on a regular basis, Sara, without knowing how to achieve it, vows to improve her life. The Sunday paper points the way. In it, she reads a story about a sweatshop girl who saved money for night school and then went to col-lege and became a schoolteacher; and she instantly knows that, despite the obstacles confronting her, she will "make for herself a person and come among people" by following the path of the woman in the story. One remembers that it was writing stories and novels that lifted Anzia Yezierska from poverty and, for a time, gave her genuine wealth.

"Schoolteacher" becomes an almost sacred word in the remainder of *Bread Givers*. In Sara's mind, it is a title that conveys a special dignity and a kind of earned nobility, and she is always aware that she could only earn it in America. Significantly, her mother, not her father, gives her the money necessary to move out of the Smolinsky household and into a dingy room that represents the door to becoming a "person."

She will be tempted away from her road to personhood by a man, Max Goldstein, who has achieved a more conventional form of the American Dream than Sara's ideal of becoming a schoolteacher.[2] During their first meeting, Goldstein initially says all the right things to entrance Sara. He praises her courage in running away from home with virtually nothing and taking an exhausting job in a laundry while attending night school: "You and I are so much alike, because I, too, wanted to make my own way in the world. And you remind me of my own beginning" (188).

He tells how, after stepping off the ship into the new world of America and into "the blowing snow of a freezing blizzard" (188), he saw men cleaning the street and grabbed a shovel and went to work with no offer from the foreman, who did, at the end of the day, pay him: "When I was paid a dollar, I felt the riches of all America in my hand" (189). Max's story recalls Benjamin Franklin and his pushing a covered wheelbarrow through the streets of Philadelphia to impress onlookers. If this story is indeed true, Max, like Franklin, understood that in America, one must take the initiative and create opportunities wherever possible.

The shoveling incident constitutes only the beginning of Max's narrative. Later, he is engaged to sell used clothes from a pushcart and, not understanding the language, yells "pay cats coals" instead of "pay cash clothes" (189). Max intuitively understood that he should not be deterred in his personal quest for the American Dream by such a minor obstacle as not speaking English. In the fashion of Horatio Alger, Max's pushcart stint leads to his becoming an actor "and earn[ing] a lot of money" (190).

Max's recounting of his personal odyssey is far from over. He adds a moral exemplum to his tale. After his success as an actor, he "began living a fast life, bumming around like a gay young feller with the women" (190), which led to a consumptive disorder. But, as in any American popular-culture success story, luck, as well as hard work, personal salesmanship, and quick thinking, plays a part. Max's consumption resulted in his doctor's prescribing that he move to California, where he sets up a stand selling imitation jewelry that, he says, "has grown to be the biggest department store in the village" (190). For Max, it is but a short step from jewelry to real estate and even more wealth.

Sara initially responds to the mixed strands of Franklinian pragmatism and entrepreneurial opportunism in Max's story. He does seem to have found in California a place where the streets, if not lined with gold, lead inevitably to it. Moreover, she is sexually attracted to him; and, after being repulsed when he takes her to a crude, exploitive show, she is exhilarated when he takes her dancing. But the temptations of hedonism wane as Max begins to speak more and more contemptuously of education and of the college-educated men he employs. Hearing him, Sara realizes that she and Max are fundamentally incompatible: "He could buy everything. To him, a wife would only be another piece of property. I grew cold at the thought how near I had been to marrying him" (199–200). With some regret, she turns to her books for consolation.

The remainder of the novel focuses primarily upon Sara's attaining her dream of being "an American schoolteacher." Especially in the context of Max's materialistic success, this goal may seem quite modest; but it does fulfill James Truslow Adams's formula for the American Dream: "It is not a dream of motor cars and high wages merely, but a dream of a social order in which each man and each woman shall be able to attain to the fullest stature of which they are innately capable, and be recognized by others for what they are, regardless of the fortuitous circumstances of birth or position" (404). Moreover, in contrast to Sara, Max emerges as an arrogant and selfish individual. That the jewelry that makes him his fortune is fake is not insignificant.

Sara's rejection of Max leads to a climactic confrontation with her father that ends in his disowning her: "I saw there was no use talking. He could never understand. He was the Old World. I was the New" (207). Only later does Sara realize and acknowledge that she owes the central element in her existence, her love of books and learning, to her father. Two key elements in their conflicted relationship had blocked that realization, his Old World gender bias and his contempt for the present.

The breaks with Max and her father force Sara into the further realization that she is now alone and must make her way without relying on others. Her alienation is intensified when she leaves New York to attend college in an unnamed small town and sees in her well-dressed, smiling fellow students "the real Americans" (210): "They had none of that terrible fight for bread and rent that I always saw in New York people's faces" (211). It is interesting that Yezierska writes "New York faces" rather than "tenement faces." It is as if she had never seen the extremely well-dressed and richly comfortable faces of uptown New York. "There was in them that sure, settled look of those who belong to the world in which they were born" (211).

The college world continues to be strange to her, especially its social dimension. She is baffled by birthday parties: "I never knew that there were people glad enough of life to celebrate the day they were born" (218). The intense difference that Sara feels from observing these middle-class students represents a momentary obstacle in Sara's quest for personhood: "Will I never lift myself to be a person among people?" (220). But it is an obstacle that she overcomes through determination and strength of will. After all, her childhood nickname was "Blood-and-Iron," and the lesson of the childhood herring incident was never lost on her.

A crucial endorsement of her re-creation of self comes after college from her dying mother: "Praise be to God! I lived to see my daughter a teacherin" (246). Ultimately she is reconciled with her father: "Deeper than love, deeper than pity, is that oneness of the flesh that's in him and in me. Who gave me the fire, the passion, to push myself up from the dirt? If I grow, if I rise, if I ever amount to something, is it not his spirit burning in me? (286). Still proclaiming the inferiority of women, the father has not changed; but, in attaining her full personhood, Sara has become more accepting and forgiving. She even finds love with the principal at the school where she teaches. Once a child obtaining food for her family by selling herring, she has become "an American teacher."

A semiautobiographical novel, *Bread Givers*, and especially the Max Goldstein incident, contains a fascinating subtext. After the publication of Yezierska's first collection of short stories, *Hungry Hearts*, in 1920, she was "discovered" by Samuel Goldwyn, who brought her to Hollywood amidst a flood of publicity, describing her as "the Sweatshop Cinderella." Goldwyn assigned her to write a screenplay, which was produced as a movie that Yezierska hated.[3] She soon left California, returned to New York and, in 1923, published her most successful novel, *Salome of the Tenements*. The rest of her life was characterized by poverty and obscurity. Yezierska did achieve, for a brief time, her version of Max Goldstein's American Dream and appropriately enough in Hollywood, America's "dream factory" (it is a little surprising that Yezierska does not have Max attain wealth in the motion-picture industry, rather through jewelry and real estate). But her painfully created identity, like Sara's, would not permit her to substitute shallow imitation for genuine creativity.

Like Yezierska, Itzok Isaac Granich also formed a new self out of the suffering of an impoverished tenement childhood. He, in fact, renamed himself Michael Gold and attained public recognition and some notoriety, primarily because of his unstinting support for Soviet dictator Joseph Stalin. In 1914, at the age of twenty-one, Gold became an editor of *The Masses*, the most prominent leftist journal in New York City. During his tenure there, he was known for his particularly strident voice, never shying away from controversy in his devotion to Marxism. But Gold's idealism had American roots. He was fascinated by the legend of Abraham Lincoln's rise from poverty and obscurity to the presidency, and he was an admirer of Walt Whitman and Ralph Waldo Emerson. Literary critic Marcus Klein writes that "Gold did plausibly succeed in becoming the kind of American who was implicit in the myths, that American who was emblematic of the culture by virtue of being initially an outcaste [sic] of the culture" (237). During his lifetime, Gold was best known for his editorial work at *The Masses* and as the author of a manifesto entitled "Towards Proletarian Art," published in *The Liberator* in 1921; but his most lasting achievement is his 1930 semiautobiographical novel *Jews without Money*.

The link between Gold and his protagonist is made apparent in the young protagonist's name, Michael; and, indeed, a major thrust of the critical conversation about *Jews without Money* concerns whether it should be described as a novel or a memoir. Its setting is essentially the same as that of *Bread Givers*, the tenements of New York's Lower East Side; but Gold focuses much more on the streets outside the home of Michael and his parents than does Yezierska. Thus, the two texts convey a claustrophobic mood in contrasting ways. Sara Smolinsky's self-creation is threatened as much by her father's self-oriented sexism as by the impoverished world in which she lives.

In contrast, from the opening chapter, *Jews without Money* is concerned with the threat to Michael's humanity from the poverty and brutality of the streets in which he grows up:

> I can never forget the East Side street where I lived as a boy. It was a block from the notorious Bowery, a tenement canyon hung with fire-escapes, bed-clothing, and faces. . . . Pimps, gamblers and red-nosed bums; peanut politicians, pugilists in sweaters; tinhorn sports. . . . Excitement, dirt, fighting, chaos! . . . The noise was always in my ears. (14–15)

For Michael, there was a strong element of "excitement" inherent in this environment, but it was of a kind that ultimately depressed and dehumanized rather than exhilarated. In such a world, one is necessarily concerned with physical and spiritual survival rather than transcendence.

Prostitution and petty crime surround Michael: "The East Side of New York was then the city's red light district, a vast . . . playground under the business management of Tammany Hall" (14). Gold's protagonist might well have turned to petty criminality under the sponsorship of Tammany Hall, a path that is taken by the two male protagonists in Kevin Baker's 1999 novel *Dreamland*. In addition to its strong element of sexism, the political incorrectness of *Jews without Money* is evident in the name of one of Michael's boyhood companions. Nigger is not African American but receives his nickname because of his dark hair and his "murky" face (42).

This character has a complex role in Gold's novel. He functions in part as Michael's guide through the ghetto, making certain that Michael witnesses the most brutal and sordid aspects of his world. It is Nigger who provides a key element in Michael's sexual initiation, taking him to spy on a prostitute and her client. Michael's reaction to what he sees is revealing. When Nigger says that "everyone does it. That's the way babies are made," Michael is outraged: "But that's like saying my mother is like that" (25–26). The characterization of Nigger fulfills a symbolic role in the novel as well; he represents the thoroughly degraded figure that Michael might have become.

Throughout the novel, the idealized figure of Michael's mother functions as a corrective force to the animalistic vision to which Nigger and the tenement world expose him. While she expresses outrage at the anti-Semitism she experienced in Europe and feels an abstract hatred for Gentiles, she is generous in her dealings with her non-Jewish fellow immigrants. A thoroughly nonpolitical figure herself, she is inextricably bound up in Michael's and, by implication, Gold's proletarianism: "Mother! Momma! . . . I must remain faithful to the poor because

I cannot be faithless to you! I believe in the poor because I have known you. The world must be made gracious for the poor! Momma, you taught me that!" (158).

While Michael's mother is always accessible to him, his dream of transformation through education often seems quite distant. When he is six, he says a "dirty word" in school and has his mouth washed out with soap by the teacher, a punishment to which his parents object "because soap is made of Christian fat, is not kosher" (36). Years later, he still hates the teacher: "I knew no English when handed to you. I was a little savage and lover of the street. I used no toothbrush. . . . I was lousy, maybe. . . . But Teacher! O Teacher for little slaves, O ruptured American virgin of fifty-five, you should not have called me 'LITTLE KIKE'" (37). In an instant of appropriate symbolism, Nigger punches the teacher in the nose after her anti-Semitic outburst: "It was Justice" (37).

Subsequently, Michael accepts and excels in school. But at the age of twelve, with his family's finances becoming ever more desperate and with the death of a treasured little sister, Michael begins feeling that "education is a luxury reserved for the well-to-do" (303). Therefore, he chooses not to enter high school and instead goes to work. Finding only the most mind-numbing and degrading forms of work and losing jobs because of prejudice against Jews, he is, on the novel's penultimate page, in a state of despair: "Jobs, jobs. I drifted from one to the other, without plan, without hope. I was one of the many. I was caught like my father in poverty's trap. I was nothing, bound for nowhere" (308).

Initially, on the final page of the novel, he is still in despair. Gold quickly summarizes Michael's adolescence, describing how, obsessed by sex, he began "drinking and whoring with Nigger's crowd" (309). Michael's dark doppelganger seems on the verge of assuming dominance at this point. But, in five short paragraphs, everything changes. Michael hears a soapbox orator proclaiming the Marxist revolution and is instantly saved: "O workers' Revolution, you brought hope to me, a lonely, suicidal boy. You are the true Messiah. . . . O great Beginning" (309).

The abruptness of this ending makes little logical or artistic sense until one puts it in the context of Michael's experiences with two mentor figures. After years of being exploited in a sweatshop, his Aunt Lena, who is absent for most of the novel, reappears, describing her participation in a strike. She has become ennobled through joining a union and fighting for the workers' rights: "It's war" (237). The centrality of Lena's new-found strength and dignity is obviously crucial to Michael's own last-page conversion to "the workers' Revolution."

The second mentor figure is Miss Barry, the teacher to whom Michael announces his intention of quitting school. Miss Barry praises Michael's skill at English composition and challenges her pupil to continue his education on his own: "It will be difficult to study at night, . . . but Abraham Lincoln did it, and other great Americans" (304). Historian Jim Cullen effectively summarizes Lincoln's centrality to one version of the American Dream: "if Franklin, Emerson, Clay, and others were [the dream of upward mobility's] prophets, then Lincoln was its Jesus Christ" (101). Miss Barry is challenging Michael to pursue the American Dream through self-education; and, in case he should miss the point, she gives him a copy of Emerson's *Essays*. Her message is that a distinctly Americanized version of self-reliance can enable him to overcome the limitations of his poverty and limited education.

The ending of *Jews without Money* begins to make sense when one reads it in the context of a tradition of American idealism centered on the American Dream. Marcus Klein discusses the significant figures who contributed to Michael Gold's Americanized version of proletarianism:

There was Buffalo Bill, who looked like the Messiah, or vice versa. . . . [and] there were literary discoveries available to him, chiefly Mark Twain and Walt Whitman. All of these were indisputably real Americans, of a certain sort: they were the American subverters of the pretensions to the

American cultural authority which was represented, for instance, by the schoolteacher . . . who addressed the young boy as "LITTLE KIKE." (235)

Remembering Aunt Lena's role in the American labor movement adds to an understanding both of *Jews without Money*'s abrupt ending and the importance of American idealism to the novel. Michael Gold's vision of Marxism was formulated in the context of the American Dream.

A grimly naturalistic text, Kevin Baker's *Dreamland* offers little of the affirmation inherent in Yezierska's and Gold's novels and especially in Antin's memoir. *Dreamland* emphasizes the corruption, brutality, and exploitation experienced by late-nineteenth and early twentieth-century Jewish immigrants in New York. Time, moreover, is not the only way in which Baker (writing at the end of the twentieth century) is distanced from his subject matter. As a Quaker, he necessarily views the Jewish American experience from the position of an outsider.

Dreamland is one of three novels that make up Baker's City of Fire trilogy, the other two being *Paradise Alley* (2002) and *Strivers' Row* (2006). Cumulatively, the trilogy can be read in part as a vision of the perversion of the American dreams of diversity, equality, and upward mobility in New York and, by extension, in the nation at large. Throughout the trilogy, fire functions as a metaphor for the violence that explodes as a result of the corruption of the American Dream.

Dreamland opens with one of its central characters, Trick the Dwarf, beginning to tell a story to some of his fellow citizens of Dreamland, the Coney Island amusement park: "It's a story about love, and jealousy, and betrayal. A story about a young man, the young woman who loved him, and a terrible villain—a story about death, and destruction, and fire . . . and the poor man's burden, and the rich man's condescension" (5). He subsequently adds, "It is a story about a great city, and a little city, and a land of dreams. And always, above all, it is a story about fire" (6).

Baker's title is taken from one of the three great amusement parks that dominated Coney Island from the 1880s to World War II. All of the parks experienced destructive fires, with Dreamland, in 1910, being destroyed first. The three amusement parts themselves represented a debased version of one particular American dream, that of cheap entertainment for the masses. A central part of Dreamland's entertainment is the Little City, inhabited solely by dwarfs. Trick, its mayor, is forced to undergo a humiliating public marriage to the queen of the miniature community, an insane woman who believes that she actually is royalty, but whom Trick nevertheless loves. Dreamland, of the three parks, was built to be impressive and even regal on the outside; but it was cheaply constructed inside, thus dangerously flammable.

Baker's Little City is a barely fictionalized version of Midget City, the featured attraction of the real Dreamland amusement park:

> Midget City was a re-creation of fifteenth-century Nuremberg built to half scale. . . . Residing there were shopkeepers, policemen, wagon drivers, and musicians, all of them dwarfs. There was a Lilliputian theater for tiny folk, a circus under a miniature tent, a livery stable, a midget Chinese laundryman, and even a midget fire department with a small steam fire engine hauled by two fat ponies. (Immerso 69)

Baker references the fact that Dreamland specialized in various kinds of "freak shows" as a metonymic reference to the grotesque debasement of the American Dream in early twentieth-century mass entertainment.

A number of unsavory historical figures associated with either New York City politics, gangs, or both appear in the novel. Two characters in the novel, Josef Kolyika and Lazar Abramowitz, are highly fictionalized versions of Kid Twist and Gyp the Blood, turn-of-the-century New York gang members recruited by Tammany Hall for secret criminal activities.

Gyp the Blood, quite succinctly described in the novel as "the most dangerous lunatic in New York," performs in various dives by taking random men across his lap and breaking their backs with an upward thrust of his knees. In an early scene, he appears in such a dive, first in the basement rat pit, in which dogs are forced to fight hordes of savage rats, and then upstairs, where he begins to demonstrate his brutal skill. He breaks the back of a clerk who has wandered into the dive out of curiosity and is about to do the same thing to a small figure that he takes to be a newsboy. In fact, the newsboy is a disguised Trick the Dwarf seeking excitement outside the Little City. Before Gyp can harm Trick, he is knocked out by Kid Twist, acting on a courageous instinct that surprises him. This begins the animosity between Gyp and the Kid that will become a dominant element in the novel's plot.

Not surprisingly, Gyp is not given to many idealistic moments. He does, though, engage in degraded fantasies based upon one popularized version of the American Dream of upward mobility. He loses, in a dice game, a nickel for the baker that his mother has entrusted with him: "He walked very slowly, thinking that something had to intervene. A nickel found in the street, an uncommonly generous stranger. . . . Maybe he could even save somebody from a runaway horse, like all those ridiculous stories about match boys and newsies on the rise." (214)

Gyp ridicules the Horatio Alger myth of upward mobility through pluck and luck, but he occasionally recalls it. Needless to say, no "generous stranger" or "runaway horse" appears to save Gyp or his nickel. It is not long after this scene that he is banished by his father from their tenement apartment: "Go to the devil with your gangster friends! Leavink the house on a Sabbath. You are *dead* to me, . . . I no longer have a son" (218). Gyp has no dream of upward mobility through education or, apart from Horatio Alger fantasies, of living what James Truslow Adams describes as a "better," "richer," "fuller" life. Abandoned on the streets, he is easy prey for Tammany Hall. Gyp represents a nightmare form of Americanization; he assimilates all the most vicious and corrupt characteristics of the new world. There is nothing left in him of the once-innocent Lazar Abramowitz; he truly has morphed into Gyp the Blood. His fate is appropriate. He is killed by an amusement park elephant that he has been tormenting.

In contrast, as shown in his rescue of Trick the Dwarf, Kid Twist, despite his experiences in both the old and the new worlds, retains an essential core of decency. As Josef Kolyika, he literally walks away from his native Polish village after his father's death and keeps walking until he finds a ship headed for America that he manages to board as a stowaway. On the ship, he studies English from a book of stories "called things like *Luck and Pluck*, or *Sink or Swim*, or *Fame or Fortune*, about a young boy with incredible luck. Sometimes the boy was called Ragged Dick, or sometimes he was Tattered Tom, or sometimes Mark the Match Boy, but his story was always the same, it was always about getting rich" (163).

Thus, Josef discovers the dream of an America of unlimited upward mobility open to anyone with "incredible luck." It is the dream of America as a land of streets paved with gold that tempted so many immigrants from Europe and Asia. His disillusionment comes very quickly. A stowaway, he jumps off the ship to avoid the immigration process and Ellis Island. His swim is not a pleasant one: "He could see, floating past him in the oily yellow light as he sank: chicken guts and horse bones, loose turds, the severed paw of a dog. Giant gray, drowned rats, floating peacefully, their heads bent over" (166). After this baptism into the new world, it is not surprising that he reappears as a Tammany Hall minion in the rat pit of a filthy, dangerous dive. At this point, Josef is close to having lost any dream of decency. But he will transcend his Kid Twist persona and finally regain his original identity as Josef Kolyika.

He is "the young man" to whom Trick refers in his introduction to his story, and the "young woman who loved him" and redeems him is Esther Abramowitz, the sister of Gyp the Blood. She works as a seamstress in the Triangle Shirtwaist Factory, where she not only endures harsh working conditions, but is also cheated in her wages. When she comes home, she is assaulted by her father, who abuses her for coming home late and condemns her as an "Amerikanerin." But, like Sara Smolinsky and Michael's Aunt Lena, she fights back against her victimization; and, although she is ultimately doomed, she finds love and attains genuine dignity before she dies.

Formal education is out of Esther's reach, but the American labor and women's movements are not. She needs a mentor figure to show her the way to struggle for advancement. She finds two, in fact: Clara, a friend from work who is active in a nascent union of women workers and who takes Esther to a meeting where she is introduced to Mrs. Perkins, a social worker who promises the women support if they decide to go out on strike. Mrs. Perkins is, of course, Frances Perkins, the legendary social activist who served as Franklin Delano Roosevelt's secretary of labor from 1933 to 1945 and who was instrumental in the enactment of minimum wage laws and reforms for women workers. Perkins serves in *Dreamland* as the personification of one aspect of the American Dream, the achievement of equality and upward mobility through collective action.

Esther, along with her friend Clara, does go on strike, is arrested and savagely beaten by police officers, then thrown into prison and tortured. Through all this, however, Esther remains proud and defiant. Like Michael's Aunt Lena in *Jews without Money*, she is ennobled by her suffering. One can envision Ester becoming a national labor leader, another Frances Perkins, until she almost certainly dies as one of the 146 victims of the 1911 Triangle Shirtwaist Factory fire, the tragedy that concludes the novel. That so many died in the fire was the result of criminal negligence by the factory owners.[4]

Taking off from a newspaper account, the concluding description of the fire reads:

> The papers said that a young man out on one of the ledges—obviously a real man—helped the girls jump to their deaths—that he held and steadied them, then lifted them out, and let them fall. And that then he held the last

woman to him, and kissed her, before he let her fall, then jumped right after, so everyone assumed she was his fiancée. (629)

The narrative voice here is Trick the Dwarf's. He goes on to speculate that the young man and his fiancée are Josef Kolyika, having shed his Kid Twist identity completely, and Esther. He further speculates that they both survive and live personally and socially productive lives together. The most probable way to read this is as an example of Trick the Dwarf's intense romanticism, but it nevertheless provides a partially affirmative note to a pessimistic, naturalistic text. Still, the fact that Dreamland was also destroyed by fire in 1910 adds to the text's apocalyptic vision of early twentieth-century American culture.

It initially seems ironic that *Dreamland*, written by an outsider more than seventy years after *Bread Givers* and *Jews without Money*, should be the most negative of the three texts. One must remember, though, that, in his City of Fire trilogy, Baker is intent on creating, from a late-twentieth-century perspective, a fictionalized account of the struggles and hard-won victories of eighteenth- and nineteenth-century Irish and Jewish immigrants, as well as by African Americans living in the north. In addition, his affirmative message in *Dreamland*, as in Gold's *Jews Without Money*, is of a collectivist realization of James Truslow Adams's American Dream of a "better," "richer," "fuller" life "with opportunity for each according to his ability or achievement" (404). Of the female protagonists in the three novels, only Sara Smolinsky can attain the dream individually through formal education.

Notes

1. Jim Cullen, in *The American Dream,* points out that Adams also wanted to call his study "The American Dream" but was overruled by his publisher. In his discussion of the centrality of *The Epic of America* to the concept, Cullen writes: "While it's not clear whether he actually coined the term or appropriated it from someone else . . . Adams invoked it over thirty times in *The Epic of America,* and the phrase rapidly entered common parlance as a byword for what he thought the country was all about" (4).

2. Cullen argues that the American Dream has traditionally had two primary strands: "commercial success" and "transformation through education" (59–60).

3. It might be added that, while she never apparently met Edward Everett Hale, Yezierska did have a romantic relationship with John Dewey.

4. For more information on the fire, see David von Drehle's book *Triangle: The Fire That Changed America* (New York: Grove, 2003). Frances Perkins witnessed the fire, which was a major inspiration in her crusade for reform.

Works Cited

Adams, James Truslow. *The Epic of America*. Safety Harbor: Simon, 2001. Print.

Antin, Mary. *The Promised Land*. New York: Penguin, 1997. Print.

Baker, Kevin. *Dreamland*. New York: Harper, 1999. Print.

Cullen, Jim. *The American Dream: A Short History of an Idea That Shaped a Nation*. Oxford: Oxford UP, 2003. Print.

Gold, Michael. *Jews without Money*. New York: Carroll & Graf, 1958. Print.

Immerso, Michael. *Coney Island: The People's Playground*. New Brunswick: Rutgers UP, 2002. Print.

Kessler-Harris, Alice. "Foreword." *Bread Givers*. New York: Persea, 1975. Print.

Klein, Marcus. *Foreigners: The Making of American Literature, 1900–1940*. Chicago: U of Chicago P, 1981. Print.

Von Drehle, David. *Triangle: The Fire That Changed America*. New York: Grove, 2003. Print.

Yezierska, Anzia. *Bread Givers*. New York: Persea, 1975. Print.

Blurring the Color Line: Race and the American Dream in *The Autobiography of an Ex-Coloured Man, Passing,* and *Cane*

Andrew Vogel

> What happens to a dream deferred?
> Does it dry up
> like a raisin in the sun?
> Or fester like a sore—
> And then run?
> Does it stink like rotten meat?
> Or crust and sugar over—
> like a syrupy sweet?
> Maybe it just sags
> like a heavy load.
> *Or does it explode?*
> (Hughes 71)

In the long poem *Montage of a Dream Deferred* (1951), Langston Hughes poses a series of deceptively simple rhetorical questions. Hughes has the American Dream in mind, which he sees as unobtainable for most African Americans, observing that the dream has "come true" for "the ones who've crossed the line / to live downtown" (257). What he means is that folks of African American descent whose skin is pale enough can move to white Manhattan to enjoy a life that folks with darker complexions cannot. As Hughes charts the boundaries of the color line, he acerbically reckons its impacts—hope shrivels up, anger festers, pain rots and turns saccharine, strength sags under constant struggle and, finally, persistent discrimination may prompt explosive uprising. The poem is thus an indictment, a challenge, a call to activism, and, ultimately, a warning to erase the color line.

Montage of a Dream Deferred was composed roughly halfway between two quintessential moments in American history—the flourishing of black arts and enterprise in the 1920s commonly known as the Harlem Renaissance, and the civil rights movement, defined most poignantly by Martin Luther King Jr.'s rousing evocation of the American Dream in his 1963 "I Have Dream" speech. When Hughes first came to Harlem in 1921, the borough was coalescing as the capital of the New Negro Movement. Black writers, artists, musicians, and entrepreneurs enjoyed the national wealth of the Roaring Twenties and organized active resistance to the discrimination and racial terrorism of the Jim Crow era in a predominantly black urban environment.

As black artists and thinkers forged a revolutionary cultural tradition by celebrating black heritage, advancing black politics, and engaging in candid self-exploration, Harlem was expected to become a great city in its own right, a robust and vital cultural capital of the global African diaspora (Watson 9). In the 1930s, however, as the Great Depression harried the borough, "the optimistic spirit eroded," and Harlem spiraled into poverty (De Jongh 75). The thriving black capital had degenerated into a dispirited ghetto, and the dream that descendants of Africa might enjoy American prosperity had been again "deferred." Riots erupted in 1935, again in 1943, and—despite King's leadership, which had culminated in the Civil Rights Act—again in 1964.

Hughes's *Montage of a Dream Deferred* revisits themes that African American writers explored throughout the Harlem Renaissance. The Civil War had brought an end to slavery, but emancipation had transformed the underlying racism that had justified slavery into more subtle forms of institutionalized racism. In the wake of Reconstruction, white fear of black power manifested in discriminatory laws designed to disenfranchise blacks. Terrorism through lynching and unjust imprisonment intimidated black populations into subservience. Segregation excluded black people from American social life and relegated many to positions of economic dependence.

The era's intense racial paranoia propelled a eugenics movement and antimiscegenation laws intended to keep the color line distinct and the American Dream secure for white people. Cultural historian Werner Sollers has suggested that antimiscegenation laws and the "one drop rule," in which someone with any amount of African blood was considered African American, were presumed necessary to national "peace and happiness" (5–6), and Daylanne K. English has argued that as "a paradigmatic modern American discourse," eugenics was considered to be essential to American progress (2). In this cultural climate, James Weldon Johnson's *The Autobiography of an Ex-Coloured Man* (1912), Nella Larsen's Passing (1929), and Jean Toomer's *Cane* (1923) all represent the ways in which the color line was excluding African Americans from the American Dream, and, thus, they question what Jennifer L. Schultz has termed "the racial contract" under which discrimination was written into the very fabric of American life (33).

Interestingly, the phrase "American Dream" first entered the national lexicon during the era in which these novels were published. The historian James Truslow Adams coined the phrase in 1931 to define the United States as "a land in which life should be better and richer and fuller for every man, with opportunity for each according to his ability or achievement" (404). More recently, historian Jim Cullen has qualified and extended Adams's definition of the dream. For Cullen, the American Dream is difficult to define precisely because by its very nature, it must adapt to the vision of the good life held by any individual. Nevertheless, Cullen argues that the promise of freedom, equality, and the pursuit of happiness for all that is articulated in the Declaration of Independence serves as a useful "charter" for the American Dream, even if the nation's actions have frequently failed to align with such ideals (58).

Like it is for Adams and Cullen, for Johnson, Larsen, and Toomer, the dream is woven together with aspirations toward family, home, security, prosperity, dignity, and freedom. Johnson, Larsen, and Toomer's books investigate the relationship between race and the dream, and they all arrive at an understanding that race is a social agreement with no basis in human nature, meaning that the color of one's skin has no significance beyond that which people decide to ascribe to it. Unfortunately, despite these authors' desires to the contrary, race in America has painful, real consequences.

Johnson, Larsen, and Toomer narrate stories of the color line to explode the concept of race itself, to criticize American racism, and to question the false promise of the American Dream. The thrust of this project is not destructive, however. It may be seen as an effort to understand and thereby dismantle the "racial thinking," as Scott Malcomson has termed it, that operates at the core of American social practice (202). It may also be seen, as George Hutchinson has argued, as an effort to refashion and reinforce American nationalism (92). In short, Johnson, Larsen, and Toomer question the American Dream in order to legitimize the claim of all citizens upon it.

Passing in *The Autobiography of an Ex-Coloured Man*

James Weldon Johnson's *The Autobiography of an Ex-Coloured Man* is a foundational text of the Harlem Renaissance. The narrative is presented as the confession of a light-skinned man who has turned away from his African American roots to enjoy the fruits of the American Dream as a presumed white man. The confession portrays the unnamed narrator's life story in order to explain his regret for his decision to sacrifice a promising musical career and pursue a more modest life passing for white. The narrator's picaresque biography carries him throughout the United States and Europe, exposing him to many facets of "the race question" (83). When he witnesses a brutal lynching in the South, he turns his back on both his musical ambitions and his black heritage. He settles in New York City, launches a business career, and eventually marries a white woman with whom he has two children. Throughout the narrative, he assails the white prejudice that alienates and humiliates African Americans, accounts for the various classes within African American society, and celebrates the accomplishments of African American culture.

Johnson's narrator is steeped in the American Dream. He speaks proudly of the home that his mother worked so hard to provide and the values that she instilled in him. He was raised to be frugal, to work hard, to be honest, and to admire ambition. He constantly endeavors to gain "the means of earning a rather fair livelihood," realizing finally the "pride and satisfaction" of earning money "by days of honest and patient work" (115, 196). He finds the squalor of certain economically distressed black neighborhoods upsetting, and he generally finds himself drawn to "the better class of coloured people," those who keep a "neat appearance" and aspire to "a fair standard of living" (74, 59, 169). He is inclined toward marriage and family, too. "It is to my children that I have devoted my life," he insists in closing, because their opportunities are the embodiment of all his sacrifice and success (210).

The narrator's success is not easily won, however. He learns what race means as he finds himself and others excluded by color from the American Dream. As a boy, he did not realize that he was different from the white children, like them taunting the "niggers" at school (15). When a teacher singles him out, and the other children understand that he is a "nigger too," he is crestfallen (16).

He begins to see himself and his mother differently. This way of seeing is the basis for segregation. Black folks, he observes, may acquire a measure of comfort in life, but only by separating themselves from whites "to live in a little world of their own" (79). Although some private comfort may be possible for African Americans, segregation still rankles because people "object to the humiliation" of it (81). Worse, the narrator learns that while white men may disagree over the treatment of African Americans in society, they vehemently agree that they would never condone their daughter "marrying a nigger" (163). Such discrimination penetrates to the very core of the narrator's personal dignity. Even though his mother maintains that his father "loved [him] and loved her very much," the fact is that his father abandoned them (38).

When as an adult the narrator recognizes his father in a theater and it dawns on him that the pretty girl beside him is his sister, a wound is opened. "Slowly the desolate loneliness of my position became clear to me," he explains. "I knew that I could not speak, but I would have given a part of my life to touch her hand . . . and call her 'sister'" (134–35). His sudden awareness casts certain childhood experiences in an ugly new light. It explains why he was "scrubbed until [his] skin ached," presumably to remove any darkening dirt that might make him look different from his father. It likewise confirms that he and his mother were forced to move away to spare his father's white bride any embarrassment (4). The pain of all this exclusion sharpens his resolve "to keep the brand from being placed upon" his children so that he can vouchsafe the dream for them (210).

The tragedy of the narrator's confession is amplified by the ambition that he sacrificed in order to pass for white and thereby achieve a perverse version of the American Dream. While listening to a recitation of an abolitionist speech in high school, the narrator recalls, "I felt leap within me pride that I was coloured; and I began to form wild dreams of bringing glory and honour to the Negro race" (46). In time, the narrator comes to realize that he can accomplish his goal by celebrating African American music. He thus aims to "voice all the joys and sorrows, the hopes and ambitions, of the American Negro, in classic musical form" (148). After he forsakes "work so glorious," his old manuscripts come to symbolize "a vanished dream, a dead ambition, a sacrificed talent." He poignantly feels, as he says, "I have chosen the lesser part. . . . I have sold my birthright for a mess of potage" (211). Whereas faith in the American Dream implies the application of talent and ambition to achieve success, the narrator's regretful confession reveals that in some abiding sense his purchase on the dream is farcical.

The narrator's motives for abandoning his ambition to pass as white are telling. His benefactor, a modern cynic, formulates the logic harshly. Although he is well aware of the social injustices black people endure, he asks, "What's the use" in trying to change things (145).

All the narrator would be doing is throwing his gifts away on a hopeless cause and sacrificing his own chance at happiness. The benefactor acidly asserts, "I can imagine no more dissatisfied human being than an educated, cultured, and refined coloured man in the United States" (145). The lynching he witnesses bring this logic home to him and unleashes "a great wave of humiliation and shame . . . that I belonged to a race that could be so dealt with; and shame for my country, that it, the great example of democracy to the world, should be the only civilized, if not the only state on earth, where a human being would be burned alive" (188). Thus stricken, he reasons that "to forsake one's race to better one's condition was no less worthy an action than to forsake one's country for the same purpose." He neither "disclaim[s] the black race nor claim[s] the white race"; rather, he tells himself that he will "let the world take me for what it would . . . [because] it was not necessary for me to go about with a label of inferiority pasted across my forehead" (191). He cynically chooses to conceal rather than claim his heritage, and, thus, doors open for him; however, his secret undercuts any comfort he might achieve.

Passing does not solve the narrator's problems; it only changes their form. While he builds his career and works his way up the social ladder, he harbors a fear of "being found out" (210). Eventually he falls in love with "the most dazzlingly white" woman he had ever seen (198). This new relation churns up self-doubt. He explains, "I began even to wonder if I really was like the men I associated with; if there was not, after all, an indefinable something which marked a difference" (200). Doubtlessly he hears echoes of the need to protect white daughters from marrying "niggers" as he stiffens his resolve to reveal the truth about himself. When he tells her he is black, she stares at him intensely. He confesses, "Under the strange light in her eyes I felt that I was growing black and thick-featured and crimp-haired" (204).

This experience recalls both the narrator's sense that as a child he maintained "a very strong aversion to being classed" with the black children (23) and his pain of seeing himself and his mother differently after discovering that they are both black. It evokes the sense that he "never exactly enjoyed the sight" of mixed-race couples (109). It reminds him of the loneliness of being abandoned by his father and being prevented from knowing his half-sister, and it highlights his benefactor's jibe that the idea of "making a Negro" out of himself is merely "sentiment" (145). His self-doubt prompts his relief when his children are born without physical features that betray their ancestry. It causes the "constant fear that [his wife] would discover in [him] some shortcoming which she would unconsciously attribute to my blood rather than to a failing of human nature" (210). Even though by all cursory measures the narrator represents the very model of the American Dream, the fact that his mother is black in a racist society poisons his enjoyment of his accomplishments. The possibility that some will see him as inferior compels him, beyond rational judgment, to see himself as inferior, and his alienation from his "mother's people" leaves him feeling incomplete despite the fact that he has achieved so much (210).

In the final analysis, the novel ridicules the very idea of race. The narrator, for example, is "amused" by the reactions of white people who take him for white but discover his color (172). Once he has fully committed to passing, he claims, "The anomaly of my social position often appealed strongly to my sense of humor" (197). As a matter of fact, his very confession strikes him as a "sort of savage and diabolical . . . practical joke on society," a joke that simultaneously confirms and taunts white fears (3). At the same time, although the narrator makes a joke of American racism, as Donald C. Goellnicht has argued, he becomes the butt of his own joke (29). His terror and shame compel him to turn his back on a heritage he admires in order to enjoy the trappings of a life in which he must always feel like an alien. Nevertheless, the confession redeems the sacrifice of his ambition to some extent. Because he is familiar with both sides of the color line, the narrator authoritatively observes, for example, that "when one has seen something of the world and human nature, one must conclude, after all, that between people in like stations of life there is very little difference the world over" (85). Still, he maintains, "So far as racial differences go, the United States puts a greater premium on colour, or, better, lack of colour, than upon anything else in the world" (155).

The narrator rebuts white supremacist logic by simply observing, "the Negro is progressing, and that disproves all arguments . . . that he is incapable of progress" (161). He sarcastically questions why the "tremendous effort" to convince descendants of Africans that they are inferior continually fails (161). Finally, exploding the supremacist faith in a "great gulf" between the races, the narrator mockingly observes that there are millions of people with the "blood of both races in their veins" (189). Laying bare the absurdity of racism, he finally suggests that transformation of mental attitude is essential to social change. He asserts, "the main difficulty of the race question does not lie so much in the actual condition of the blacks as it does in the mental attitude of the whites; and a mental attitude, especially one not based in truth, can be changed more easily than actual conditions" (166). The trouble and the tragedy are that mental attitudes, including his own, are not so mutable; nevertheless, the novel's persuasive power lies in its candid blurring of exactly that aspect of the color line.

The Black and White Worlds of *Passing*

Like *The Autobiography of an Ex-Coloured Man*, Nella Larsen's exquisitely crafted *Passing* incisively questions racial discrimination and the anguish it causes. The narrative revolves around the reunion of two childhood neighbors and friends, Clare and Irene. Both women are pale enough to pass for white, and they bump into one another in a restaurant atop the exclusive Drayton Hotel. Irene, the protagonist, who is married to a black doctor, discovers that Clare has completely passed into the white world, marrying a white man who is an incorrigible bigot and thereby walling herself off from any interaction with black people. The chance encounter reminds Clare how much she has missed the African American community of her childhood, and she imposes upon Irene to reconnect her with "Negro society" (24).

Clare's desire extends beyond polite company, and Irene eventually discovers that Clare is having an affair with her husband, Brian. Irene had always been apprehensive about Clare, but the affair proves that Clare is a threat to Irene's security. When Clare's husband tracks her to a mixed party, confirming his suspicions that she is a "black scrimy devil," Irene rushes to Clare, who falls to her death (40). Witnesses offer multiple interpretations of the tragedy, and while Clare's ambiguous end suggests suicide, it is as likely that Irene pushed her to protect herself and her family. As the events unfold before Irene, the novel questions issues of racial identity, racial discrimination, and desire that hinder the characters' pursuit of the American Dream.

Irene lives the bourgeois American Dream. She is married to a successful doctor with whom she has two children. They live comfortably and can afford to travel. They organize charity functions and host tea parties in the home that Irene has arranged "with a sparingness that was almost chaste" (91). She and Brian maintain a polite, respectable appearance, teasing each other for occasional lapses of decorum and arguing over their boys' education (52–53). Irene has worked hard to create "the smooth routine of her household," and she enjoys a "security of place and substance" (58, 61). For Irene, "security was the most important and desired thing in life," and she tells Clare, "I know very well that I take being a mother rather seriously. I *am* wrapped up in my boys and the running of my house. I can't help it. And, really, I don't think it's anything to laugh at" (81).

Despite her accomplishments, Irene had always struggled to hold this life together. Although Irene is committed to living in the United States, Brian dislikes living in a racist country. The distance between them sparks differences in their approaches to child rearing. Irene wants to protect her children from premature exposure to racism, but Brian insists that if she is "so determined, they've got to live in this damned country, [the boys] better find out what sort of thing they're up against as soon as possible" (103). Although Irene is "unable to grasp" why "the easy monotony" of their life is "so hateful to him," she is painfully aware that Brian's unhappiness with living in United States constitutes an ever-present threat to their household (60). She exhausts herself anxiously wondering what will happen to her and the boys if she cannot "make up to him that one loss" (64). As the months pass, Brain seems more irritable and remote. In a flash, Irene realizes that he is having an affair with Clare and connects it to his "old longing" to be free of American racism (97). Whatever else she may symbolize, Clare represents a direct threat to Irene's hold on the dream.

Irene feels that she and Clare are "strangers in their desires and ambitions. Strangers even in their racial consciousness" (63). Nevertheless, they are more alike than Irene would allow. After struggling to understand a strange look that Clare gives her, "partly mocking" and "partly menacing," Irene realizes that Clare's weapon is the mask that she wears to protect her "dark secret" (45, 73). Irene also wears a mask to get what she wants. When Clare ambushes her with an introduction to her bigoted husband, who launches into a racist tirade, "outwardly" Irene remains "calm" (41). Later, when Irene bumps into Clare's husband on the street while she is out shopping with a black friend, "instinctively . . . her face had become a mask" (99). When Irene discovers Brian's affair with Clare, she suppresses her feelings and politely navigates the tea party she is hosting. Finally, when Clare dies, Irene covers her own possible culpability with an easy lie and feigned grief: "Irene struggled against the sob of thankfulness that rose in her throat. Choked down, it turned to a whimper" (113). The masks that Clare and Irene use to pursue their ambitions are portrayed as necessary to their security and attainments in a race-conscious society.

Larsen's questioning of the significance of physical characteristics, and especially of color, ignites the novel's critique of the color line. Character descriptions frequently highlight "red patches" in Irene's "warm olive" cheeks, Brian's "deep copper," and Clare's "ivory mask" (11, 24). As Steve Pile maintains, the novel is "saturated" with "a rich spectrum" of skin colors (32). Clare's features in particular are scrutinized by Irene—her "tempting mouth," her cheeks and forehead that are "a trifle too wide," the "soft lustre" of her "ivory skin," and above all her "magnificent" eyes. "Surely," Irene thinks, "They were Negro eyes" because "there was about them something exotic" (29).

Similar interest in Clare prompts Hugh, a white friend, to ask Irene to explain interracial desire. Irene speculates that it is nothing more than "emotional excitement" related to being in the presence of "something strange" and even perhaps "a bit repugnant" because it is opposed to "all your accustomed notions of beauty" (76). Moreover, the novel subtly suggests that Clare's husband is not as disgusted by African Americans as he pretends. His pet name for Clare is "Nig," which he has given her because "she's gettin' darker and darker," possibly turning "into a nigger" (39). His refusal to really see Clare seems almost voluntary once he is forced to acknowledge that she has black friends, and when she dies he groans "like a beast in agony," proving he loves her whether or not he could admit (or because he could not admit) to himself that she is biracial (111). Such questioning and confusion suggests that all the characters would prefer color and race to be insignificant, but they cannot prevent them from being determining facets of American life.

Passing, and the curiosity surrounding it, serves, therefore, a dual function in the novel. It reinforces racial boundaries by revealing the ways in which black and white Americans are obsessively fascinated by their differences while it simultaneously undermines those boundaries. Irene believes white people are "stupid" about passing, but she insists that black people can tell when someone is passing, not by anything "definite or tangible . . . just something. A thing that couldn't be registered" (77).

Irene hints that subtle cues rooted in the sensitivity to prejudice expose passers. Although Irene has some experience with passing for convenience's sake, sitting across from Clare, she becomes deeply curious about "this hazardous business" (24). She had always considered Clare "glamorous" and wants to understand the impulse to reject the "familiar and friendly to take one's chance in another environment, not entirely strange, perhaps, but certainly not entirely friendly" (19, 24). She wants to know especially how one felt when one met "other Negroes" (24). For her own part, Clare wonders why "more coloured girls . . . never 'passed' over" because it's "frightfully easy" (25). The ambiguity of Clare's "frightfully" plays ironically against Irene's sense that passing is dangerous. Brian maintains, "they always come back," despite the risks. When Irene demands to know why, Brian responds, "If I knew that I'd know what race is" (55).

Although he thinks it an "unhealthy business," Brian presumes that passing is related to the "instinct of the race to survive and expand," but Irene knows that Clare's motives are more acquisitive and that she harbors scant interest in motherhood. Irene comes to understand that Clare longs for black society because she is lonely (56). She recognizes that Clare could never show the slightest sympathy for any black person lest she reveal her secret, and thus Irene feels a duty to protect Clare. She feels "bound to her by those very ties of race, which, for all her repudiation of them, Clare had been unable to completely sever" (52). At the decisive moment of the novel, Irene feels "caught between two allegiances . . . Herself. Her Race" (98). Though she never had before, she now feels bound and suffocated by race, wishing "for the first time in her life, that she had not been born a Negro" (98). Her wish reveals the infection of the American Dream by the obsession with race, and as Josh Toth has pointed out, Clare's passing sabotages the necessity of maintaining relationships invested in racial affinities (65). In its exploration of the various ways in which people internalize racial thinking, *Passing* charts the color line in order to show that it is completely imaginary in spite of its real consequences.

Despite the tragedy of the novel, *Passing* fundamentally questions the intersection of race and the American Dream by treating passing as a great joke. Brian, for example, reminds Irene of "its humorous side," which Irene grants (55). However, Clare sees the joke in a far more penetrating light. She decided to pass after her father died and she was taken in by pious white aunts who treated her like a servant. Because

Clare was denied the things that other girls had, her cynical approach to life seems as reasonable as it does tragic. When Clare introduces her husband, Irene detects a "mocking . . . menacing" look in Clare's eye. These looks reveal "some secret joke" that Clare evidently hides behind her ivory mask (81). It is a joke that Irene accepts implicitly. "The sardony of it!" she thinks while examining her position with regard to Clare (52). Later, trying to dismiss Clare's charms, Irene observes to Brian that she thinks Clare is "intelligent," but she adds, ironically, "eighteenth-century France would have been a marvelous setting for her, or the old South if she hadn't made the mistake of being born a Negro" (88). This ugly joke reveals Irene's growing antipathy for Clare, but it also exposes her understanding of the conditions of race that have determined Clare's (and her own) response to life. Once she has discovered the affair, she must control her emotions and hide her knowledge. Nevertheless, she shatters a tea cup and explains it to her friend Hugh:

> Did you notice that cup? Well you're lucky. It was the ugliest thing your ancestors, the charming Confederates ever owned. I've forgotten how many thousands of years ago it was that Brian's great-great-grand-uncle owned it. But it has, or had, a good old hoary history. It was brought North by way of the subway. Oh, all right! Be English if you want to and call it the underground. What I'm coming to is the fact that I've never figured out a way of getting rid of it until about five minutes ago. I had an inspiration. I had only to break it, and I was rid of it for ever. So simple! And I'd never thought of it before. (94)

Irene is not talking about the cup. The terms of her speech suggest she is sarcastically referring to prejudice. She seems to be suggesting that the repulsive legacy of racism is so fragile that it could easily be destroyed, but it survives because Americans cherish and protect it. Of all her friends, Hugh, a man of "devastating irony," would comprehend what she now recognizes in Clare's features. When Clare's husband breaks into the party, screaming Clare's secret, "So you're a damned dirty nigger," Irene recognizes the "faint smile" on her face, which ignites the "terror" and "ferocity" that impel her to rush at Clare, who is standing by an open window (111). All Clare's actions seem to Irene to be "rather a joke" that she was making out of her thoroughly American values, especially the twin investments in family and race (44). Clare's death resolves the immediate threat to Irene's household, but not the underlying canard of wedding race to security that the color line enforces and passing disrupts.

Nature, Sex, Violence, and Race in *Cane*

Jean Toomer's *Cane* also charts the color line's impact on the American Dream. As an experimental, multigenre text, *Cane* weaves together poetry and prose to show that North and South are fundamentally bound together in the construction of an idea of race that shapes the social experience of every citizen.

The twenty-nine separate pieces of *Cane* are woven together by recurrent themes. Nature imagery blends shared experiences of African Americans into racial sympathy, which is the basis for the folk songs that give voice to the black experience. Nature is further represented as the force behind the drive for physical intimacy that often culminates in racial mixing. The color line is drawn by the talk of others and solidified by racial discrimination and terrorism. Nevertheless, Africa's children meet such social forces with a grim defiance. All the while, the will to achieve respectability is undercut by the orphans and broken homes that result from racial violence and discrimination, and, therefore, the American Dream is spoken of with contempt.

Thenature imagery in *Cane* is powerfully haunting, and it is linked to the artistic expression of black people. In "Carma," for example, Toomer depicts the slow setting of the sun and associates it with song: "The sun is hammered to a band of gold. Pine needles, like mazda, are brilliantly aglow," until, "Dusk takes the polish from the rails. Lights twinkle in scattered houses. From far away, a sad strong song" (10).

Similarly, the moonrise in the story "Blood-Burning Moon" is represented thus: "Up from the dusk the full moon came. Glowing like a fired pine knot, it illumined the great door and soft showered the Negro shanties. . . . Negro women improvised songs against its spell" (28). In the poem "Georgia Dusk," "The sky lazily disdaining to pursue / The setting sun, too indolent to hold / A lengthened tournament for flashing gold, / Passively darkens for night's barbeque." In the night, men carrying "Race memories . . . Go singing through the footpaths of the swamp" (13). Throughout *Cane*, African Americans are represented as ambivalently weighted down and buoyed up by the terrain and natural beauty of the South, by "the soil of one's ancestors" (17).

The potent nature imagery in *Cane* is also associated with human sexuality, particularly interracial sex. In "Georgia Dusk," "the sacred whisper of the pines" inspires "virgin lips" to be given to "cornfield concubines" (13). In "Theater," the young show girl, Dorris, dances seductively for the manager to a song "of canebrake loves and mangrove feastings" (53). The story "Becky" centers on "the white woman who had two negro sons" (5). In "Bona and Paul," Bona desires Paul because "He is a harvest moon. He is an autumn leaf. He is a nigger" (70). While Paul watches Bona, he pictures a pastoral scene in which "a Negress chants a lullaby beneath the mate-eyes of a southern planter" (76). In "Esther," the "lil milk-white gal" desires Barlo, who is "magnetically" black, with an intensity that drives her mad. In "Blood-Burning Moon," Louisa, whose skin "was the color of oak leaves on young trees in fall" is loved by Bob Stone, the scion of a powerful white family (28). Nature, sex, and the whole spectrum of variations of skin tone are blended together in *Cane*, challenging the national impulse to maintain racial purity.

Cane's emphasis on interracial desire demonstrates that all efforts to segregate the races are but an absurd custom partially enforced by talk. Becky, the white mother of two black sons, is ostracized by her town: "The white folks said they'd have no more to do with her. And black folks, they too joined hands to cast her out" (5). In "Esther," the "loose women" break Esther's seductive spell by teasing, "So thats how th dictie niggers does it" (25). In "Blood-Burning Moon," the men provoke Tom Burwell by talking "about Louisa and Bob Stone, about the silk stockings she must have gotten from him" (29). Burwell complains, "Niggers always tryin t make something out a nothin" (30). For his part, Bob Stone blushes at the thought that "his friends up North" would be shocked and "repulsed" if they discovered he loved a black woman, but he goes to her anyway (31). Similarly, even though the other girls in the dormitory speculate on Paul's ancestry, Bona "dont give a damn," going out with Paul anyway (72). As Bona and Paul dance together at the cabaret, Paul draws uncomfortable looks: "Suddenly he knew that people saw, not attractiveness in his dark skin, but difference" (75). As the couple hurries out of the cabaret, the black doorman's "eye's are knowing" (78). He knows that, as all the poems and stories in *Cane* demonstrate, sexual attraction can be a more powerful force than the customs that enforce segregation.

Cane also demonstrates that because segregation is built on shaky ground, it must be buttressed with racial violence. The poem "Portrait in Georgia" hauntingly describes the beauty of a woman after she has been lynched and all that remains is "her slim body, white as the ash / of black flesh after flame" (27). After Tom Burwell cuts Bob's throat in a fight over Louisa, he is lynched by a mob. The scene is described in spare, evocative terms, "Stench of burning flesh soaked the air. Tom's eyes popped. His head settled downward. The mob yelled" (34).

Ralph Kabnis politely lies to Southern friends when he says, "there's lots of northern exaggeration about the South. It's not half the terror they picture it," but later the same evening, after his friends have told him the story of the worst lynching "round these parts," he flees in horror when he believes he has been threatened if he does not leave town (90). The lynching they describe is of a woman whose unborn child is cut from her and impaled on a knife stabbed into a tree. Stories of violence limn the tensions between attraction and repulsion that define the color line, and as Joel B. Peckham has observed, *Cane* "exposes false dichotomies and separation that are both literary and social" (276). The violence indexes the cultural energy necessary to keep the color line distinct and thus questions its relevance, hinting at the pleasures of integration.

African Americans' quest to achieve the American Dream floats like a bubble on the surface of racial discrimination and violence, as the maintenance of homes, businesses, and respectability shows, but the pursuit of the dream is constantly disrupted by the color line. Many of *Cane*'s characters—Karintha, Becky, Fernie, Dorris, Dan Moore, and Kabnis, for example—are orphaned in a world that does not want them because they are on the wrong side of the color line, and their refusal to conform to American values and morality demonstrates a deep-seated contempt. Dark-skinned Karintha, for instance, learns how to love in a two-room Georgia Home, where folks cook and eat in one room and love and sleep in the other. After Karintha "played 'home'" with a boy, the "interest" of men pressed her into prostitution. She "married many times" but she holds nothing but "contempt" for the men who bring her money, and she abandons her illegitimate child on "a bed of pine needles in the forest" (1–2).

Becky's life and death likewise cast doubt on the American Dream. Becky is abandoned by the entire community for bearing black children, and her house collapses to prove the awful results of miscegenation; ironically, however, "the Bible flaps its leaves with an aimless rustle on her mound" (7). The Christian commitment to charity is flouted by the supposed monstrousness of miscegenation, leaving Becky and her boys to fend for themselves in a world that despises them.

In "Theater," while Dorris dances for John, she wonders, "Maybe he'd love. I've heard 'em say that men who look like him . . . will marry if they love. O will you love me? And give me kids, and a home, and everything? (I'd like to make your nest, and honest, hon, I wouldn't run out on you.) You will if I make you. Just watch me" (52). However, Doris and John's possible relationship miscarries on the very racialized assumptions that draw them together, and they remain isolated. For all the orphans of *Cane*, the American Dream is hopelessly out of reach.

The same frustration is visible in the broken homes and the general contempt for American conformity presented by the characters. For example, Tom Burwell loves Louisa because she is young, beautiful, and "goes t church" (30). He woos her by bragging, "next year if ole Ston'll trust me, I'll have a farm. My own. My bales will buy yo what y gets from white folks now" (30). Louisa is attracted to both Tom and Bob Stone, but she could never marry Bob, and whatever chance at happiness she may have had with Tom is destroyed by the mob that burns him alive.

Even achieving a home is no guarantee of happiness. Mrs. Pribby, in "Box Seat," keeps an elegant parlor in a nice house, and she presses Muriel, a boarder, to keep good manners and live a moral life. Dan, Muriel's love, knows this, and he sees the houses, the parlors, and the billeted seats of the theater as locking people into a sort of slavery. Muriel wants Dan "to get a good job and settle down" (59). She pleads with him to "get along," but he fires back, "Mussel-heads get along, Muriel . . . there is more to you than that." In the end, Muriel fears the "root-life" he represents (59).

Ralph Kabnis also wrestles with respectability and fails. His boss, Hanby, is "a well-dressed, smooth, rich, black-skinned Negro who . . . affects the manners of a wealthy white planter [and] lets it be known that his ideas are those of the best New England tradition" (93). When he fires Kabnis, Hanby explains, "the progress of the negro race is jeopardized whenever the personal habits and examples set by its guides and mentors fall below the acknowledged and hard won standard of its average member" (93). Kabnis mounts an ineffectual revolt against Hanby's morality as he struggles to find an artistic voice that can announce his frustrations with the pressure to conform but he accepts exclusion. His friend Lewis formulates the problem curtly: Black Americans are a "muted folk who feel their way upward to a life that crushes or absorbs them" (105). Halsey puts it this way: "give me a good job an sure pay an I aint far from being satisfied, so far as satisfaction goes. Prejudice is everywheres about this country. An a nigger aint much standin anywheres" (109). Halsey's shabby claim on satisfaction barely conceals his deeper repudiation. *Cane* unearths this feeling, giving voice to its implicit contempt. However, as Gino Pellegrini has observed, *Cane* voices a "mixed race sensibility" that could be "grasped and appreciated by the American public" (1). The contempt with which the book represents both bourgeois respectability and the color line intimates that only a "mixed race sensibility" can salvage the relevance of the American Dream.

Conclusion

"Harlem of the bitter dream," Hughes wrote in *Montage of a Dream Deferred,* because passing reinforces the color line even as it transgresses it. Toomer, Johnson, and Larsen, like Hughes, all candidly depict the struggles of mixed-race characters during a historical moment when white supremacists were mounting a campaign of terror to maintain white racial purity and power. Rallying to the New Negro Movement, they participated in fomenting a tradition of black pride, yet they also derided the culture of the color line. In this historical context, mixed-race individuals, especially those who could pass in both cultures, were perceived as a monstrous threat to racial purity, clear racial boundaries, and, crucially, the racialized American Dream. However, Johnson, Larsen, and Toomer's books represent mixed-race individuals as monstrous only because they both reflect and discredit the monstrousness of racial thinking. The narratives of the color line in these books think through and beyond a United States defined by racial difference. They expose the preposterous basis of racial ideology. They highlight the mutual presence of blackness in white identity and whiteness in black identity. By blurring the color line that the United States was so desperately trying to parse, they suggest that biological and cultural hybridity are both inevitable and related. They demonstrate, further, that although racial mixing generates confusion, pain, and strife, it need not be feared. To simply ignore race will not make it go away; rather, these books suggest that people need to understand what racial thinking is in order to stop thinking in racialized ways.

Johnson, Larsen, and Toomer assiduously confronted the legacies of racial thought in the United States and asked whether they were worth perpetuating. Their answer is a unanimous and resounding "no," because for them, the American Dream is an idea that is valuable in its own right. It is an idea worth preserving, if the idea of color could be removed from it, so that all Americans could enjoy access to the pride and prosperity that the American way of life can afford. In the final analysis, the sarcasm with which Hughes, Johnson, Larsen, and Toomer address the color line instigates a legitimate criticism of American acts but not of the American Dream. These stories of the color line argue that if the American Dream cannot be enjoyed by every citizen, then it cannot be claimed, it cannot be respected, and it does not really exist for any citizen.

Works Cited

Adams, James Truslow. *The Epic of America*. Boston: Little, 1931. Print.

Cullen, Jim. *The American Dream: A Short History of an Idea That Shaped a Nation*. New York: Oxford UP, 2003. Print.

De Jongh, James. *Vicious Modernism: Black Harlem and the Literary Imagination*. New York: Cambridge UP, 1990. Print.

English, Daylanne K. *Unnatural Selections: Eugenics in American Modernism and the Harlem Renaissance*. Chapel Hill: U of North Carolina P, 2004. Print.

Goellnicht, Donald C. "Passing and Autobiography: James Weldon Johnson's *Autobiography of an Ex-Coloured Man*." *African American Review* 30.1 (Spring 1996): 17–33. Print.

Hughes, Langston. *Montage of a Dream Deferred*. New York: Holt, 1951. Print.

Hutchinson, George. *The Harlem Renaissance in Black and White*. Cambridge: Belknap-Harvard UP, 1995. Print.

Johnson, James Weldon. *The Autobiography of an Ex-Coloured Man*. New York: Hill, 1960. Print.

Larsen, Nella. *Passing*. Ed. Thadious M. Davis. New York: Penguin, 1997. Print.

Malcomson, Scott. *One Drop of Blood: The American Misadventure of Race*. New York: Farrar, 2000. Print.

Peckham, Joel B. "Jean Toomer's *Cane*: Self as Montage and the Drive Toward Integration." *American Literature* 72.2 (June 2000): 275–90. Print.

Pellegrini, Gino Michael. "Jean Toomer and *Cane*: 'Mixed-Blood' Impossibilities." *Arizona Quarterly* 64.4 (Winter 2008): 1–20. Print.

Pile, Steve. "Skin, Race, and Space: The Clash of Bodily Schemas in Frantz Fanon's *Black Skins, White Masks* and Nella Larsen's *Passing*." *Cultural Geographies* 18.1 (Jan. 2011): 25–41. Print.

Schultz, Jennifer L. "Restaging the Racial Contract: James Weldon Johnson's Signatory Strategies." *American Literature* 74.1 (Mar. 2002): 31–58. Print.

Sollers, Werner. *Interracialism: Black-White Intermarriage in American History, Literature, and Law*. Oxford UP, 2000. Print.

Toomer, Jean. *Cane*. Ed. Darwin T. Turner. New York: Norton, 1975. Print.

Toth, Josh. "Deauthenticating Community: The Passing Intrusion of Clare Kendry in Nella Larsen's *Passing*." *MELUS* 33.1 (Spring 2008): 55–73. Print.

Watson, Steven. *The Harlem Renaissance: Hub of African American Culture, 1920–1930*. New York: Pantheon, 1995. Print.

After Auschwitz, Connecticut?: Dreams and Disappointments in Mid-Twentieth-Century American Literature_____

Tiffany Gilbert

On its surface, the juxtaposition of the state of Connecticut and the con-centration camp Auschwitz seems dangerously cavalier and improper, as the travails of Northeastern life simply do not compare in scope to the terrors of government-sponsored mass murder across Europe and Russia. I invoke this unlikely juxtaposition not to minimize the events that transpired, but to help us imagine the dilemma contempo-rary Americans faced at the end of World War II: squaring together an irrevocable past with a gleaming present that urged forward progress and prosperity. The title of this essay evokes the maxim, "No poetry af-ter Auschwitz," a truncation of Theodor Adorno's brutal assessment in "Cultural Criticism and Society" (1951) that such luxuries of the mind as poetry and art were no longer valid or even possible in a world that had not only witnessed the horrors of the concentration camps, but had also produced such barbarism in the first place. After Auschwitz, and later Hiroshima and Nagasaki, Adorno implied that beauty itself risked becoming an extinct beast fossilized in the sediments of memory. In-deed, as far as the future itself was concerned, what dreams could have survived the nightmarish conflagration of the Holocaust and the atomic bomb?

The United States home front, with the exception of Japan's surprise attack on Pearl Harbor in December 1941, remained largely unscarred by the war. Psychological and physical trauma existed, to be sure, but contemporary politics and media encouraged a swift return to normal-cy; routine was salvation for many Americans, who responded vigor-ously to their postwar circumstances by funneling their energies and anxieties into a renewed pursuit of happiness. Holding out the promise of plenty, the American Dream translated into the lingua franca of de-ferment, the promise that hard work would pay off someday.

In the years immediately following the end of World War II in 1945, however, "someday" no longer sufficed. Many young men sought refuge from traumatizing battlefield memories in marriage and in bucolic suburbia. Compelled by the "return to normalcy" ideology that was promoted by advertisers on New York's Madison Avenue and politicians in Washington, DC, Americans subscribed to a consumer-driven economy that whetted materialist appetites for all things new and modern. The GI Bill enabled returning soldiers to earn college degrees, thereby optimizing their chances at landing lucrative jobs in the private sector and increasing their earning potential to support the demands and desires of their families. Once combatants of Nazis and Japanese, these men traded foxholes for the boardrooms of corporate giants like General Electric and IBM. In exchange, their wives, many of whom had worked out of necessity and patriotism in factories during the war, returned to the home—away from the city. Here, on the outskirts, in William Levitt–designed developments, amid the glimmering linoleum and the polished chrome of the latest Sunbeam appliance, Americans sought to live out their lives in opulent predictability.

Fought on two fronts—domestic and corporate—the battle to redefine the American Dream escalated into an existential crisis in the 1950s. Mindless consumerism resulted in more dissatisfaction. The home, once treasured as a sanctuary, now weighed heavily on both husbands and wives: a money pit for him, a prison for her. More painful than mortgages for these mid-century American dreamers, however, was the realization that they—unlike their country, which believed completely in its "exceptionalism"—were not special. They were simply average, conducting lives as prefabricated and unoriginal as Levitt's tract houses. In many ways, then, the crushing banality and predictability of postwar American life, initially an enormous relief from wartime uncertainty, proved to be an indomitable new nemesis.

This low-grade discontentment that simmered in suburbia eventually bubbled to the surface and finally broke into the literature of the period. This essay examines the American Dream after Auschwitz as it was diagnosed in narrative, verse, and drama by authors as diverse as Sloan Wilson, Tennessee Williams, Lorraine Hansberry, and Frank O'Hara. Confronting the unsustainably indulgent nature of the American Dream and its enervating effects on the American psyche, these authors, as well as contemporaries Richard Yates and Allen Ginsberg, chronicled the moment in the modern vernacular of aspiration and angst.

Tempest in a Cul-de-Sac: Wilson's *The Man in the Gray Flannel Suit* (1955) and Yates's *Revolutionary Road* (1961)

Just a train ride away from New York City, an elegant home in Connecticut represented the apex of bourgeois domestic success throughout the early 1950s. By mid-decade, however, this image had begun to sprout weeds. In the opening paragraphs of Sloan Wilson's first novel, *The Man in the Gray Flannel Suit*, the author introduces his protagonist, Tom Rath, by describing the mediocre home he shares with his family. "By the time they had lived seven years in the little house on Greentree Avenue in Westport, Connecticut, they both detested it. There were many reasons," Wilson writes, "none of them logical, but all of them compelling. For one thing, the house had a kind of evil genius for displaying proof of their weaknesses and wiping out all traces of their strengths" (1). Its "evil genius" manifests itself in a question mark-shaped crack that curves toward the ceiling in the living room. The crack, caused by a vase Tom throws in frustration over his wife Betsy's spending, daily reminds them that they have grown weary with the business of adulthood—working, raising children, and managing a household. The house, once considered their "starter home," has become a cheerless burden:

> It took them five years to realize that the expense of raising three children
> was likely to increase at least as fast as Tom's salary at a charitable foun-
> dation. If Tom and Betsy had been entirely reasonable, this might have

caused them to start painting the place like crazy, but it had the reverse effect. Without talking about it much, they both began to think of the house as a trap, and they no more enjoyed refurbishing it than a prisoner would delight in shining up the bars of the cell. Both of them were aware that their feelings about the house were not admirable. (3)

Tom and Betsy, in their less-than-charitable attitudes toward the house, renege on their tacit agreement as postwar Americans to prosper without complaint. Drifting from day to day, they merely endure their lives, believing "something would have to happen" (3).

By locating the source of Tom and Betsy Rath's dissatisfaction in the home, Wilson targets a central pillar in America's sociopolitical strategy after World War II. After the war's end in 1945, President Harry S. Truman implemented a multidimensional foreign policy of "containment" to protect the country from communist invasion and other threats. Domestically, the US government mounted a "soft" defensive campaign that enlisted the American family in the cause, encouraging homeownership and large families. To ensure the external security of the nation, the internal networks of marriage and family were positioned on the front lines of the emerging Cold War. Domesticity, according to historian Elaine Tyler May, offered tranquility and safety to men and women who still harbored fears about the future (18).[1] Couples were encouraged to unite in matrimony and restore prewar gender divisions—all in the name of normalcy, of course. These commitments were glorified as reaffirmations of citizenship that would deliver tremendous emotional and political dividends.

In the world of *The Man in the Gray Flannel Suit*, however, Wilson depicts the fallout when the safety net guaranteed by these commitments begins to fray. Betsy accuses Tom of having "no guts." To better his family's living situation, Tom applies for a higher-paying job as a public-relations consultant for a mental illness awareness campaign. Part of the application process requires Tom to write an essay in which he describes "the most significant fact about me" (11). He struggles a while before reducing his life to an innocuous paragraph that scantly covers vital statistics, military record, and work history. The ambivalence Tom now experiences as a job applicant opposes his decisiveness on the battlefield, where survival mattered; *how* he survived was a separate issue. One fact about Tom's life, however, is incontrovertible: seventeen, the number of men he killed.

> Plenty of men had been dropped behind the enemy lines, as Tom had been on five different occasions, and they had had to do some of their killing silently, with blackjacks and knives. They had known what they were doing, and most of them were healthy enough not to be morbid about it, and not to be proud of it, and not to be ashamed of it. Such things were merely part of the war, the war before the Korean one. It was no longer fashionable to talk about the war, and certainly it had never been fashionable to talk about the number of men one had killed. Tom couldn't forget the number, "seventeen," but it didn't seem real any more; it was just a small, isolated statistic that nobody wanted. (13)

Indeed, Tom cannot forget the war. Much of *The Man in the Gray Flannel Suit* takes place in 1944, almost ten years before the novel's start, where the exigencies of war in Italy influence much, if not all, of Tom's actions. There, Tom, though he is married to Betsy, falls in love with Maria, a girl from the village where he and his fellow soldiers enjoy a reprieve from fighting. Quickly, they fall into the casual habits of domesticity, forming "a suburban community, with the men all working for the same big corporation" (82). Tom and Maria's romance results in pregnancy, but he receives transfer orders to New Guinea before the child is born; he never sees Maria again.

Notwithstanding his indiscretion with Maria, the paradigmatic event that splits Tom's life in two is his inadvertent killing of his war buddy, Hank Mahoney, during a melee with the Japanese. Mahoney's brutal death, which Tom causes by throwing a grenade prematurely, triggers a mental breakdown—the effects of which still haunt Tom. Indeed, the peripatetic structure of Wilson's novel underscores Tom's tenuous control over his circumstances. Tom's flashbacks reveal that he has not reconciled his guilt over the accident. He chastises himself for this perceived weakness, for indulging in self-pity when his family's future is at stake. "No, Tom thought, I mustn't go on like this. Between peace and war a clear line must be drawn. The past is something best forgotten; only in theory is it the father of the present. In practice, it is only a wildly unrelated dream, a chamber of horrors. . . . The past is gone, Tom thought, and I will not brood about it. I've got to be tough. I am not the type to have a nervous breakdown. I can't afford it. I have too many responsibilities" (97). Wilson's irony is hardly subtle: The man in charge of promoting mental-health awareness verges on the edge of psychological collapse.

Despite its confident tone, Tom's inner monologue rings hollow; his toughness is just talk. He clings to his gray flannel suit, which becomes his corporate uniform, as though it were a life preserver. And, in many ways, it is. "I will go to my new job, and I will be cheerful, and I will be industrious, and I will be matter-of-fact. I will keep my gray flannel suit spotless. I will have a sense of humor. I will have guts—I'm not the type to start crying now," he tells himself (98). The gray flannel suit identifies Tom as a rank-and-file member of the commuter class, marking him as man of the times, not a vestige of "the war before the Korean one." Moreover, it announces his intention to claim his share of the American Dream. One caveat, however: Tom no longer believes in the American Dream—especially if it means only a steady parade of useless acquisitions and empty accolades. He muses that "the trouble hadn't been only that he didn't believe in the dream any more; it was that he didn't even find it interesting or sad in its improbability. Like an old man, he had been preoccupied with the past, not the future" (Wilson 173). After living on the brink for so long during the war, a desk job hardly suffices; the corporate routine itself now becomes a kind of living death.

What began as an excoriation of suburbia in *The Man in the Gray Flannel Suit* finds itself in a much different territory by its end. Inasmuch as Tom's malaise shows the adverse effects of the manic self-corporatization that afflicted many postwar Americans, the novel stops short of a full-frontal assault on the sociocultural "Dream" machinery that churned up these white-collar fantasies in the first place. Tom and Betsy, for all their protests about the house and their dull suburban lives, ultimately embrace safety over subversion. Homeowner-turned-landlord, Tom plans to rezone his grandmother's property for a housing development project he is spearheading. In New York, he vacates his position with the demanding mental-health campaign, citing the importance of honesty. He explains to his boss, "I'm trying to be honest about this. I want the money. Nobody likes money better than I do. . . . I can't get myself convinced that my work is the most important thing in the world" (251). At home, this need for honesty compels Tom to confess the truth of his affair and child to Betsy, who is outraged and storms out the house. Her subsequent return signals not only their reconciliation, but also Tom's recognition of the "gray flannel" charade he performed:

> I really don't know what I was looking for when I got back from the war, but it seemed as though all I could see was a lot of bright young men in gray flannel suits rushing around New York in a frantic parade to nowhere. They seemed to me to be pursuing neither ideals nor happiness—they were pursuing a routine. For a long while I thought I was on the side lines watching that parade, and it was quite a shock to glance down and see that I too was wearing a gray flannel suit. (272)

If Tom and Betsy Rath begrudgingly accept the suburban routines of the American Dream, Frank and April Wheeler in Richard Yates's *Revolutionary Road* choke on its blandness. The novel opens auspiciously with April's performance in a disastrous local production of *The Petrified Forest*. With her disappointment at what she assumed would be her moment in the spotlight, Yates taps into his work's emotional center of gravity: the realization of one's ordinariness in a world that valorizes exceptionalism. On the way home, April's self-pity infuriates Frank:

> It strikes me . . . that there's a considerable amount of bullshit going on here. I mean you seem to be doing a pretty good imitation of Madame Bovary here, and there's one or two points I'd like to clear up. Number one, it's not my fault the play was lousy. Number two, it's sure as hell not my fault you didn't turn out to be an actress, and the sooner you get over *that* little piece of soap opera the better off we're all going to be. Number three, I don't happen to fit the role of the dumb, insensitive suburban husband; you've been trying to hang that one on me ever since we moved *out* here, and I'm damned if I'll wear it. (26)

Frank's comparison of April to Gustave Flaubert's desperate housewife Emma Bovary is an apt one. Just as Madame Bovary indulged her bourgeois fantasies by trying to transform her country-doctor husband into a world-class surgeon, conducting affairs with wealthy playboys, and shopping her way into debt, so too does April imagine herself as woman whose tastes and opinions are far more sophisticated than her neighbors'. In her mind, she *deserves* better—whether or not she has the means or talent.

"Better," of course, begins with a new house. Like Tom and Betsy Rath's in *The Man in the Gray Flannel Suit*, Frank and April's house on Revolutionary Road functions as a kind of avatar, registering happiness or discontent in its architecture. During their house hunt, Mrs. Givings, an officious realtor, champions the house as an exception; its charm lies in its difference from the other houses that surround it. Unlike the "great hulking split levels [painted] in nauseous pastels," the one they eventually purchase, she effuses, "has absolutely no connection with that. One of our nice little local builders put it up right after the war, you see, before all the really awful building began. . . . Simple, clean lines, good lawns, marvelous for children" (30). Notwithstanding Mrs. Givings's hard sell, Frank and April scoff at the presence of a picture window, a common feature of suburban housing. While April concedes that the house is "nice," Frank's response is prescient: "Still, I don't suppose one picture window is necessarily going to destroy our personalities" (31).

Spoken in jest, Frank's comment about the window reveals his and April's intensifying anxiety over the survival of their identities as they age. Over weekly cocktails with friends—a provincial habit they believed they were too good to adopt—they mask their own petrification with insults and superiority. On one occasion, Frank, his confidence stoked by liquor, lectures April and their guests on the problems with America:

This country's probably the psychiatric, psychoanalytical capital of the world. Old Freud himself could never've dreamed up a more devoted bunch of disciples than the population of the United States—isn't that right? Our whole damn culture is geared to it; it's the new religion; it's everybody's intellectual and spiritual sugar-tit. . . . It's as if everybody'd made this tacit agreement to live in a state of total self-deception. The hell with reality! Let's have a whole bunch of cute little winding roads and cute little houses painted white and pink and baby blue; let's all be good consumers and have a lot of Togetherness and bring our children up in a bath of sentimentality—Daddy's a great man because he makes a living, Mummy's a great woman because she's stuck by Daddy all these years—and if old reality ever does pop out and say Boo we'll all get busy and pretend it never happened. (Yates 69)

Frank's speech strikes down the major culprits of mid-century anomie and despair—the suburbs, mass consumerism, reactivated gender binaries, the nuclear family. It is a boozy call to action, which later inspires April to propose that the family cut their American ties and move to France. But, in their haste to leave behind their mediocre lives, and joy in planning their future, Frank and April make love without taking precautions against pregnancy.

The tragedy of *Revolutionary Road* is not that Frank and April Wheeler never travel to France, or even that April dies after terminating the pregnancy on her own. Rather, Frank and April allegorize the failure of America's fundamental scripts that preached the virtues of individualism and freedom, and viewed happiness as an entitlement. By the time Frank and April wake up from their reality, the American Dream—at least as they conceived it—has passed.

The Wages of Inheritance: Williams's *Cat on a Hot Tin Roof* (1955) and Hansberry's *A Raisin in the Sun* (1959)

Disguising geopolitical ambitions in the domestic rhetoric that positioned the home as ground zero in the emerging Cold War, the American Dream of the 1950s left little room for the individual. American security would not be achieved through conquest and land grab, but through the economic and emotional aggrandizement of the nuclear family, which represented a new frontier for modern nation-building efforts. Playwright Tennessee Williams avoided dramaturgy that consciously engaged in socioeconomic debate or critiqued America's materialist appetites (Gilbert 186); yet, within the context of a Southern family drama that deals with such weighty themes as death and homosexual panic, Williams interrogates the dynastic implications of the American Dream and the repercussions for the individual in his play *Cat on a Hot Tin Roof.*

Set on the occasion of Big Daddy Pollitt's birthday, *Cat* opens with the beautiful yet childless Maggie Pollitt complaining to her husband, Brick, about the raucous antics of their nieces and nephews, whom she calls "no-neck monsters":

Hear them? Hear them screaming? I don't know where their voice-boxes are located since they don't have necks. . . . I said to your charming sister-in-law, Mae, honey, couldn't you feed those precious little things at a separate table with an oilcloth cover? . . . She made enormous eyes at me and said, 'Ohhh, noooooo! On Big Daddy's birthday? Why, he would never forgive me!' Well, I want you to know, Big Daddy hadn't been at the table two minutes with those five no-neck monsters slobbering and drooling over their food before he threw down his fork an' shouted, 'Fo' God's sake, Gooper, why don't you put them pigs at a trough in th' kitchen?'—Well, I swear, I simply could have di-ieed! (884)

Through Maggie's monologue, Williams presents a tableau of familial dysfunction: loud, ill-mannered grandchildren, sycophantic in-laws, and a dying patriarch who calls his own heirs "pigs." Instead of names given them at birth, the children respond to what Maggie terms "dawgs' names"—Dixie, Trixie, Buster, Sonny, and Polly (896). With five already and another baby on the way, their parents, Gooper and Mae, enact the American Dream's reproductive mandate that led to the baby boom of the 1950s. Maggie scoffs at Mae's rampant fecundity. "That monster of fertility, Mae; she's downright odious to him!" Maggie says. "Know how I know? By little expressions that flicker over his face when that woman is holding fo'th on one of her choice topics such as—how she refused twilight sleep!—when the twins were delivered! Because she feels motherhood's an experience that a woman ought to experience fully!—in order to fully appreciate the wonder and beauty of it! HAH!" (887). For her part, Maggie masks her "mother envy" by calling her nieces and nephews "no-neck monsters," but still she feels the sting of Gooper and his wife Mae's gossip. She reports to Brick, "It goes on all the time, along with constant little remarks and innuendos about the fact that you and I have not produced any children, are totally childless and therefore totally useless" (884). Without heirs, Maggie and Brick jeopardize the future of Big Daddy's empire, as well as forfeit their opportunity to advance according the American Dream narrative.

In the mid-century version of the American Dream, maternity equates with relevance. But, Maggie's dreams of motherhood and Big

Daddy's vision of a Pollitt dynasty come at the expense of individual choice for Brick. Much of the scholarship surrounding Brick's character has focused on his sexual indifference to Maggie and the romantic nature of his relationship with his dead friend Skipper. David Savran, for example, has suggested that Brick's quandary evolves from an internalized conflict between the gay and straight masculinities Skipper and Big Daddy respectively embody. However, fixating on Brick's sexuality minimizes the play's focus on the larger cultural inheritance—and burden—the American Dream poses. Even Big Daddy, his bravado notwithstanding, chafes under his familial and social obligations: Gooper, Mae, and their band of "screechers" annoy him; Big Mama is repulsive; church "bores the Bejesus out of" him; and the clubs are "crap" (941). Literally and metaphorically, these things gnaw at Big Daddy's core. Indeed, it would not be excessive to read his malignant cancer as a kind of cultural diagnostic—the dream as disease.

Where does a man like Brick fit in proscriptive contexts of the American Dream? Disgusted with his limited options, Brick sulks, jumps hurdles while drunk at the high school track where he was once a star, and steeps in his grief over Skipper. To avoid conversations, he blasts music from the stereo console, which Williams calls in the production notes, the "monumental monstrosity peculiar to our times" (880). Big Daddy encourages his son to return to sports announcing, but Brick declines: "Sit in a glass box watching games I can't play? Describing what I can't do while players do it? Sweating out their disgust and confusion in contests I'm not fit for? Drinkin' a coke, half bourbon, so I can stand it?" (944).

Brick can no longer abide the pretense of "standing it." Mendacity, as he calls all "lies and liars," taints every relationship in the Pollitt family. Yet it props up the charade that they are an American Dream success story. Ironically, a lie allows Maggie to realize her dream of becoming a mother. In the first ending Williams composed for *Cat*, Maggie leverages Brick's weakness for liquor in exchange for sex. She reiterates her love for him, but he is not convinced. With "charming sadness," he questions, "Wouldn't it be funny if that was true?" (976). In the Broadway version of the play, Brick exhibits more agency. When Maggie conceives the lie that she is pregnant to preserve Brick's stake in the Pollitt fortune, he corroborates her story. With his own desires still unarticulated, Brick subordinates them to Maggie's wish for a baby, and to the family's dynastic ambitions.

Like *Cat on a Hot Tin Roof*, Lorraine Hansberry's *A Raisin in the Sun* centers on the nexus of the American Dream, individual desire, and the conflicts created by collective inheritance. The play, the first by an African American woman to win the Pulitzer Prize, tracks the Younger family's anticipation and plans for a hefty insurance check resulting from Walter Lee Sr.'s death. His son and namesake, Walter, a chauffeur by trade, lives with his wife Ruth, their son Travis, his sister Beneatha, and his mother, Lena, in a cramped apartment in the projects on Chicago's South Side. Here, the Youngers disagree over how to spend the insurance money: Should Mama make a deposit on a larger home in a better neighborhood and open an account for Beneatha's college education, or give it to Walter to invest in a liquor store? Hansberry's dialogue conveys the daily pressure the American Dream exerts upon the Younger family. It has, in fact, invaded the morning ritual, as Walter and Ruth argue yet again about their future during breakfast. Walter says:

> There you are. Man say to his woman: I got me a dream. His woman say: Eat your eggs. (*Sadly, but gaining in power*) Man say: I got to take hold of this here world, baby! And a woman will say: Eat your eggs and go to work. (*Passionately now*) Man say: I got to change my life, I'm choking to death, baby! And his woman say—(*In utter anguish as he brings his fists down on his thighs*)—Your eggs is getting cold! (556)

Walter's predicament is clear: As a black man, he is powerless to pursue his own destiny in a nation that throws up barriers in front of him every step of the way, and yet he struggles for validation within his own family. Exasperated with Walter's dream talk, Ruth anchors herself in the simple reality of breakfast. She too aspires for something better but recognizes the futility of his building castles in the air. (*"Wearily*) Honey, you never say nothing new," Ruth tells Walter. "I listen to you every day, every night and every morning, and you never say nothing new. (*Shrugging*) So you would rather *be* Mr. Arnold than be his chauffeur. So—I would *rather* be living in Buckingham Palace" (557). Ruth's palace fantasies suffocate in the "rat trap" she and her family call home (562).

Drawing from her own family's legal battle against housing discrimination, Hansberry skewers the American Dream's claims of fairness and equal opportunity in the subplot centering on Mama's wish for her own home and backyard for a garden.[2] The Chicago tenement was supposed to be temporary, until she and her husband could save enough money to purchase a proper home. The time never arrived for her husband, who could only hope for a chance; in reality, the contemporary American Dream rhetoric implicitly, if not blatantly, excluded black and brown Americans from its promise. A second-generation beneficiary of America's cold shoulder, Walter bristles with rage over seeing "white boys" his age broker deals and toss money around like it is nothing. His selfish arguments over the money sadden Mama, who fled to the North to escape a violent South.

WALTER: Mama—sometimes when I'm downtown and I pass them cool, quiet-looking restaurants where them white boys are sitting back and talking 'bout things . . . sitting there turning deals worth millions of dollars . . . sometimes I see guys don't look much older than me—

MAMA: In my time we was worried about not being lynched and getting to the North if we could and how to stay alive and still have a pinch of dignity too. Now here come you and Beneatha—talking 'bout things we ain't never even thought about hardly, me and your daddy. You ain't satisfied or proud of nothing we done. I mean that you had a home; that we kept you

---

After Auschwitz, Connecticut?

out of trouble till you was grown; that you don't have to ride to work on the back of nobody's streetcar—You my children—but how different we done become. (582)

The play takes a decisive turn when Mama places a deposit on a small home in a predominantly white neighborhood outside the city. She gives Walter the remainder to purchase a stake in the liquor store and save in the bank for Beneatha's education. But the American Dream she believes in is used against her to dissuade the family from moving. When Mr. Lindner, a representative of the Clybourne Park neighborhood, visits, he laces his appeals against integrated housing with Dream rhetoric. "Well—you see our community is made up of people who've worked hard as the dickens for years to build up that little community," he demurs. "They're not rich and fancy people; just hard-working, honest people who don't really have much but those little homes and a dream of the kind of community they want to raise their children in" (606). With this polite rejection, he could easily be describing the Younger family and their aspirations; worse still, he offers to buy the home Mama has chosen for more than she paid. Acting on his mother's behalf, Walter throws Mr. Lindner out of the apartment.

Hansberry balances this scene of triumph with a subsequent one that depicts Walter's ambitions, completing the diptych of aspiration and defeat that the play actively sketches. Instead of depositing Beneatha's share of the money, Walter gives the entire sum—more than six thousand dollars—to business partners, Willy and Bobo, to close the deal on the store. But Willy, as Bobo later informs the family, disappears with all of the money. Mama, remembering her husband "working and working and working like somebody's old horse," slaps Walter repeatedly in the face for his selfishness, and prays for strength (615).

A Raisin in the Sun concludes without the ambivalence of *The Man in the Gray Flannel Suit* or *Cat on a Hot Tin Roof*, or the despair of

Revolutionary Road. The play reestablishes the family as the engine that drives the American Dream. Walter, whose entrepreneurial plans nearly destroyed the family, considers Lindner's payoff after the terrible blow to his own dreams. Recovering his authority, however, Walter refuses to exchange his family's dignity for profit. According to Margaret Wilkerson, who examines early drafts and production notes of the play in her essay "*A Raisin in the Sun*: Anniversary of an American Classic," Hansberry initially intended to end the play by depicting the Youngers in their new living room bracing for white retaliation, but ultimately opted to give the play a more optimistic, yet ambiguous conclusion.

Living the Dream: Ginsberg's *Howl* (1956) and O'Hara's *Lunch Poems* (1964)

At once an island of dreams and a cauldron of nightmares, New York City lies at the center of the American Dream's literary cartography. In "Howl," Allen Ginsberg creates an urban landscape littered with the detritus of human suffering, pummeling the American Dream in a verbal tour de force that, in his introduction to the poem, William Carlos Williams likened to hell (8). The three-part poem and its addendum "Footnote to 'Howl'" draw power from anaphoric refrains, incantatory pacing, and shocking use of vernacular and profanity. Reminiscent of Whitman's "Song of Myself," Ginsberg catalogues an array of lost souls, the casualties of the consumerist decade. Madison Avenue, hub of the nation's advertising industry, mutates into an American Hiroshima. Here, "the best minds of my generation"

> who were burned alive in their innocent flannel suits on Madison
> Avenue amid blasts of leaden verse & the tanked-up clatter of the
> iron regiments of fashion & the nitroglycerine shrieks of the fairies
> of advertising & the mustard gas of sinister intelligent editors, or
> were run down by the drunken taxicabs of Absolute Reality. (16)

More vitriolic in his cultural critique than Sloan Wilson, Ginsberg transforms the signature apparel of postwar ambition—the gray flannel suit—into a burning death shroud. Advertising dulls individual minds with "leaden verse," turning America into a nation of sheep. Instead of spontaneity, Ginsberg sees nothing but regimented dehumanization: men and women ferried about in "drunken taxicabs" in pursuit of some elusive dream or, worse, reality itself.

In terms at once material and cannibalistic, Ginsberg asks in Part Two, "What sphinx of cement and aluminum bashed open their skulls and ate up their brains and imagination?" (21). The ancient sacrificial god Moloch operates as shorthand for what he views as the scourges of modernity; that is, the destructive military-industrial complex, soulless conformity, and rampant consumerism. In one memorable stanza, the poem virtually shouts via Ginsberg's prolific use of exclamation points:

> Moloch! Moloch! Robot apartments! Invisible suburbs! skeleton
> treasuries! blind capitals! demonic industries! spectral nations!
> invincible mad houses! granite cocks! monstrous bombs! (22)

Moloch functions as an anti-mantra that elevates the unholy and profane. Mental institutions housing countless numbers are hidden from view while monuments—"granite cocks"—are erected to honor the powerful elite, and "blind capitals" look the other way. Everywhere in "Howl," men and women sacrifice themselves to Moloch, breaking their backs, plunging off bridges, or going insane.

But the poem should not be dismissed as a mere rant against the American Dream. Departing in spirit and tone from the litany against a spectral Moloch, Part Three addresses an individual: Carl Solomon, the writer Ginsberg met in a psychiatric hospital and to whom he dedicates "Howl." Between verses that dramatize Solomon's plight, a melodic refrain stresses Ginsberg's allegiance to Solomon, and lulls the reader into sympathizing as well:

> I'm with you in Rockland
>> where you bang on the catatonic piano the soul is innocent and
>>> immortal it should never die ungodly in an armed madhouse
>> I'm with you in Rockland
>> where fifty more shocks will never return your soul to its body again
>>> from its pilgrimage to a cross in the void. (25)

These insidious psychiatric treatments cannot alter Solomon's soul, which remains "innocent and immortal." Ginsberg extends this benediction to the "Footnote," where he recites a litany of people and things—fellow Beats Neal Cassady and Jack Kerouac, typewriters, exotic locales, and jazz—naming them as the ingredients for his art. Floating these images upon the poem's anaphoric structure, he declares them all "holy! holy! holy!"

If the American Dream sustains an attack in "Howl," Frank O'Hara's slim volume *Lunch Poems* revels in the dream's byproducts: modern art, movies, traffic. O'Hara, who composed many of these poems on his breaks from his job at New York's Museum of Modern Art, curates his daily experiences with verve. Significantly, neither resentment nor lassitude marks these poems. Even though he acknowledges in "Music," which inaugurates the collection, that "the season / of distress and clarity" has arrived, he is undeterred (7).

Indeed, he is open to everything. In "A Step Away from Them," he revels in the city's sights, enumerating them as if the reader is on the walk with him:

> It's my lunch hour, so I go
> for a walk among the hum-colored
> cabs. First, down the sidewalk
> where laborers feed their dirty
> glistening torsos sandwiches
> and Coca-Cola, with yellow helmets

on. They protect them from falling
bricks, I guess. Then onto the
avenue where skirts are flipping
above heels and blow up over
grates. The sun is hot, but the
cabs stir up the air. I look
at bargains in wristwatches. There
are cats playing in sawdust. (18)

O'Hara elevates the ordinary lunch break into an afternoon esca-
pade. The city, with its synesthetic "hum-colored" taxis, vibrates
around him. In search of a cheeseburger, he imbues every one he sees
with importance; hot, dirty construction workers appear as "glisten-
ing" sculpture. The casual joie de vivre of this summer day is apparent
in the image of skirts "flipping / above heels." A timestamp included in
the second stanza—"it is 12:40 of / a Thursday"—reminds us that this
is not a recollection, but a live recording of the day's events. Even on a
day like this, where "There are several Puerto / Ricans on the avenue,
which / makes it beautiful and warm," he sadly remembers recently de-
ceased friends, the painter Jackson Pollock and lyricist John Latouche.
But O'Hara does not dwell in the past or fret over the future—after all,
lunch is brief, and he must return to work.

Instead of waiting on the right job, a move to Paris, or the arrival
of an insurance check, forward progress, O'Hara insists, is the only
option. Indeed, in *Lunch Poems*, the American Dream is in the doing—
buying a watchband, editing an art exhibit, or recalling Billie Holiday
singing at the 5 Spot. The poem "Adieu to Norman, Bon Jour to Joan
and Jean-Paul" contains what well may be an antidote to the American Dream's legacy of festering hopes and dissatisfaction. Musing on
friends like Allen Ginsberg, who "is back talking about god a lot," and
his own lingering hangover, he resolves:

we are all happy and young and toothless

it is the same as old age

the only thing to do is simply continue

is that simple

yes, it is simple because it is the only thing to do

can you do it

yes, you can because it is the only thing to do. (O'Hara 36)

Despite O'Hara's certainty, "continuing" in the postwar American Dreamscape was no easy task. Encouraged to distance themselves from the horrors of Pearl Harbor, Nazism, and atomic bombs, men and women bartered present-day satisfaction and tranquility for the hope of a dazzling, secure future. In the emerging consumer economy, the two-story colonial house, a well-paying job, and a prospering family loomed as irresistible talismans in the acquisitive American imagination. Sure, the Connecticut fantasy may have distracted Americans from the ghosts of Auschwitz and World War II, if only by creating the white noise of ambition. In their place, however, as these mid-century writers poignantly demonstrate, melancholy and discontentment filled the void, taking residence in the weary suburbanite's heart.

Notes

1. In addition to May's fine social history on the impact of containment on postwar American families, see also Jurca, Castronovo, Halberstam, Riesman, and Mills below.

2. In 1940, the Supreme Court adjudicated the class-action lawsuit *Hansberry v. Lee*, in which Lorraine Hansberry's father, Carl, challenged the racially restrictive covenants of the white Chicago neighborhood in which he desired to purchase a home. For a complete transcript of the court's decision, see http://supreme.justia.com/cases/federal/us/311/32/

Works Cited

Adorno, Theodor. "Cultural Criticism and Society." *Can One Live after Auschwitz? A Philosophical Reader*. Ed. Rolf Tiedemann. Stanford: Stanford UP, 2003. Print.

Castronovo, David. *Beyond the Gray Flannel Suit: Books from the 1950s That Made American Culture*. New York: Continuum, 2004. Print.

Gilbert, James. *Men in the Middle: Searching for Masculinity in the 1950s*. Chicago: U of Chicago P, 2005. Print.

Ginsberg, Allen. *Howl and Other Poems*. San Francisco: City Lights, 1956. Print.

Halberstam, David. *The Fifties*. New York: Ballantine, 1994. Print.

Hansberry, Lorraine. "A Raisin in the Sun." *Plays of Our Time*. Ed. Bennett Cerf. New York: Random House, 1967. Print.

Jurca, Catherine. *White Diaspora: The Suburbs and the Twentieth-Century American Novel*. Princeton: Princeton UP, 2001. Print.

May, Elaine Tyler. *Homeward Bound: American Families in the Cold War Era*. New York: Basic, 1999. Print.

Mills, C. Wright. *White Collar: The American Middle Classes*. New York: Oxford UP, 1953. Print.

O'Hara, Frank. *Lunch Poems*. San Francisco: City Lights, 1964. Print.

Riesman, David, Nathan Glazer, and Reuel Denney. *The Lonely Crowd: A Study of the Changing American Character*. New York: Doubleday, 1953. Print.

Savran, David. "'By Coming Suddenly into a Room That I Thought Was Empty': Mapping the Closet with Tennessee Williams." *Studies in the Literary Imagination* 24.2 (1991): 57–74. Print.

Wilkerson, Margaret. "*A Raisin in the Sun*: Anniversary of an American Classic." *Performing Feminisms: Feminist Critical Theory and Theatre*. Ed. Sue-Ellen Case. Baltimore: Johns Hopkins UP, 1990. 119–30. Print.

Williams, Tennessee. *Plays, 1937–1955*. Ed. Mel Gussow and Kenneth Holditch. New York: Library of America, 2000. Print.

Wilson, Sloan. *The Man in the Gray Flannel Suit*. New York: Thunder's Mouth, 1955. Print.

Yates, Richard. *Revolutionary Road*. New York: Vintage, 1961. Print.

The Assimilated and Unassimilated in Bernard Malamud's *The Assistant*_____

Quentin Martin

Frank Alpine, the protagonist in Bernard Malamud's novel *The Assistant* (1957), is a migratory near-bum in the Depression-era United States whose schemes for success involve robbery and petty thievery; it is his way of compensating for the deprivations of his orphaned and abusive childhood in the West. Having come to Brooklyn armed with a hostile attitude and a recently purchased gun, he teams with an equally abused and crime-prone young man, Ward Minogue, who adds to the mix an inveterate anti-Semitism. Wanting to get back at a Jewish classmate and father who, Ward believes, targeted him in school (72), and who now have made a success of their family liquor business, Ward recruits Frank to help him rob the store. However, as they approach, the vigilant father, Julius Karp, quickly locks up. Undeterred, Ward persuades Frank to simply move the operations next door to a grocery store owned by Morris Bober, on the grounds that "a Jew is a Jew" (70).

It is by these roundabout means that the novel's core collision occurs between the native-born, Italian Catholic Frank, with his rootless ideas and behavior, and the rooted principles of the Yiddish-accented Jewish immigrant Morris. The culmination is Frank's religious conversion—in the novel's celebrated last words, Frank "became a Jew" (246)—completing a series of conversions that ripple through the novel. Taken together, they represent an inversion of the usual immigrant saga of a foreign people (in this case, Morris and his daughter, Helen) slowly assimilating and acculturating to their new American environment; instead, the plot is largely driven by the American Frank's immersion into and embrace of the principles and behaviors of the unassimilated Jewish immigrant. However, Frank and the Bobers' resistance to assimilation comes with a steep cost: social and financial marginalization.

The "novel turns on a paradox" (Hershinow 34), in that in order to attain the moral and spiritual success of the unassimilated, one has to endure social and financial failure. By extension, the book also renders the concept of the American Dream a paradox, or at least highly problematic. The trumpeted benefits of achieving the dream turn out to be riddled with unexpected consequences. In short, both resisting assimilation and embracing it cause forms of misery. The Bobers' lack of money and social ostracism are obvious forms of misery, while the misery of the assimilated Jewish neighbors is the result of materialism and moral blindness, hidden by wealth and social approval. Nothing comes easy in the world of *The Assistant*.

That Frank is converted, if not saved, by his own crime victim is another unexpected paradox of the story (highlighted by Malamud's withholding of the information until nearly one-third of the way through the novel that Morris's new assistant is the same man who had assaulted him). However, though Morris and Helen's role in converting Frank is paramount, Frank came to the Bobers ready, in his vague and impractical way, to mend himself. He knows that his life has been a series of failures and that he needs direction, if not a model. He had not only failed to achieve the conventional American Dream of upward mobility and social success, but is also unsure if it was even a worthy goal. He tells Morris during their first full conversation that "sooner or later everything I think is worth having gets away from me in some way or other. . . . With me one wrong thing leads to another and it ends in a trap" (36). Morris listens sympathetically and even identifies with the young man because his own life has become a "trap" as a result of his failing grocery store. Frank, though, wants more than sympathy from Morris—he wants nothing less than for Morris "to tell him how to live his life" (37).

Frank's surprising introspection and desire for change is subtly signaled throughout the novel by his habit of looking at himself in a mirror; these looks usually reflect his own failed state (Siegel 123–24). Even on the night of the robbery, while Ward threatens Morris with the gun (and ultimately hits him twice), Frank "turned to stare" into the "cracked mirror" that hangs over a sink in the back room of the grocery (25). Later, as Frank still wrestles with his impulse to steal money and goods from Morris's store, "he was afraid to look into the mirror for fear it would split apart and drop into the sink" (85). The night of his drunken and chaotic rape of Helen, which occurs after (and probably as a result of) being fired by Morris for the thefts, Frank looks at his face in a bar mirror and feels a "nose-thumbing revulsion" for having committed another "wrong thing" and fallen into a "trap" after seeming so close to attaining a regenerated life (174). As Ben Siegel notes, these "partial, deflected glimpses . . . intensify his inadequacies and frustrations," but they also signal some crucial self-awareness (123).

Frank's yearning to surmount his own revulsion-producing behavior and create a "new life" for himself—as he says in another self-reflective moment while standing in front of a window (60)—seemingly stems from his youthful fascination with his namesake, Francis of Assisi (Saint Francis), the thirteenth-century founder of the Franciscan Order. "An old priest used to come to the orphans' home where I was raised," he says, "and every time he came he read us a different story about St. Francis. They are clear in my mind to this day" (30). Saint Francis's conversion from materialistic hedonism to a "new life" of self-abnegating poverty and tireless care for the poor resulted not only in his canonization two years after his death but also in his ability to inspire Catholics and non-Catholics alike through the centuries. Immortalized in scores of paintings, sculptures, and stories, including one in which he supposedly preached to the birds (he believed all things on Earth were worthy of reverence since they were created by God), Saint Francis set an example through life-changing conversion, tireless dedication, and Christlike love for the despised of the earth, attributes that became staples of Catholic thought, trickling down to the abused and abandoned child, Frank Alpine, leading him on his own path toward a different definition of success than one enshrined as the American Dream.

When Frank first appears on Morris's block after the robbery—casing the area not for crime but for expiation—he is seen by another Jewish storekeeper, Sam Pearl, staring "for five minutes" at a picture of Saint Francis: "[a] thin-faced, dark-bearded monk in a coarse brown garment, standing barefooted on a sunny country road. His skinny, hairy arms were raised to a flock of birds that dipped over his head. In the background was a grove of leafy trees; and in the far distance a church in sunlight" (30). This description clearly aligns the two as much as their shared name and shared Italian roots do, in that Frank is "dark-bearded" and wears "an old brown rain-stained hat" (29). In addition, Frank is from the most famous city named after Saint Francis, San Francisco, California, as he specifically says twice (33, 81). (These connections have been pointed out by many critics; see Hays 224–25 for example.) Jeffrey Helterman also claims that Malamud most likely used the word "assistant" for both Frank and the title of the novel, rather than "apprentice"—as the novel was originally titled (Davis 114)—or any other reasonable alternative, to help cement the link between the two through the first five letters of their identifying tags, Assisi and Assistant (10).

However, Saint Francis's inner principles, rather than his outward appearance and his name, are what Frank wants to integrate into his own life. He tells the hovering storekeeper Sam Pearl—another Jewish merchant on the street, which serves as a sort of Jewish ghetto surrounded by an often antagonistic Gentile neighborhood—that Saint Francis "was born good, which is a talent if you have it" (31). Clearly, Frank feels he needs to learn to acquire goodness, since he, despite all his superficial links to Saint Francis, was born without it (Hays 220). In the grocery store, as he looks across the way from Sam Pearl's shop, he finds his path to that quality.

Morris Bober has owned his declining, decaying grocery store for twenty-one years. Though his store is never as prosperous as Julius Karp's liquor store, at least it provided a living before the Great Depression, an event that pushes him and his business to the brink of collapse.[1] The depressed times have been accelerated by the recent nearby opening of a well-stocked grocery store run by an "energetic German" (12). With this grievous multiplication of his problems, "all times were bad" (11). Even loyal customers, including the Bobers' upstairs tenants, the young Italian couple Nick and Tessie Fuso, have begun patronizing the new store. The novel opens in early November, and the growing seasonal darkness and "clawing" wind clearly have more than climatic significance for Morris and his store: They represent "a world in which the long shadow of suffering still blotted out the sun" (Rosen vii).

Morris's first customer on this dark morning in these dark times is his usual one: a strange, "sour-faced" Polish woman who seems to sneer at Morris and even mock his Jewishness. That Morris would get up at 6 a.m. every day for her measly three-cent purchase—especially since she is often the only customer for hours, is perhaps anti-Semitic, and complains if Morris is a few minutes late—is the first and perhaps most important key to Morris's rooted principles that so appeal to and overwhelm Frank. Instinctively, through his devotion to Jewish law, Morris has one simple code: feel every "schmerz" (pain), not just your own but everyone's (7), and if possible, return hate with love. This self-defined Jewish principle, though with clear correlatives to Jesus and Saint Francis, has profound implications. It requires Morris not only to suffer through the early working hours every day for no real financial benefit, but also to expose himself to the ridicule of others for his financial backwardness, including that of his less-than-sympathetic wife, and the affluent Jewish merchants, especially Julius Karp. In assimilated American culture, with its capitalistic grail of profit, one is "crazy" (as Ida calls Morris) to work for nothing, to give things away. Morris, though, with his unassimilated, Old World principles, does not calculate value with their typical cash-register formula: Feeling for others, giving to others in need, and doing good in return for evil is as automatic as breathing, though it costs him the financial success the more conventional, assimilated grocer might attain. When Frank, for example, tells him about the common tricks he has observed in his vagabond working career, Morris says:

> "It's easy to fool people."
>
> "Why don't you try a couple of those tricks yourself, Morris? Your amount of profit is small."
>
> Morris looked at him in surprise. "Why should I steal from my customers? Do they steal from me?"
>
> "They would if they could."
>
> "When a man is honest he don't worry when he sleeps. This is more important than to steal a nickel." (84)

It is not just peace of mind that Morris gains from valuing honesty over profit, however. He also gains from potential enemies a return of trust, if not affection. Even the oddball and potentially anti-Semitic Polish woman shows a sort of dedication to Morris. She is not one of those who deserts him when flashy competitors appear and she is honest with Morris in return. The one roll she buys every morning is in a bag outside the doorway in the morning, and she stands there, in the dark and cold, waiting for Morris to arrive so that she can pay him for something with which she could easily walk away (3). On Morris's return from a week's bed rest after his initial injury, she is again waiting, and she pays him six pennies instead of three because she presumably did take one roll during his absence (32).

As a grocer, Morris feeds many, including the poor, a Christlike role (Helterman 11, 51) that Saint Francis had also played. Just as Saint Francis "gave everything away that he owned, every cent, all his clothes off his back," as Frank says, Morris goes through pain and privation to "feed" the Polish woman for the nominal three cents (31). If a customer has no money, Morris gives his food away.

Morris's second customer of the day, on the same cold November morning that opens the novel, is a girl of ten who comes begging for more credit on behalf of her mother. With his own mounting bills and enforced penny-pinching life, Morris initially refuses, his "heart held no welcome for her," but when the girl "burst into tears," he gives in and increases the debt, though marking the figure at $1.61 (rather than its true amount of $2.03). Again, money has less importance in Morris's code than a child's distress and his own self-estimation. "His peace—the little he lived with—was worth forty-two cents" (4).

Morris even tends the sick. His supplier of paper products, Al Marcus, is dying of cancer yet continues to work in order to stay connected to life. For this man, "no matter how bad business was, Morris tried to have some kind of little order waiting for him" (86). To the unassimilated Morris, charity and love trump the calculations of business and profit. Furthermore, Morris, as he does with others, gives Marcus his time, as they routinely "stand around a few minutes, making small talk" (87). Time is not money for Morris.

Morris's habit of feeding the poor and tending to the sick continues in his treatment of Frank, who was actively anti-Semitic. However, such matters do not concern Morris. Before Frank begins working as Morris's assistant, he has hidden out and slept in the grocery cellar, stealing milk and rolls. However, Morris reacts not with recrimination and outrage but with compassion. Seeing Frank's "drawn and haggard face" (50), Morris wonders, "How can you sleep in such a cold and drafty cellar?" He then asks Frank if he is still hungry and, finding that he is, makes him sandwiches and soup, which Frank "ate with great hunger, his hand trembling as he brought the spoon to his mouth. The grocer had to look away" (51).

Frank's education in the charity of the unassimilated is furthered when he hears Ida complain to Morris that Frank's problems "ain't my business." Morris responds that people such as Frank who land at their door are in fact their—or, at least, his—business (52). Morris takes for granted that he is his brother's keeper, asking Ida, "Where you want him to go?" After complaining further, Ida reluctantly gives in, though she shouts, "Morris, you crazy" (53). Later, in their bedroom while Frank sleeps on the couch in the store below, Ida continues:

"He will clean out the store."

"Where is his truck?" Morris asked, smiling. Seriously he said, "He's a poor boy. I feel sorry for him." (53)

Aside from occasionally fantasizing about Saint Francis, Frank has never encountered a man like Morris. Though fully aware of her father's financial failures, Helen says, "he knew, at least, what was good" (230). Frank wonders if Morris's goodness has something to do with being Jewish; as they become better acquainted and then coworkers, Frank asks Morris: "What is a Jew anyway?" (123). When Morris responds that "to be a Jew all you need is a good heart" and that "a Jew must believe in the Law" (124), Frank is a bit skeptical because he has noticed that Morris does not go to synagogue, handles pork, and opens his store on Jewish holidays. He says of Morris's claim that he is a Jew, "I can give you an argument that you aren't." Ashamed and a bit defensive, Morris counters that such matters are trivial; the key point is to remember "the Law," which he says "means to do what is right, to be honest, to be good" (124). Frank, trying to get to the singularity of Jewishness, argues that "other religions have those ideas too," so the quality that makes Jews different, he concludes, is that they "suffer so damn much." Morris's response startles Frank and is perhaps a turning point in his learning and converting to Morris's (and Saint Francis's) principles:

"They suffer because they are Jews" [Morris says].

"That's what I mean, they suffer more than they have to."

"If you live, you suffer. Some people suffer more, but not because they want. But I think if a Jew don't suffer for the Law, he will suffer for nothing."

"What do you suffer for, Morris?" Frank said.

"I suffer for you," Morris said calmly.

Frank laid his knife down on the table. His mouth ached. (125)

Those simple words constitute a revelation for Frank and make him realize that Saint Francis's spirit lives in the twentieth century, even in a run-down Jewish grocery store in backwater Brooklyn. Morris is a "flesh and blood" incarnation of Francis (Abramson 29). In her perceptive overview of post–World War II Jewish American fiction, Dorothy S. Bilik points out that the older immigrant characters in these writings are often "the embodiment of the history and tradition of European Jews . . . imbued with the moral power and the will to preserve and transmit in the American Diaspora that Jewish heritage that was tragically destroyed in Europe" (5). Characters such as Morris, she continues, are "often modern, secular versions of the *tsadik* (pious, saintly man) of traditional Yiddish and Hebrew literature, who acts as teacher and moral example to others" (5). Thus, from two ancient sources, Catholic Saint Francis and the Jewish *tsadik*, fused in the present in the person of Morris, Frank is able to move toward "moral or perceptual" change (Bilik 18).

Part of Morris's "suffering" over and concern for Frank's condition derives from him equating his long-dead son Ephraim with Frank. Had he lived, Ephraim would have been about Frank's age of twenty-five. In the course of the novel, Frank becomes Morris's lost son, whom he reclaims. As in the famous Gospel story of the Prodigal Son—in a parallel also pointed out by Sheldon Hershinow (46)—Morris's loving acceptance and embrace of his "son," regardless of past behavior, illustrates the godly quality of unconditional love, as well as the healing power of such love. This is especially evident, by way of contrast, with another key father-son relationship in the novel, that of Ward and his father, a police detective (who is simply called by his last name, Minogue). Ward's fate shows what would have happened to Frank if he had never found his "father" (Helterman 47, 50). Ward remains Ward (partly because he is not loved unconditionally by his father), while Frank becomes Francis.

Like Frank, Ward misbehaved as a youth in ways that evoke the behavior of the Prodigal Son: He was a "wild boy, always in trouble for manhandling girls" (49). His father's response was to "regularly beat up his son," and when Ward was later fired from a job for stealing (in an exact parallel of Frank's behavior), "his father beat him sick and bloody with his billy [club] and drove him out of the neighborhood." Ward's father's pattern of brutal response "didn't do much good" (49)—a typical narrative understatement that is easily missed but that underscores the contrast being set up. Whereas Frank is tutored and ultimately changed by Morris's loving acceptance and help, Ward continues to decline; he adopts other behaviors of the Prodigal Son, including eating and drinking to the point of nausea and living in the same type of squalor that the Prodigal Son eventually does. Reduced to this swinish condition, Ward makes one final, pitiful attempt to reunite with his father and evoke some remnants of love, even as his father fires his pistol at him. Ward "ran into his father's arms" and "pleaded with the detective not to hurt him," but "his father beat him mercilessly with his billy until Ward collapsed" (216). Ward vows to kill him if he ever appears again. Bloody, concussed, and nauseous, Ward performs his final misdeeds: stealing alcohol from his original target, Julius Karp's liquor store and then setting the store on fire, dying in its flames (217–18).

Ward's actions contrast with those of Frank, who in the preceding section puts out a fire at the grocery store and saves Morris's life. (Morris, in a panic of financial desperation, set the fire with the thought of collecting insurance money but then immediately regretted his act and clumsily tried to put out the fire.) By this point, despite his own grievous misdeeds and backward slips, Frank has nearly finished his conversion to Francis. He runs the store as Morris did, wearing Morris's apron (54), getting up in the dark to feed the Polish woman, and, by the end, performing all the charitable functions that Morris had. The novel's final scenes are a almost exact replicas of the opening ones, down to making lemon tea for the downcast and impoverished light-bulb peddler, Breitbart, who has troubles with his own son (6, 245). To employ the symbolic implications of his last name rather than his first, Frank has climbed the "alpine" mountain to a new identity (Bilik 55; Freedman 162).

Frank's ascent was also made possible by Morris's daughter, Helen, who further instructs Frank about doing "what is right, to be honest, to be good" (124). Holding to such behaviors makes the twenty-three-year-old, second-generation American, unaccented Helen even more of a subject of ridicule than her father. The fully assimilated Ned Pearl, the son of the candy-store owner, who is seen as highly desirable because of his looks, intelligence, and prospects, tells Helen, "You've got some old-fashioned values about some things." He wonders how "anybody [could] have such a hot and heavy conscience in these times," informing her that "people are freer in the twentieth century" (109). All Helen can say about her unassimilated, premodern ways is that "my values are my values." Another failed suitor of Helen, Louis Karp, the son of Julius Karp, is equally puzzled and upset by Helen's self-imposed restraints; after she resists his advances, he mockingly predicts she will become a "dried-up prune of an old maid" (45). With Frank, though she feels herself falling in love with him (130), she continues to adhere to her "values" of not engaging in hasty sex even while lying in his bed; she says, "I want to be disciplined," to which Frank, still not yet Francis, replies, "Crap" (140).

This conversation proves to be a turning point, for Frank realizes Helen's use of the word "disciplined" links to his deepest desires. Suddenly, "the idea seized him" that acquiring discipline is actually a powerful and difficult concept that, if mastered, would provide a key to his whole future (Freedman 163). It becomes as powerful a talisman as the image of Saint Francis; the linked words "discipline," "self-control" and "will" are as enticing as the image of Saint Francis preaching to the birds. "With the idea of self-control," he later reflects, "came the feeling of the beauty of it—the beauty of a person able to do things the way he wanted to, to do good if he wanted" (157). He would, he resolves, "change and live in a worthwhile way" (158). However, such a demanding, life-changing principle is not donned like a robe, and he continues to backslide, including his sexual attack on Helen, his petty thieving from the store, and his spying on Helen while she showers. When the fruits of his efforts do come, when he manages to integrate all Morris and Helen have shown and taught him, the shift is so profound he cannot even articulate or fully understand it. "One day, for no reason he could give, though the reason felt familiar, he stopped climbing up the air shaft to peek at Helen, and he was honest in the store" (242).

As Iska Alter points out, Helen has also educated Frank about what constitutes real and false value in their cash-based American culture. Helen has come to her own understanding of the distinction because, as an attractive, marriageable young woman, she has had to resist attempts to convert her own body into a commodifiable object, perhaps as signaled by her work at "Levenspiel's Louisville Panties and Bras" (106), since those body parts are "the most obvious tokens of feminine identification used by men to signify the woman as an erotic product" (Alter 99). The summer before the story opens, Helen had an affair with Nat Pearl, but while Helen had wanted "a future in love" with him, all Nat "wanted without too much trouble [was] a lay" (14). Feeling at the time that love was possible, Helen had given up her virginity and slept with him. As the novel opens, she fully understands Nat and what he really valued in her; consequently, she is depressed and has to fight off "self-hatred" (15). She realizes "how little he wanted. Not her, Helen Bober." In all, she had been "valued under her expectations" (14).

The well-off Karps also attempt to put a price on Helen. Though the son, Louis, has always struck out with her, the father, Julius, wealthy and fully assimilated to the moneymaking philosophy, knows better (Alter 10). All he has to do is give a good offer and the impoverished Bobers, like any weaker party in a business negotiation, will jump. "Karp felt he could ease his son's way to Helen by making Morris a proposition" about rescuing the Bober store in exchange for the Bober daughter. Karp "would describe Louis' prospects after marriage in terms of cold cash . . . and suggest that Morris speak to Helen on the subject" (151). Karp himself would "talk turkey" with Helen, confident that "she would listen to reason and appreciate the good life he was offering her" (152). In short, he is offering her the American Dream of wealth and upward mobility. However, this "cash register" approach is not the kind to woo the unassimilated Bobers. Even when Karp applies additional pressure by telling Morris he is bringing in another highly competitive grocer, Morris explodes in profanity, both at Karp's repeated backstabbing and his attempted commodification of Helen (155).

In his first approaches to Helen before he has been changed, Frank, falls into the same pattern as Nat and the Karps: He sees Helen as a commodity he can appraise and buy. Feeling shame over the former because he was "making her into a thing" (75), and rejected in the latter because Helen knows that "for gifts you pay" (112), Frank once again is required to learn a new way and to understand value as the unassimilated Bobers define it. Patiently, carefully, and thoughtfully, he grows to see both the complete Helen, in which Nat had no interest, and how much his and Helen's interior lives correspond: their shared loneliness, thirst for education, and dreams of new and better lives. Frank recognizes that they are both broken, a notion communicated repeatedly throughout the novel by their most defining outward characteristics—Frank's misshapen nose and Helen's bowed legs; thus, both search for healing. Eventually, Frank views her bowed legs as beautiful and enticing, and she comes to see that his nose "fitted his face and his face fitted him. It stayed on straight" (130). He was, Helen continues to reflect, "gentle, waiting for whatever he awaited with a grace she respected" (130). He "valued her more than she was altogether sure she wanted to be" (131), the exact reversal of Nat's and the Karps' more conventional valuations.

The loving patience and humanistic valuation that Frank originally learned from Morris in his treatment of the Polish woman and others (including himself), carries Frank through both the aftermath of drunken rape on the day he was fired by Morris and his long-delayed confession to Helen that he was one of the men who robbed her father. Frank's way back derives from his deep understanding and identification with Helen, which allows him to intuit her inward resolve after her father's death: While weeping over his poverty-pinched life and endless sacrifices, Helen "felt she must do something for herself, accomplish some worthwhile thing or suffer his fate. Only by growing in *value* as a person could she make Morris's life meaningful" (234, italics added). The value, she believes, will be reached only by going back to college and earning her degree. Soon after her realization, Frank has a "thought so extraordinary it made the hair on the back of his neck stiffen. He figured the best thing he could do was help her get the college education she had always wanted" (235). When he speaks to her about this, "her heart moved violently. . . . His staying power mystified and frightened her" (238–39). When she refuses, still hateful over his behavior, he says the only "magic word[s]" (237) possible: Do it, he says, "in your father's name. If not for you, then for him" (239).

These key breakthrough moments are so shattering that they are registered physically rather than mentally—Frank's mouth ached over Morris's definition of Jewishness and suffering, he cannot put into words his own conversion to disciplined honesty, his hair stands on end as he finally realizes Helen's deepest core need and value, and Helen's heart lurches at the "mystifying" ability of Frank to look so deeply into her and her father. The unassimilated Bober principles get at the core of human experience, beyond the reach of conventional verbal formulations. It is in these cases that the benefits of the unassimilated Bober ethic are most prominent.

Frank's having "changed into somebody else" (243), and Helen's recognition of such, is illustrated by a new kind of gift he gives her. After repeatedly failing to atone for his sexual attack and her resultant abhorrence for him, he dreams that he is standing outside her window in the icy snow of deep winter, which is reflective of both her mood and the state of his prospects. He stands there so long the snow piles up on his head, and she, "moved by pity," opens the window and throws a delicate white flower down to him, which he catches in his hand (185). The dream ends and, fully awake, the flower is gone and the window "sealed with ice" (185). Some days later, he finds a rough two-by-four in the cellar and begins to carve "the first [thing] he had ever made" (192): first a bird (a symbol that echoes the Saint Francis story) and then a "delicate" flower—a miracle of transformation from rough wood to delicate flower that parallels his own (192–93).

At the novel's close, in a sort of religious vision, Frank (while reading the Bible in the grocery) sees his very own Saint Francis "come dancing out of the woods in his brown rags, a couple of scrawny birds flying around over his head" (245). The man approaches the store, reaches into the garbage for the carved flower Helen had dumped, and then tosses it into the air, where it transforms into a real flower; Saint Francis then offers it to Helen with the gentle words, "Little sister, here is your little sister the rose" (245–46). This time, Helen takes it, "although it was with the love and best wishes of Frank Alpine" (246). The improved ending of this vision reflects a shift in Helen. Seeing him transformed to one who does not think her principles are "crap," who sees her as a whole being and not just a body, and who knows the value of nonassimilation, has also transformed her. "She had, she thought, changed in changing him" (130).

The culmination of Morris's and Helen's education occurs at the book's close: Frank undergoes circumcision to become a full Jew. In another crucial paradox, the pain of the procedure both "enraged and inspired" him (246), which represents another key to Frank's understanding and integrating of the Bober system of values: that genuine insight and humanity come from suffering (Alter 17–18), and the inverse, that a lack of suffering creates moral blindness, also holds. While Morris feels every *schmerz*, the candy-store owner Sam Pearl, for example, floats above life's darkest realities in his gaming and money-making obsessions (Alter 12). Though they nod and wave to each other occasionally, the two men "never bothered to talk. What did [Morris] know about race horses? What did the other know of the tragic quality of life? Wisdom flew over his hard head" (17–18). Hershinow further explains this concept of knowledge through suffering:

> Suffering is central to Morris's identity; he needs it, expects it, and receives it in generous doses. But suffering is also an essential part of his goodness—if he were not a good man, Malamud implies, he would not be subject to suffering in such overwhelming onslaughts. . . . Morris is doomed to a material suffering that plays a counterpoint to an arduously won but genuine spiritual triumph. (34)

Frank's own spiritual triumph by way of suffering creates a link, once again, to his original model, Saint Francis of Assisi. As a sign of his spiritual growth—in inverse proportion to his material well-being— Saint Francis was granted the stigmata of Christ (the five wounds Christ received during the Passion). As Helterman points out (39), Frank acquires stigmata-like wounds: the self-punishing marks he makes with his own "thick nails" (like the nails of the cross) for his continued thieving (69) and the cutting of his own palms (like the nails through Christ's palms) over his failed early attempts to buy Helen's favor (112). These and other physical and emotional wounds (including circumcision) are signs of God's favor. Frank has become, all at once, a Jew, a Bober, the son of Morris, Morris himself, and Saint Francis, which is reinforced toward the end—his clothes become rags and his frame becomes "scrawny" through virtual starvation (240, 241). Just as he replicates Morris's behavior in the store, he replicates Saint Francis's steps toward saintliness.

A final crucial point is that the Bober system that Frank has embraced and will carry forward is poorly suited to the American system of profit over honesty and the pursuit of financial, rather than moral and ethical, rewards. The Bobers of the United States are generally "failures" because of their lack of material possessions and income. Alter says: "This paradox is an indication that such virtues as honor, duty, responsibility, and goodness are a hindrance in an aggressive society addicted to the pursuit of externally determined success, not its internal reality; that morality and ethical behavior are signs marking only the failed, the lost." (9). Morris and Helen's Jewishness, Edward Abramson adds, "is starkly contrasted with the values of modern America" (26). Therefore, while the novel celebrates the Bobers' principles, it also makes clear the costs of such a lifestyle.

The people with the "right" attitudes, by society's standards, get rewarded, as seen in the character of Julius Karp, the greatest financial success in the novel. After Prohibition ends, he manages to get a liquor license, though "when asked how, winked a heavy-lidded eye and answered nothing" (16)—a sign that something underhanded, probably a bribe or an exchange of favors, was involved. His business, furthermore, depends on being in the middle of an impoverished area where people buy cheap booze to dull their reality; as Morris says, "a business for drunken bums" (9). That Karp gets rich selling liquor, while Morris becomes poor providing food, is a further "reflection of American values" (Abramson 41). These values—which reward fraud and bribes—have an even more direct impact on Morris earlier in his working life because of the machinations of his former partner, Charlie Sobeloff. Through a roundabout scheme, Sobeloff had driven Morris out of their business, costing Morris his hard-earned four-thousand-dollar investment, and then reopened as the sole owner, becoming wealthy. The "cross-eyed but clever conniver" (204) was rewarded by a system that must discourage and financially punish Bober probity.

By the end of his life, before contracting double pneumonia, Morris realizes that he has perhaps immigrated to the wrong country. Having risked everything to escape military service in czarist Russia, "he had hoped for much in America and got little" (27). Despite his endless labor, he has failed because he did not adopt or assimilate to the financial-social system of his new country, where wealth is the determiner of value and all is fair in its accumulation. "What had he escaped to here?" (206), he asks himself, but the answer by this point is clear:

an unsuited environment, "where good and decent people are not honored" (Abramson 27). Morris is unable to emulate or understand the Karps and Sobeloffs of the world. He has no envy for their kind of "value": "For Karp . . . what was there to envy? He would allow the liquor dealer his bottles and gelt [money] just not to be him" (23), and "he would not envy Charlie Sobeloff his dishonest wealth" (207). The Karps and Sobeloffs have been conditioned to believe money equals a meaningful life, a confusion the Bobers avoid through "old-fashioned" beliefs (10). Though at the same time, even Helen sees that her father's ways, while abstractly admirable, are problematic. She wonders, "What was the good of such honesty if he couldn't exist in this world? . . . He made himself a victim" (230).

Nonetheless, Frank embraces the Bobers' unassimilated principles and adopts them regardless of the social and economic costs. For him, they transmit a way of life as old as both Jewish law and the teachings of Saint Francis, one that is morally superior to the American Dream philosophy to which Julius Karp and Charlie Sobeloff adhere. The Jewish and Catholic principles, even with all the suffering they entail, are the key to Frank's ability to finally find his way. Abjuring the American Dream may not get him gelt, but pursuing the "Bober Dream" raises hair on the skin and cause hearts to lurch.

Notes

1. The novel is never precisely dated, and some critics—as well as Malamud, who does so in marginal notes for an earlier draft (Davis 132)—set the story in the late 1940s or see it as purposely undated, thereby lending it a timeless quality. However, the "hard-times" mood of the novel, as well as the specific mention of "bad" and "unhappy times" (87, 132); references to the ending of Prohibition (9, 16); and Ida's job sewing military epaulettes (233) make a strong case to many critics for dating the novel in the late 1930s at the beginning of World War II. (See Bilik 56 and Langer 120, for example.)

Works Cited

Abramson, Edward A. *Bernard Malamud Revisited*. New York: Twayne, 1993. Print.

Alter, Iska. *The Good Man's Dilemma: Social Criticism in the Fiction of Bernard Malamud*. New York: AMS, 1981. Print.

Bilik, Dorothy S. *Immigrant Survivors: Post-Holocaust Consciousness in Recent Jewish-American Fiction*. Middletown, CT: Wesleyan UP, 1981. Print.

Davis, Philip. *Bernard Malamud: A Writer's Life*. New York: Oxford UP, 2007. Print.

Freedman, William. "From Bernard Malamud, with Discipline and with Love." *Bernard Malamud: A Collection of Critical Essays*. Ed. Leslie A. Field and Joyce W. Field. Englewood Cliffs, NJ: Prentice-Hall, 1975. 156–85. Print.

Hays, Peter L. "The Complex Pattern of Redemption." *Bernard Malamud and the Critics*. Ed. Leslie A. Field and Joyce W. Field. New York: New York UP, 1970. 219–33. Print.

Helterman, Jeffrey. *Understanding Bernard Malamud*. Columbia: U of South Carolina P, 1985. Print.

Hershinow, Sheldon. *Bernard Malamud*. New York: Ungar, 1980. Print.

Langer, Lawrence L. "Malamud's Jews and the Holocaust Experience." *Critical Essays on Bernard Malamud*. Ed. Joel Salzberg. Boston: Hall, 1987. 115–25. Print.

Malamud, Bernard. *The Assistant*. New York: Farrar, 1957. Print.

Rosen, Jonathan. Introduction. *The Assistant*, by Bernard Malamud. New York: Farrar, 2003. vii–xi. Print.

Siegel, Ben. "Through a Glass Darkly: Bernard Malamud's Painful Views of the Self." *The Fiction of Bernard Malamud*. Ed. Richard Astro and Jackson J. Benson. Corvallis: Oregon State UP, 1977. 117–47. Print.

American Indians and the American Dream: "A World in Which We Had No Part"_____

Lee Schweninger

In the poem "The Man from Washington," celebrated Blackfeet–Gros Ventre poet and novelist James Welch (1940–2003) demonstrates that what mainstream society enjoys as the fruits of the American Dream have been essentially inaccessible to the indigenous peoples of North America. According to the poem, a man representing the US government

> promised
> that life would go on as usual,
> that treaties would be signed, and everyone—
> man, woman and child—would be inoculated
> against a world in which we had no part,
> a world of money, promise and disease. (lines 8–13)

Part of the power of these lines comes from the ironic suggestion that along with promise and the hope of money—staple components of the American Dream—came disease for Native Americans. In one sense, the line suggests that such promise and money are diseases in themselves. In another sense, the poem powerfully alludes to the millions of indigenous North Americans who died as a result of European diseases against which they had no immunity.

The list of indigenous people who have asserted that the American Dream has been inaccessible and exclusionary is long, and it is not restricted to modern writers such as Welch. Several nineteenth- and early twentieth-century American Indians, such as Pontiac (Ottawa), Tecumseh (Shawnee), and Luther Standing Bear (Sioux), articulated their misgivings about Indians' access to the promises of the American Dream. Following their lead, contemporary Spokane–Coeur d'Alene writer Sherman Alexie (b. 1966) exposes the limitations of the dream throughout his fiction and poetry, perhaps most notably in his novel *The Absolutely True Diary of a Part-Time Indian* (2007).

In her essay "What I See When I Look at the $20 Bill," Cherokee writer Sarah Vowell (b. 1969) contrasts the idealized portrayal of Jacksonian democracy with the reality of the Indian Removal Act of 1830. Vowell examines the triumphs of Andrew Jackson's presidency, particularly the promise of Manifest Destiny and the expansion of suffrage to nearly all adult white males, against his exclusionary policies regarding American Indians, highlighting the inherent contradictions of the American Dream. All of these writers suggest ways in which the dream has offered very little in the way of promise or hope for Native Americans.

The American Dream, which is often invoked to refer to the promise of material wealth, can also be said to include the ideals articulated in the Declaration of Independence (1776) and the Bill of Rights (ratified 1791), particularly the rights to equal opportunity and the pursuit of happiness. In the context of American Indian history specifically, the American Dream highlights such contradictions as the freedom to worship in accordance with tribal custom, the freedom to retain and use the land of one's ancestors and to move freely across that land, and to enjoy in the inalienable rights of life and liberty. Paralleling the history of the countless instances of white Americans pursuing and often realizing their dreams is the inverse history of indigenous peoples—a history of massacre, extermination, exile, confinement to reservations, mandatory boarding school attendance, land allotment, and forced relocation. At every turn, despite the promises from Washington, American Indians were deprived of their treaty rights, their political rights, and the opportunity to pursue and achieve the American Dream.

In an opinion piece he wrote for the *New York Times* in 1988, "For the Indians, No Thanksgiving," novelist and journalist Michael Dorris (1945–1997) describes the stereotypes that have come to be associated with the American Indians who may have been present at the first Thanksgiving in 1621. Dorris argues that the Indians had little to be thankful for and less to look forward to as they stood at the edges of that feast. He concludes by observing that even in the late twentieth century,

> A majority of reservation Indians reside in among the most impoverished counties in the nation. They constitute the ethnic group at the wrong peak of every scale: most undernourished, most short-lived, least educated, least healthy.
>
> For them, that long ago Thanksgiving was not a milestone, not a promise. It was the last full meal. (201)

The opening moments of the film *Skins* (2002), directed by Cheyenne-Arapaho filmmaker Chris Eyre (b. 1968), makes much the same point. Utilizing a documentary-style opening sequence, this narrative fiction film begins with a series of flyover shots of the Pine Ridge Indian Reservation in South Dakota, one of the poorest counties in the United States. Accompanying the aerials is a voice-over narration explaining that 40 percent of Pine Ridge residents live in substandard housing, that the unemployment rate there is 75 percent, and that the life expectancy of people on Pine Ridge is fifteen years less than the national average. The film cuts to a close-up of a Pine Ridge man being interviewed who articulates the gap between the American Dream and the reality: "I believe that America is big enough; it's powerful enough; it's rich enough, you know, to really deal with the American Indian in the way it should be done."

These two works by American Indian artists—an opinion piece looking back nearly four hundred years and a film set in contemporary America—depict rather explicitly and forcefully that what mainstream Americans think of as the American Dream has been and remains an untenable mirage for indigenous peoples in North America. Dorris's reference to the Pilgrims at Plymouth Colony giving thanks to their god is fitting, in that one of the long-standing clichés of the American Dream is that it includes the right to worship freely. Ten years after the

Pilgrims' arrival on Cape Cod, another group seeking religious freedom arrived, the Puritans. Their leader, John Winthrop (1588–1649), offered a shipboard "lay sermon" aboard the *Arbella* upon departing England to sail to Massachusetts in 1630. In this sermon he lauded the character of his fellow Puritans, insisting that their mission in the New World was to establish a "true" church and that their society would become a model for future settlements: "Wee must Consider that wee shall be as a Citty vpon a Hill, the eies of all people are vppon us" (Winthrop 199). The US Congress would not pass the American *Indian Religious Freedom Act* for another 348 years.

In conjunction with religious freedom, protected by the First Amendment of the US Constitution (and granted to American Indians only in 1978), came political freedom, especially those ideal political freedoms articulated in the Declaration of Independence. The personal history of Thomas Jefferson (1743–1826), the Declaration's primary author, embodies one of the contradictions inherent in the American Dream. He advocated that it was self-evident that all men deserved "life, liberty, and the pursuit of happiness," yet the author of that declaration thrived economically by participating in the institution of chattel slavery, an institution that necessarily deprived slaves of their liberty and the pursuit of happiness. This contradiction inherent in Jefferson's politics translates into the American Dream, which insists on the right and freedom for some individuals to pursue economic success at any cost, a freedom that devolved into a form of laissez-faire capitalism.

Another element of the American Dream is the right to own land. One of the great attractions to European colonists in North America was the availability of land, which to them appeared to be empty because it was not under European-style cultivation and development. The settlement of the American West, especially during the late nineteenth century, was in large measure about owning one's own piece of the earth. The US government facilitated this worldview along with the land grab it created in passing the Homestead Act of 1862, which made available to prospective homesteaders vast tracts of land, up to 160 acres at $1.25 per acre, with the mere requirement that the homesteader live on the land and make improvements. Concurrent with this and similar federal land acts came the establishment of reservations and Indian removal policies affecting those who, for generations, had lived on the very land offered by the government to "American" citizens. (Native Americans were not granted US citizenship until 1924.)

Along with the dreams of religious, political, and economic freedoms and the dream of land ownership, the American Dream insists that anyone can rise above the socioeconomic class into which he or she was born. This promise grew out of a refutation of rigid European class systems in which people were essentially confined for life to the class they were born into. In America, in contrast, the dream promises that anyone—including peanut farmers and actors—can become a president or a millionaire. To substantiate their beliefs, mainstream Americans have cultivated and embraced the idea of a grassroots Jacksonian democracy and the parallel myth of an Abe Lincoln growing up in an obscure cabin in the wilds of Illinois. They have also long treasured the countless Horatio Alger–type rags-to-riches stories.

The American Dream can also be said to include the right to an education. Yet education, which is understood as an opportunity and a means to achieve the dream for mainstream Americans, has often been a horror for Native Americans. Rather than a choice, for Indians, an education often meant being forcibly taken from one's family and culture and required to conform to non-Indian life, language, culture, and dress. It meant giving up one's name and identity.

Thus, not everyone in America has been able to share in this dream. Not everyone has been able to gain access to the economic, social, and material wealth that the dream promises regardless of an individual's heritage and ethnicity. Indeed, much of the American Dream has been and continues to be built upon the land of American Indians.

As early as the eighteenth, nineteenth, and early twentieth centuries, several American Indians responded to elements of what mainstream Americans have since called the American Dream. In the middle of the eighteenth century, for example, the Ottawa leader Pontiac (c. 1720–1769) urged his people to resist the allure of the material wealth and materialist culture of the European colonists well before there was any uniform articulation of an American Dream. In a speech in 1763, he reminds his people of its dangers: "You have bought guns, knives, kettles, and blankets from the white men, until you can no longer do without them; and what is worse, you have drunk the poison firewater, which turns you into fools. Fling all these things away; live as your wise forefathers lived before you" (Pontiac 147). Pontiac also urges his people to repel the English militarily in order to achieve happiness and prosperity. Although his motives were most immediately militaristic, in that he wanted to encourage armed resistance, one can certainly argue that he foresaw the danger of pursuing a dream that creates a reliance on material goods. Pontiac's uprising finally failed, and he was assassinated in 1769. His name lives on as a Michigan town and as an automobile brand, a vehicle that sported an Indian-head hood ornament from its beginning in 1926 until 1957.

Another eighteenth-century leader, the Shawnee Tecumseh (1768–1813), made a similar speech, also designed to provoke armed defense of his homeland, the Ohio River valley. Tecumseh warns that in pursuit of their Dream, the colonists would take and destroy the land that was home to Shawnee, Choctaws, and Chickasaws: the forests "will be cut down to fence in the land which the white intruders dare to call their own. Soon their broad roads will pass over the grave of your fathers. . . . Your people . . . will soon be as falling leaves and scattering clouds before their blighting breath. You, too, will be driven away from your native land and ancient domains." "Before the palefaces came among us," he continues, "we enjoyed the happiness of unbounded freedom, and were acquainted with neither riches, wants nor oppression. How is it now? Wants and oppression are our lot" (Tecumseh 149). Much of the motivation behind Tecumseh's plea to his Choctaw and Chickasaw neighbors is grounded in the realization that, as a result of their rapaciousness and greed, the white settlers have deprived the Indians of their land, liberty, and happiness, three inalienable and fundamental attributes of the American Dream.

Mainstream Americans believed that they had the sanction of their god, that they enjoyed a Manifest Destiny to march westward and establish farms and cities, railroads and factories. They saw American Indians as impediments rather than as fellow dreamers because these European American settlers felt they had a god-given right to the land that these Native peoples were living on. The story is told and retold countless times: European Americans found gold in the hills around Dahlonega, Georgia, in the 1820s, so Georgians and US government officials forced the Cherokee inhabitants into exile. They established farms, ranches, and timber claims across the Midwest, and so European Americans received the sanction and protection of the United States Army, protection that resulted in countless battles and massacres such as the Sand Creek Massacre in Colorado (1864) and the Wounded Knee Massacre in South Dakota (1890). They discovered gold in California, more gold in the Black Hills of the Dakotas, gold and silver in Colorado, and more gold still in the Klondike, Yukon Territory. They found oil in Oklahoma, and uranium in Arizona, New Mexico, and Idaho. In each instance the pursuit of these minerals resulted in the removal and exploitation of the Native inhabitants. In the twenty-first century, there is an ironic "giving back" in the ever-present push to use Indian reservation lands, which do not have the same health and environmental protections as the rest of the United States, as sites for hazardous waste disposal.

If the opportunity of acquiring an education is part of the American Dream, it has long been somewhat perverted in the case of American Indians. During the nineteenth century and well into the twentieth, reservation Indians were conscripted to boarding schools. The man behind the boarding school initiative, Richard Henry Pratt (1840–1924), is infamous for his slogan, "Kill the Indian; save the man." His idea was that an "education" away from family and culture could effectively create a generation of American Indians who were no longer "Indian."

Thus Native children were either taken or volunteered to leave home and family to attend boarding schools far from the reservations. The Lakota Sioux writer Luther Standing Bear (1868–1939) recounts his experience in his memoir *Land of the Spotted Eagle* (1933). He recalls being transported some 1,500 miles from his home in the Dakotas to Carlisle, Pennsylvania, where he was confined to a boarding-school dormitory and school grounds. He had his hair forcibly cut; he was not allowed to speak his own language; he was made to eat a foreign diet; he was forced to wear Western clothing he found uncomfortable. And he was obligated to choose a "Christian name." Thus, Luther Standing Bear writes that "the change in clothing, housing, food, and confinement combined with lonesomeness was too much, and in three years nearly one half of the children from the Plains were dead and through with all earthly schools. In the graveyard at Carlisle most of the graves are those of little ones" (Standing Bear 234). Kill the Indian, indeed.

In her poem "Los Angeles, 1980," Laguna Pueblo writer Paula Gunn Allen (1939–2008) critiques the materialism that has come to be associated with the American Dream. She lumps mainstream Americans pursuing the Dream into what she calls the "dying generation." In other instances in the poem she refers to the Dreamers as the "death culture" and the "death society":

> The dying generation moves purposefully:
> well-dressed in Jantzen and Wrangler,
> Gucci and Adidas, clothes, bodies,
> smiles gleaming cool in the practiced
> superiority of well-cut, natural fiber
> clothes and vitamin-drenched consciousness,
> they live their truth. They cannot count
> the cost. (234)

But Allen's poem is not just about the availability of name-brand clothing for those who can afford the latest fashions. It is also very much about the failure of equality and the great cost to everyone in pursuing their exclusionary Dream. In large measure the theme of her poem is that all people, Indian and non-Indian alike, ultimately face the same fate and the same polluted air that is an unspoken consequence of the freedoms the Dream promises. Ultimately, she argues, this pollution covers and obscures "our brightest dreams":

> The death people do not know
> what they create, or how they hide
> from the consequences of their dreams.
> Wanting the good they slide
> into an unforgiving destiny. (234)

Allen's evocation of consumerism in Los Angeles is reminiscent of a scene in the Pulitzer Prize–winning novel *House Made of Dawn* by Kiowa writer N. Scott Momaday (b. 1934). The author creates the Navajo character Ben Benally, who has moved from his reservation home in Arizona and is living in the city in the 1950s. Benally describes the difficulties relocated Indians face in attempting to share in the American Dream. For them, the urban culture is new and foreign and virtually impossible to participate in. As he explains, "you *want* to do it, because you can see how good it is. It's better than anything you've ever had; it's money and clothes and having plans and going someplace fast. You can *see* what it's like, but you don't know how to get into it; there's too much of it and it's all around you and you can't get hold of it because it's going too fast" (139). It is perhaps no accident that both Allen and Momaday set their critiques of the American Dream in Los Angeles, the city of angels, perched as it is on the very western edge of the continent. Believing in Manifest Destiny, European American settlers felt they had a god-given right to reach and settle on this coast. Ironically, that part of the American Dream necessarily excluded American Indians, many who came to Los Angeles involuntarily as a result of the government's relocation policies.

In what is often classified as juvenile or adolescent fiction, Sherman Alexie's *The Absolutely True Diary of a Part-Time Indian* (2007) can be seen as instructive in the context of American Indians and the American Dream even though as a novel it suffers from the restrictions and limitations of its genre. The novel tells the story of a young American Indian man named Junior who leaves his Spokane reservation home every day to attend an otherwise all-white high school called Reardan. Because he is the only non-European American at an otherwise all-white school, he calls himself a "part-time Indian." He travels to the "rich, white farm town that sits in the wheat fields exactly twenty-two miles away from the rez . . . [a town that] has one of the best small schools in the state" (45–46). Early in the novel, Junior transfers to the off-reservation "white" school because he feels that there is no chance of doing well or of ever achieving his dreams if he stays at the reservation high school. Indeed, in a chapter called "Hope against Hope," the teacher at the reservation school explains the limitations: "All these kids have given up," he says. "All your friends. All the bullies. And their mothers and fathers have given up, too. And their grandparents gave up and their grandparents before them. And me and every other teacher here. We're all defeated" (42). But he says to Junior, "I don't want you to fail. I don't want you to fade away. You deserve better" (40). So Junior decides to attend the off-reservation high school. And the character, like the author himself, does indeed succeed, as the protagonist of young-adult fiction often does.

In contrast to the narrator, an older sister who also has great potential actually dies in pursuit of her dream: "Mary was a bright and shining star . . . And then she faded year by year until you could barely see her anymore" (40). She runs away from the reservation. "She was trying to live out her dream," the brother tells the reader: "I just kept thinking that my sister's spirit hadn't been killed. She hadn't given up. This reservation tried to suffocate her, had kept her trapped in a basement, and now she was out roaming the huge grassy fields of Montana" (91). But as the reader finds out, before her death she does not roam the grassy fields; rather, she lives in a trailer, is unemployed, and gets drunk daily. She dies when she burns to death in a fire set accidentally by a drunken guest at her trailer. Junior's father explains what happened: "your sister and her husband passed out in the back bedroom . . . [someone accidentally started a fire] and the trailer burned down quick. . . . The police say your sister never even woke up. . . . She was way too drunk" (205).

The novel is replete with instances of death, and the narrator calls attention to the fact that Indians are dying much more often than the friends and family members of his white classmates:

> I'm fourteen years old and I've been to forty-two funerals.
>
> That's really the biggest difference between Indians and white people. . . .
>
> All my white friends can count their deaths on one hand.
>
> I can count my fingers, toes, arms, legs, eyes, ears, nose, penis, butt cheeks, and nipples, and still not get close to my deaths. (200–01)

The narrator's grandmother dies; his father's best friend Eugene is shot and killed by his good friend and drinking buddy Bobby in a drunken brawl; Bobby then hangs himself in prison; and then his sister and brother-in-law die. After the sister's death, Junior retains the pride he felt for her: "she was amazing. It was courageous of her to leave the basement and move to Montana. She went searching for her dreams, and she didn't find them, but she made the attempt" (216). And at the same time, he blames himself for her death. He thinks that if he had not left the reservation to pursue his own dream, she would not have left: "she only . . . left the rez because I had left the rez first. She was only living in Montana in a cheap trailer house because I had gone to school in Reardan. She had burned to death because I had decided that I wanted to spend my life with white people" (211).

Mary and Junior's example offers three different perspectives of Native Americans' pursuit of the American Dream: 1.) One can stay on the reservation and live without opportunity. Sherman Alexie makes clear that as far as the narrator and his sister are concerned, the reservation is a dead end. There is no hope. 2.) Or one can leave a reservation for another as the narrator's sister essentially does. She runs away from the reservation, but that does not work because she essentially takes her reservation lifestyle and its limitations with her. 3.) Or one can take the path that the narrator takes: leave the reservation but in so doing ultimately abandon one's family, friends, heritage, and lifestyle. Leaving is worth the sacrifice, Junior insists, because not to leave would be disastrous: "staying on the rez would have killed me" (216). But leaving also has its pitfalls and drawbacks: "Some Indians think you have to act white to make yourself better. Some Indians think you become white if you try to make your life better" (131). In an invocation of boarding school history, it is nevertheless the path that the narrator chooses and that the plot of the novel follows.

Junior considers his parents' input as he considers whether he should transfer from the reservation school to the white school in Reardan. He asks his parents a question:

"Who has the most hope?" I asked. . . .
   "Come on," I said. "Who has the most hope?"
   "White people," my parents said at the same time.
   That's exactly what I thought they were going to say. (45)

The question offers a telling indication of why he wants to transfer, and it indicates clearly the differences in opportunity afforded white people as opposed to Indians.

The narrator prides himself on his drawings, and his diary is littered with them (the book's actual artist is Ellen Forney). In one drawing, the narrator depicts a boy with a line drawn vertically right down his middle: the left half is labeled "WHITE" and the right half, "INDIAN." The white half wears a Ralph Lauren shirt, khaki trousers, and Air Jordan shoes; he has "a bright future," "positive role models," and "hope." The Indian half wears a "Kmart T-shirt" and "Sears blue jeans." Instead of an ergonomic backpack, the Indian half carries a "garbage book bag." He has "a vanishing past," and he faces a "bone-crushing reality" (57).

Standing Rock Sioux writer Susan Power (b. 1961) describes a similar conundrum in her novel *The Grass Dancer* (1994). Power introduces a character who, like Junior, also wants to pursue her dreams, and to do so she must leave behind not only her home but her culture and worldview as well. In her application letter to Stanford University, in fact, she describes the great cost of pursuing her dreams as an American Indian. Besides leaving home and family, she writes, "I know I am committed to a college education because I am willing to go to great lengths to earn one. I will have to put aside one worldview—perhaps only temporarily—to take up another. From what I have learned so far, I know the two are not complementary but rather incompatible, and melodramatic as it may sound, I sometimes feel I am risking my soul by leaving the Indian community" (24). This character dies in a car wreck at the very beginning of her quest to pursue her dream, and her death implies emphatically that the fruits of her dream are unavailable to her.

The requirements of the genre in Alexie's young-adult fiction insist that the protagonist not only survive but that he succeed. He has left the reservation to go to high school, and he discovers that his leaving puts him immediately in a difficult situation with his friends and family: "You can't just betray your tribe and then change your mind ten minutes later. I was on a one-way bridge. There was no way to turn around, even if I wanted to" (55). In the novel's final pages Junior and his best friend Rowdy back on the reservation (the two friends had a falling out over Junior's leaving but have reconciled) talk about the fact that he will leave the reservation again, for good, unlike any other Indian either of them knows (except for the sister who has died pursuing her dream).

The narrator does not believe in the possibility of achieving his dreams, but he does try to find common ground with Penelope, a white girl at the school who talks about her own dreams:

"Why don't you quit talking in dreams and tell me what you really want to do with your life," I said. "Make it simple."

"I want to go to Stanford and study architecture."

"Wow, that's cool," I said . . .

And I couldn't make fun of her for that dream. It was my dream, too. And Indian boys weren't supposed to dream like that. (111–12)

Despite Junior's repeated insistence that Indians should not dream or hope, he himself is extremely hopeful and ultimately successful: he does transfer; he makes the basketball team as a freshman and becomes a star player; he makes many non-Indian friends at school and dates one of the most popular girls; he gets excellent grades. He also has the unflagging love and support of his mother and father, as well as a renewed bond with his best friend back on the reservation. Despite all his successes, however, the narrator continues to insist, repeating over and over, that he has no options and that Indians in general exist in a world without hope or possibility of participating in the American Dream. Late in the novel he articulates this negative attitude pointedly: "I figured any nightmare would be better than my reality" (208).

To a certain extent, the fact that the narrator is successful at the white high school belies the argument that he has no hope or lacks opportunity. The subtext of the novel is arguably that anyone, even an Indian, can actually have and then take advantage of a situation and make the most of every opportunity to improve oneself and pursue one's dreams and to some extent achieve them. The basketball coach's favorite aphorism applies as much to the Indian narrator as to anyone else in the school. The coach loves to quote Vince Lombardi, one-time coach of the professional football team Green Bay Packers: "The quality of a man's life is in direct proportion to his commitment to excellence, regardless of his chosen field of endeavor" (148). But, according to Alexie, not regardless of his ethnic heritage.

Another of Junior's drawings depicts one of those clichéd directional signs: to the left in one direction according to the sign is the

"Rez" and "Home"; in the other direction, toward the right, is "Hope" and "???," suggesting potential; to the right of the hopeful indicators is the narrator himself facing away from home, away from the Rez and in the direction of hope and potential (43). The clear indication is that an Indian must leave the reservation and home in order to pursue his dreams, and to do so one risks either literal death (the sister) or symbolic, cultural death (Junior). In other words, Alexie seems to be reiterating the dangerous belief that one must kill the Indian to save the man. Ultimately, that is, the plot complicates the novel's primary theme that American Indians have exceedingly few opportunities and are thus doomed to a desperate life of poverty on the reservation.

Cherokee writer and public radio personality Sarah Vowell articulates her awareness of the irony inherent in her own professional successes and her achievements, especially as a Cherokee woman whose ancestors were forced to travel the Trail of Tears. She writes about that Cherokee removal of the 1830s in a personal essay entitled "What I See When I Look at the Face on the $20 Bill" (2000). The title refers, of course, to the image of Andrew Jackson, president of the United States from 1829 to 1837. His administration is infamous for having legislated and adjudicated the implementation of the forced removal of the Cherokees from their homelands as well as several other American Indian tribes, including the Seminoles, the Choctaws, the Chickasaws, and the Creeks.

Alexie's character Junior also makes reference to the twenty-dollar bill, but neither the author nor character give any indication of being mindful of the implications of this former president being so honored and remembered. Alexie's character refers to the bill simply as a way to establish the fact that for reservation Indians there is rarely enough food to eat or money to buy food with. "I wish I could draw a peanut butter and jelly sandwich," exclaims the narrator, "or a fist full of twenty dollar bills, and perform some magic trick and make it real" (Alexie 7).

The immediate occasion for Vowell's essay is her own trip (in a rental car) along the route that her Cherokee ancestors were forced to march from northern Georgia to eastern Oklahoma. She intertwines the narrative account of her own trip with that of the 1838 trek of the Cherokees. Some sixteen thousand Cherokees were forced to travel approximately 1,200 miles from their homelands to a new reservation in Indian Territory, a march that has come to be called the Trail of Tears. The trip took about eight months (from June 1838 to January 1839), occurred during an especially bitter winter season, and resulted ultimately in the deaths of approximately four thousand Cherokee people. Fully one-fourth of those forced to relocate from their homelands died before arriving in Indian Territory.

Vowell shares her awareness of some of the ironies of her trip: "I can't go more than a few miles without agonizing and picking apart every symbolic nuance of every fact at my disposal." One of those nuances is her recognition that the farms she sees in Kentucky seem so perfect that they make her think of clip art: "we drive past farms that look so cliché they're practically pictographs—barns straight out of clip art. . . . I convince myself that we're on a normal road trip. Be we're not. We're on a death trip" (148). The existence of these Kentucky farms along the Trail is ironic in that they so neatly epitomize the reality of the American Dream for some people. In all their splendor, these farms make manifest the Dream: the unseen farmers represent the facts that land ownership, the opportunity to cultivate that land, and the freedom to prosper are dreams come true. Vowell contrasts the pastoral reality of these farms with the stark reality of the historical removal. At one commemorative stop along the way, for example, Vowell notes that a brochure acknowledges the inequality evident in the treatment of the Indians: "These cracks in the sidewalks, they are symbolic of broken promises," says Vowell's sister and travel companion; she then reads: "Some of the pavers are cracked to symbolize the broken promises made to the Indians" (138). The intentional cracks in the sidewalk also imply the disparity between the American Dream and the circumstances of the Cherokees, underscoring the limited potential for the American Indians on whose land European Americans have lived out their Dream.

Before removal, the Cherokees were especially deserving of being considered "civilized" by mainstream American standards. According to Vowell, "More than any other Native American tribe, the Cherokee adopted the religious, cultural, and political ideals of the United States" (132). As Vowell adroitly explains, the Cherokees "had always taken an interest in the more useful innovations of white culture. . . . By the early nineteenth century, they launched a series of initiatives directly imitating the new American republic. In one decade, they created a written language, started a free press, ratified a constitution, and founded a capital city" (130). Moreover, the Cherokee Nation "sought to emulate not just the democratic structures of the United States government . . . but the best ideals of the American republic" (131). This belief and faith in the republic's ideas and ideals are evident in their very constitution, modeled closely on the US Constitution. One hears the echoes immediately in the preamble: "We, the Representatives of the people of the Cherokee Nation in Convention assembled, in order to establish justice, ensure tranquility, promote our common welfare, and secure to ourselves and our posterity the blessings of liberty." (qtd. in Vowell: 131). These words express the same hopes and desires, the same dreams that mainstream Americans have cherished for well over two centuries.

In addition to the political characteristics that mirrored those of the US federal government, the Cherokees had translated the Christian Bible into the Cherokee language and wealthy Cherokee plantation owners even participated fully in the system of chattel slavery. According to Vowell, the principal chief of the Cherokee Nation, John Ross, "was a Jeffersonian figure in almost every sense. . . . who cribbed from Jefferson in writing the Cherokee Constitution. Like Jefferson, he preached liberty while owning slaves" (134). Vowell writes that Ross "was caught between two nations. He believed in the possibilities of the American Constitution enough to make sure the Cherokee had one too. He believed in the liberties the Declaration of Independence promises, and the civil rights the Constitution insures" (157). But he was of course inevitably disappointed because as it turned out those possibilities and liberties, those promises of civil rights did not apply to him or any Cherokee people. Those were aspects of the Dream reserved for non-Indians, for European Americans. Rather than enjoying the rights and freedoms guaranteed by the Constitution and promised in the Declaration, Ross, his immediate family, and the people for whom he served as elected chief were forced into exile. Ross himself wrote, "Treated like dogs, we find ourselves fugitives, vagrants, and strangers in our own country" (qtd. in Vowell: 135). Despite being considered "civilized," and despite modeling their government, religion, and economic system on mainstream America's, they were ultimately without the right to the land they farmed, the land they had lived on for generations.

Vowell describes the conundrum she herself faces: "I want to hate Andrew Jackson because it's convenient." She continues, adding, "no matter what horrific Jackson administration policy I point out, I can't escape the symbolism of Jackson's election. The American Dream that anyone can become president begins with him" (144). Jackson was a relatively uneducated, common man rather than an aristocrat; he was an orphan, and he had what can be considered a working-class background. Thus, he embodies an important element of the American Dream. At the same time, however, as Vowell recalls, his anti-Indian policies are therefore all the grimmer: "That Jackson's election was a triumph of populism still does not negate his responsibility for the Trail of Tears. If anything, it makes the story that much darker. Isn't it more horrible when a so-called man of the people sends so many people to their deaths? One expects that of despots, not democrats" (145).

One particular statement made by Jackson demonstrates the vast difference between how pursuit of the American Dream differs from one group to another. While mainstream Americans were busy settling the hills of northern Georgia and the American West and enjoying the freedoms of commerce and property, American Indians were very literally under the gun, being relocated or massacred. Jackson asked rhetorically: "Can it be cruel in the government, when, by events which it cannot control, the Indian is made discontented in his ancient home to purchase his lands, to give him a new and extensive territory, to pay the expense of his removal, and support home a year in his new abode. How many thousands of our own people would gladly embrace the opportunity of removing to the West on such conditions?" (qtd. in Vowell: 143).

In this passage Jackson fallaciously compares "the *removal* of Indians from their land with the *opportunity* of his generation to just go out west" (143). As Vowell points out, such a comparison makes evident the worlds of difference between those who were in a position to embrace such a possibility and those who were forced, against their will and with military escort, to walk those 1,200 miles. It can be argued that one of the most cherished aspects of the American Dream is the freedom to possess and cultivate one's own land. But in their removal, this freedom was denied the Cherokee people and other tribes in the American southeast. One of the mainstays of American democracy, and thus part of the American Dream, is the idea that all people are equal in the eyes of the law. This equality was denied the Cherokee people. The non-Indian settlers had the legal and moral sanction of the federal government as they moved onto Indian land and, in some cases, into Indian homes in pursuit of their Dream. Meanwhile, the Cherokee were pursued by the most terrifying of nightmares.

It is important to state explicitly by way of conclusion that American Indians in the twenty-first century are neither tragic figures nor victims. Thus there is a contradiction at the heart of Native writing about the American Dream. In the novel *Winter in the Blood* (1974) James Welch, himself a highly accomplished author, depicts an Indian character who is able to achieve the Dream. Welch simultaneously praises and mocks the character's successes: "Lame Bull had married 360 acres of hay land, all irrigated, leveled, some of the best land in the valley, as well as a 2,000-acre grazing lease. And he had married a T-Y brand stamped high on the left ribs of every beef on the place. And, of course, he had married Teresa" (10). The character Lame Bull does indeed become a landowner, and he even "had taken to grinning now that he was a proprietor" (18). Similarly, both Sherman Alexie and Sarah Vowell are highly successful writers. Through their successes they embody the contradiction at the heart of the discrepancies between the promise of the Dream and the limitations experienced by Indian peoples generally. Vowell acknowledges the irony of her success in the face of such general inequality: "I have this tiny, petty thought—an embarrassingly selfish gratitude for the Trail of Tears, because without it, my sister and I wouldn't exist" (150). An earlier confession epitomizes the contradiction: "I wonder if we should be embarrassed by certain discrepancies between our trail and theirs. We're weak, we're decadent, we're Americans" (136). In the poem "Riding the Earthboy 40" Welch writes that "Dirt is where the dreams must end" (32), but before the dirt and elsewhere, one can keep dreaming.

Works Cited

Alexie, Sherman. *The Absolutely True Diary of a Part-Time Indian.* New York: Little, 2007. Print.

Allen, Paula Gunn. *Shadow Country.* Los Angeles: Amer. Indian Studies Center, 1982. Print.

Dorris, Michael. "For the Indians, No Thanksgiving." *Crossing Cultures: Readings for Composition.* 3rd ed. Ed. Henry Knepler and Myrna Knepler. New York: Macmillan, 1991. 199–201. Print.

Momaday, N. Scott. *House Made of Dawn.* 1968. New York: Harper, 1999. Print.

Pontiac. "Pontiac's Allegory." *American Indian Literature: An Anthology.* Rev. ed. Ed. Alan R. Velie. Norman: U of Oklahoma P, 1991. 145–47. Print.

Power, Susan. *The Grass Dancer.* New York: Putnam, 1994. Print.

Standing Bear, Luther. *Land of the Spotted Eagle.* 1933. Lincoln: U of Nebraska P, 1978. Print.

Skins. Dir. Chris Eyre. Perf. Graham Greene and Eric Schweig. First Look Media, 2002. Film.

Tecumseh. "Tecumseh's Plea to the Choctaws and Chickasaws." *American Indian Literature: An Anthology.* Rev. ed. Ed. Alan R. Velie. Norman: U of Oklahoma P, 1991. 148–51. Print.

Vowell, Sarah. "What I See When I Look at the Face on the $20 Bill." *Take the Cannoli.* New York: Simon, 2000. 127–58. Print.

Welch, James. "The Man from Washington." *Riding the Earthboy 40*. 1971. Pittsburgh: Carnegie Mellon UP, 1997. 35. Print.

---. *Winter in the Blood*. 1974. New York: Penguin, 2008. Print.

Winthrop, John. "A Modell of Christian Charity." *The Puritans: A Sourcebook of Their Writings*. Rev. ed. Ed. Perry Miller and Thomas H. Johnson. New York: Harper, 1963. 195–99. Print.

Mexican Americans Encounter the American Dream: *George Washington Gómez*

Ramón J. Guerra

In Américo Paredes's *George Washington Gómez*, a novel written during the 1930s but not published until 1990, the culminating event is the message sent to the title character and all of his fellow Mexican American students upon their graduation from a high school along the Texas border in the early twentieth century. That message: They have graduated only because of their willingness to redefine and realign their cultural identities through the educational system. The speaker for the graduation event, K. Hank Harvey (who was "considered the foremost authority on the Mexicans of Texas" [270]), addresses the graduating class collectively, not distinguishing between Anglos and Mexicans, but instead assigning all of them a generic Anglo identity. This helps Harvey match the students with a brief, one-sided perspective of Texas history and its Anglo "heroes." Harvey tells the class and the audience gathered:

> "May they never forget the names of Sam Houston, James Bowie, and Davey Crockett. May they remember the Alamo wherever they go. . . . When our forefathers rose on their hindlegs and demanded independence," he continued, "when they arose with a mighty shout and forever erased Mexican cruelty and tyranny from this fair land . . . They set an example which younger, weaker generations would do well to follow. Girls and boys, I give you the world; it is at your feet as young Americans and as Texans." (274)

By verbally assaulting "Mexican cruelty and tyranny," Harvey's message implies that a successful Mexican American in a graduating high school class should have willfully abandoned any and all connections to ancestral, familial, or cultural ties that he or she has to Mexico. He also assumes that the crowd gathered for his speech accepts one truth about Texas history and subsequently one truth about success: They must be "young Americans and Texans" rather than young Mexican Americans or Mexican Texans.

Harvey's speech essentially invites graduates to pursue the construction of the American Dream of success in the United States that requires individuals to subscribe to the identity standards that Harvey has laid out ("American" and "Texan"). The young protagonist, nicknamed Guálinto, reacts to the speech with confusion, anger, and built-up frustration. He glares at the man giving him his diploma and shrugs off his lifelong ambition to go to college.

Paredes depicts Guálinto on the verge of an ultimate question of how to succeed in the United States as a Mexican American. At the time of the novel, access to the American Dream for Mexican Americans was limited to the prescribed narrative of assimilation and acquiescence. In the United States during the 1930s there was no version of Mexican American–based success from which Guálinto could receive inspiration, direction, and guidance. This absence of a model leads to frustration and plants doubt about whether he should strive for "success" in the United States. In order to reframe the mythical dream, as Paredes suggests, changes in self-determination, cultural nationalism, and basic civil rights would be required, in the form of what became known a few decades later as the Chicano movement.

The American Dream and the Mexican American

In order to discuss the American Dream and its relationship to Mexican Americans in the twentieth century, an understanding of how that promise was conceptualized and transmitted to people is required. In *American Dream, American Nightmare: Fiction since 1960* (2000), Kathryn Hume describes how the American Dream has appeared to immigrants:

> People have . . . hoped to enjoy certain liberties in America: freedom of worship, justice in the courts, and a classless society (or at least one where the class barriers were permeable to those who educated themselves). That

all men are held to be created equal in the Declaration of Independence has encouraged those who have suffered from cultural and racial scorn to hope that they, too, could make good. (3–4)

For Mexican Americans living in the United States in the early part of the twentieth century, the ideas and goals laid out in Hume's reading of the American Dream were a large component of an ongoing negotiation of identity—namely, to what extent could the hopes of Mexican Americans be fulfilled, and at what price? One element that most characterizations of the American Dream carry is the vague quality of effort, or rather, the idea that the benefits of the dream are inherently reserved (and seemingly available) for those who work hard and make the correct choices. In order to enjoy the fruits of the American Dream, certain aspects of one's identity must be highlighted: the willingness to recognize the opportunities in the United States, the acumen to develop a plan to pursue those opportunities, and the perseverance to remain devoted to the plan through hardship and setback. In addition to these requirements, Mexican Americans have historically encountered the narrative of the American Dream with certain prescriptions for their identity and development. Historically, these directions have come with a heavy sense of cultural hegemony (or an imposed set of cultural norms such as not speaking Spanish and changing one's name) that insists upon assimilation prior to achieving any success or benefits of the American Dream.

Many Latino studies scholars break down the twentieth-century development of Mexican American identity into broad eras that help to define the values and cultural markers associated with, among other issues, their relationship to immigrant assimilation. By examining Mexican Americans' desires and interpretations of the American Dream narrative over the course of the twentieth century, one can see how different periods of time are indicative of a growing sense of self-determination among the community.

For Latinos, there was a prolonged shift from the pre–World War II desire to be culturally "American" to the desire in the Chicano movement era (1960s and 1970s) to point out that the American Dream was a myth that was not fully available to all. Within this shift there was also a steady realization by young Mexican Americans that they should not have to assimilate (negating their cultural heritage) in order to find the opportunities or benefits offered by the American Dream.

Mario T. García offers a brief chronicle of three eras that define the perspective of Mexicans in the United States in the twentieth century by highlighting the different ways Mexican Americans chose to align themselves with an established set of norms for "success." García divides the century into three periods: the immigrant era, from the turn of the century to the Great Depression; the Mexican American era, between 1930 and 1960; and the Chicano era of the 1960s and 1970s (10). Through this division, García and others indicate that the sense of "American" self that Mexican Americans have held at one time or another may be largely dependent on their degree of separation (both geographically and temporally) from Mexico.

The immigrant era at the beginning of the twentieth century is marked by several common identity factors, including leaving Mexico in the wake of economic dissolution after the Mexican Revolution that began in 1910, a sense of nationalism represented by the phrase "México de Afuera" ("Mexico outside"), a desire to return to Mexico, and a wariness of Americanization. During the Mexican American era a generation later, Mexican Americans began to seek full inclusion as American citizens and establish permanence in the United States. There was an increased focus on integration, although in a limited, strategic sense, by acquiring political presence and fostering the idea of biculturalism.

Finally, the Chicano era of the 1960s and 1970s highlights several key components of what can broadly be termed "cultural sovereignty." These traits include a decrease of accommodation to European American cultural and historical norms, self-determination in the realms of politics and culture, an ongoing focus on the struggles of the working class (of which a predominant number of Mexican Americans were a part), policy reforms for issues such as immigration and bilingual education, and, finally, the construction of a dual identity that builds on and strengthens the preceding generation's focus on biculturalism by promoting a validation of one's cross-cultural existence. The area between these last two eras (the Mexican American and the Chicano) provides an opportunity to reconsider the American Dream as it has been sold to Mexican Americans.

Within this transition period, several notable works of Mexican American/Chicano literature that illustrate a shift in developmental perception were published. For example, Luis Pérez's little-known autobiographical novel *El Coyote: The Rebel* (1947) was written and published at a time when immigrant achievement and the golden opportunities of the United States were celebrated as potentially available for all. The protagonist, Luis, is a young Mexican revolutionary soldier who escapes to the United States and, through a series of foolhardy but determined adventures, achieves an immigrant success story: education, American citizenship, and the potential to acquire an American fiancé.

José Antonio Villarreal's better-known *Pocho* (1959), published just prior to the onset of the Chicano movement, more directly challenges the "golden" nature of the immigrant story of potential success. Protagonist Richard Rubio's negotiation of his Americanness deals with the questions of his allegiance, assimilation, and eventual decision to join the US Navy after the attack on Pearl Harbor—searching for a statement of who he is as an American. The influence of *Pocho* on the ensuing production of Chicano literature is significant because it arguably presents one of the earliest complex depictions of the Mexican American perspective. Paredes's *George Washington Gómez*—written some fifteen to twenty years prior to the two examples just listed—provides an illuminating perspective on the development of a Mexican American take on the American Dream.

George Washington Gómez

George Washington Gómez is an account of the fictional George Washington "Guálinto" Gómez that reflects many of the sociocultural impressions taken in by Mexican Americans of this time along the US-Mexican border. The novel follows Guálinto's growth from 1915 through the Depression-era 1930s and into his post-World War II career in the US Army, stationed along that same border on which he grew up. Guálinto's early upbringing reflects Paredes's own experiences. As a result, throughout the novel, the question of where Guálinto saw his future in the United States consistently surfaces: among the Anglos and their representation of "success" or among the Mexican American population whom he repeatedly learns to subconsciously ridicule and shame.

Guálinto is faced with the outwardly impossible task of negotiating his access to the American Dream as a Mexican American, specifically during the 1920s and the 1930s, when the modern idea of civil rights was still some twenty or thirty years away. Guálinto tries to achieve what his family and community have set before him: to become a "leader of his people." This phrase, which Paredes bestows upon his protagonist as his destiny and repeats at various points throughout the novel, characterizes an immense sense of pressure hanging over the heads of young Mexican Americans. Paredes's novel examines this pressure and the way that the American Dream was often preached to and interpreted by Mexican Americans during the first half of the twentieth century. Thus, Paredes raises questions about Mexican Americans' efforts to "succeed" in the United States: Was it then (and is it now) possible to achieve a prominent role in the country—one of leadership, status, and power—while continuing to remain tied to the cultural-historical concerns of one's ethnic group? Paredes's fictional but semiautobiographical account of a young Mexican American is his way of expressing his frustrations, and no doubt his own firsthand encounters, with such an issue.

The Significance of the Chicano Movement Consciousness

Paredes began writing his novel during the 1930s and it was based on many of the experiences that he encountered in his own youth growing up in the Rio Grande Valley of Texas. During the Mexican American era, in which a formula of work ethic and gradual assimilation was emphasized to those seeking inclusion in the American Dream, many Mexican Americans were driven by the goals of that dream to accelerate their inclusion into the dominant American culture and to achieve success by embracing their Americanness.

As one primary example of attempted inclusion, in the 1940s, during World War II, many Mexican Americans (some reports say up to 750,000) proudly served overseas in the armed forces, a prominent display of patriotism as well as an indirect effort to reduce discrimination in the United States (Rivas-Rodriguez). While this concerted effort helped Mexican Americans make some strides toward social equality and served as a source of pride, it was and has been largely ignored and underreported. During this time, Mexican Americans experienced discriminatory assaults in policy, in the media, and as verbal and physical acts of violence. For example, in the Zoot Suit Riots of 1943 in Los Angeles, Mexican American youths dressed in the stylish "zoot suits" of the time were dragged into the streets and beaten by US military serviceman who targeted them as "un-American" and "extravagant" during a time of war and purported national unity. In the wartime atmosphere, this act and newspapers' coverage of it effectively portrayed all Mexican Americans—either immigrants or children of immigrants— as disloyal and undeserving of "American" status (Mazon and Pagán).

Even so, the sense of hope represented by the American Dream was prevalent during the rise of the Mexican American era. As F. Arturo Rosales writes about the spirit of this time, "In the Mexican American era of civil rights, the extent of racism and oppression was either denied or masked over by an overly optimistic appraisal of access to the US opportunity structure" (xvi). The primary goal for many Mexican

---

Americans was to achieve success in the United States by acquiring education and material wealth or through political or social engagement. Rosales goes on to describe how this approach was reconsidered during the rise of the Chicano movement:

> Mexican Americans now [in the 1940s and 1950s] attempted to resolve problems with faith in education, electoral politics, litigation and a claim to being white Americans. By the 1960s Chicano activists categorically rejected the assimilationist and racial identity aspects of this ideology— that "belonging" meant being just another white American—but advanced most of the other ideals. (90)

This concept of faith in the established system began to wear on generations of Mexican Americans who often did not have any direct ties to Mexico and who began to develop the ideals and strong political presence of resistance that signified the Chicano movement. They remained committed to the ideals of the Mexican American era, but they also realized that the promises and opportunities laid out in the description of the American Dream, which drove the faith and optimism of the previous generation, had been largely smoke and mirrors.

The genesis of the Chicano movement[1] (or *Movimiento Chicano*) really began to develop in the aftermath of World War II. Even though Mexican American veterans felt patriotic because of their service, they began to see the limitations placed on them in their home country: the problems of underrepresentation in politics and education, the unfair labor situations of the working class, and continued suppression of non-Anglo cultural identity as a precursor to achieving any type of success. Mexican American war veterans were angered by the ongoing discrimination and outright racism to which they returned. This anger drove them to achieve political power and to voice their opinions. During this time of supposed great advancements in American national culture, Mexican Americans (along with many other minorities) were "still subjected to segregation or barred from public facilities in schools, theaters, swimming pools, restaurants and housing tracts" (Rosales 97).

As young Mexican Americans shifted their focus from trying to "become American" (or the dominant version of "American" that was portrayed) to recognizing their differences and benefitting from them, they began to think in a different way about how to identify themselves and about what disparities they would strive to transform. The Chicano movement emerged with three general concerns: labor and workers' rights, political and social presence, and youth and education. In addressing these issues by highlighting rather than bypassing the issue of ethnicity, the movement accelerated those areas of concern previously addressed by Mexican American leaders. Also of importance, the Chicano movement aimed to reinvigorate the Mexican American era quest to identify and assert a positive place in American society, albeit with the newly refined concept of "cultural sovereignty" or "cultural nationalism."

The prominent voices of the Chicano movement, such as Cesar Chavez, Reies Lopez Tijerina, and Rodolfo "Corky" Gonzáles,[2] were driven by the needs both to secure justice and equality and to determine the cultural identity and history of their people by their own accord—hence the term "cultural sovereignty." The movement was built upon these premises and strove to reform the conditions for working-class laborers through unions, to develop a political presence through organized voter presence and political parties, and to address the education and empowerment of the youth through college-campus presence and curriculum reform. Rosales describes these motivations and actions of the early movement: "The new organizations, especially the ones in California, departed from traditional Mexican Americanism in two ways. One, they diluted the notion that mainly a lack of education made Mexicans vulnerable and, two, they regularly employed the rhetoric of racism as a source of problems" (108). It should be obvious that Rosales's appraisal of this shift recognizes that limited access to the American Dream would no longer simply be blamed on a "lack of education" or other lack of effort, but instead would be reexamined with a focus on the issues of race and racism that were underlying and often unspoken detriments to accessing the American Dream.

Finally, in charting the rise of the Chicano movement and its effect on Mexican American youth, cultural identity, and self-determination, there is a decidedly radical voice that emerges. Along with other concurrent civil rights movements, the Chicano movement of the 1960s and 1970s held fast to certain beliefs of empowerment through pointing out inconsistencies in the narrative of equality for all Americans. The need to challenge Americans' overt belief in their country as a "land of opportunity" fell to a newly charged, culturally sovereign generation of Mexican Americans. The evolution from an acquiescent faith in the existent system to the far-reaching and outspoken voice of the Chicano youth was influenced by other contemporary civil rights groups.

In the Mexican American era, most of the leadership came from middle-class reformers who favored assimilation tactics. As young black leaders and other activists emerged with a focus on youth and the working class, Chicano leaders followed suit. This shift away from compliance toward cultural sovereignty, which marks the onset of the Chicano movement era, is made even distinct because, in the dominant culture, in order for Mexican Americans to be perceived as "American" prior to the movement, they were required to surrender specific parts of their cultural identity through assimilation. Paredes had the foresight not to see this as success and indicated that perhaps the existent American Dream narrative was flawed because of the surrender of cultural identity. He also hinted that in the future a new culturally centered success story— one in which the Mexican American could identify as both Mexican and American—would be a possibility with some advancements.

Race/Ethnicity and the Call for Assimilation

One prominent way in which Paredes illustrates the inaccessibility of the American Dream for Mexican Americans during the 1930s is through his depiction of the Great Depression. During this moment in history, Mexican Americans were given fewer jobs, less assistance, and were often deported even if they were legal citizens, simply to keep the few jobs there were open to Anglos. During this time there were laws passed to enforce and legalize the deportations. The Texas Cotton Acreage Control Law of 1931–32 and the Agricultural Adjustment Act of 1933 were two such laws that led to the displacement of a large number of Mexicans. Both laws allowed and encouraged landlords to evict Mexican farm workers who lived on the land where they worked. Most of these workers returned to Mexico because of both the increased pressure from Anglos and anti-Mexican sentiment (Balderrama and Rodriguez). However, when their work was eventually needed again (for a fractional bargain), programs were established to institute their presence back in the United States.[3]

Paredes carefully illustrates this duality in Mexican Americans' lack of control and subsequent lack of power, thereby increasing the need to dismiss any "Mexicanness" on the way toward the American Dream. At one point, when describing the labor situation and the issue of loyalty during this hard time, Paredes writes, "The MexicoTexan has a conveniently dual personality. When he is called upon to do his duty for his country he is an American. When benefits are passed around he is a Mexican and always last in line" (195).

The forced development of the dual nature of Mexican Americans indicates the control of the dominant class in the United States and also helps construct the system to which a Mexican American "dreamer" can be prepared to subscribe. In Paredes's reading, the pretense is made that the Mexican voice will reside alongside the world of power and success but ultimately it is only a ruse to ensure continued success for those already in power. When jobs are few and Mexican cheap labor is unnecessary, the case is similar. The path to Mexican American success in the United States is depicted as only temporary and built out of a necessity for their labor, votes, or support.

A common reaction to this lack of accessibility was to weigh the benefits of assimilation. In his analysis of Chicano film narratives,

Charles Ramírez Berg dissects the formulaic portrayals of assimilation and describes them as a semigenre of "assimilation narrative." Berg argues that the depictions of assimilation follow a formula because there does not appear to be any other option: "In this formula, success is defined in upwardly mobile, professional, and socioeconomic terms and goes hand in hand with mainstream assimilation. (There is no success outside the dominant.)" (32).

Berg's description suitably defines the environment of the 1930s and 1940s in which Guálinto seeks success. The pressure of a dominant, one-sided model of success eventually overtakes Guálinto and results in complete assimilation and outright rejection of his people and his past. Guálinto is an intelligent child and will seemingly achieve success through education. However, that education is geared toward only one interpretation of success, similar to the formulaic manner that Berg writes concerning a determination by immigrants to work hard (often in undesirable jobs) and to adopt the cultural norms of their new nation as quickly and adeptly as possible. Harvey's graduation address at Guálinto's school illustrates that in the eyes of the dominant culture who have constructed the qualifications for achievement, assimilation is the only acceptable means for immigrants seeking access to the American Dream.

In the opening of the novel, Guálinto's father, Gummersindo, who has been fatally wounded, implores his brother-in-law, Feliciano, to watch over his son and ensure his safety. Gummersindo's thoughts immediately turn not just to the boy's safety and well-being but, more significantly, to the purpose or role of the child's life. Essentially, Gummersindo wants to prevent his son from being mired in a life of hatred. Rather than insist that his son seek vengeance against the Texas Rangers who shot him, Gummersindo seems to possess a higher, if vague, vision of how to create change in the future. He says to Feliciano, "My son. Mustn't know. Ever. No hate, no hate" (21), which Feliciano pledges to uphold, perhaps unwittingly setting Guálinto's assimilative future in motion.

From this moment, Feliciano becomes the guardian of not only Guálinto, his mother, and his two sisters but also Guálinto's destiny as a "leader of his people"—the phrase used to describe him ever since his father dubiously named him "George Washington" so he might be a "great man among the Gringos" (16). Early in the novel, the measure of Guálinto's success is left to conjecture. Even the members of Guálinto's family speculate as to how he will grow up and help their people: perhaps as a great orator or lawyer. Throughout the novel, Paredes implicitly questions whether there exists a possibility for Guálinto to achieve traditional success represented by the American Dream while also embracing the principal language, history, and other cultural markers that the traditional model has deemed undesirable or, worse, "un-American."

During a crucial scene in the middle of the novel, Paredes positions Guálinto at the center of an encounter that demands a response, an act of self-identification and affirmation. The scene comes as he and his fellow high school students attend their class party after earning money and reserving a restaurant on the outskirts of town for the entire class. Guálinto's girlfriend María Elena (of a relatively well-off family and of questionable devotion to Guálinto) asks him if the two of them could ride with her friends rather than in the car with Guálinto's Mexican American friends. Guálinto concedes, and the two ride in the car with her friends, who represent a higher social class than Guálinto's working-class Mexican American friends. At the party, three of Guálinto's Mexican American friends are stopped at the door of the restaurant and accused of attempting to "crash the party," implying that they are not welcome because they are Mexican. Guálinto steps in and tells the doorman that his friends are part of the reserved party and should be let in. The doorman looks over Guálinto and tells him that nobody is stopping him; he is allowed to go in to the party. Guálinto maintains his loyalty to his friends, restating that he will not go in unless his friends are also allowed.

Up to this point Guálinto's display of principles reflect friendship and fairness—the others had raised money for the party and had been part of the reservation ahead of time, so he felt that they deserved to go in. However, the moment becomes more serious when Guálinto's own identity is directly questioned by the doorman:

> The bouncer was looking at Guálinto with interest. "Are you Mexican?" he asked.
> "I am," Guálinto answered.
> "He's not," María Elena said, tugging at his arm. "He's a Spaniard. Can't you see he's white?"
> "I'm a Mexican," Guálinto said. María Elena released his arm. (173)

This is the first time in the novel that Guálinto readily identifies himself as a Mexican. It is also the first time he has been directly questioned about his identity. Having been set up with the possibility of two outcomes, one with a "positive" product and one with a "negative" product, Guálinto decides upon the one that limits him or prevents him from doing or gaining something. María Elena's urging that he identify himself as Spanish, and therefore European, with all the privileges that it entails (in this case, entrance into the party), is not enough to persuade him to deny his and his friends' Mexican heritage. His two-word response to the question of identity—"I am"—reveals his strength of mind. It is not difficult to see the parallel between Guálinto's Mexican identity limiting his "access" and Paredes's larger statement about ethnic/racial identity leading to the denial or limitations of the American Dream.

Guálinto's statement that "I am a Mexican" may only serve to indicate that he can name "who he is" and "whom he should side with" when questioned. The real stakes of identity affirmation will be revealed later when he discovers that this position may result in limitations when it comes to achieving success in the United States in the traditional sense—when there is even more at stake than a high school party and a girlfriend. Once the repercussions are heightened, the call of assimilation eventually strikes out at those of this pre-Chicano era, like Guálinto, who may make statements or acts of identity conviction and then begin to realize that there is no way to attain access to both the world of success and the world of Mexican Americans. In the party scene, Guálinto essentially declines the world of access and achievement in exchange for the other world where he displays his Mexicanness. He later feels similar pressure with higher stakes and ultimately chooses the option of access. Guálinto ultimately succumbs to the "either/or" assimilation model, but Paredes implies that Guálinto regrets doing so.

Rejection of Cultural Identity and the "Dream" Fulfilled?

The final section of *George Washington Gómez*, in which Guálinto returns home nine years after having left (which puts the final scene somewhere around the year 1942), begins by describing him slowly, unveiling to the reader the choices that he has made and their subsequent results. Guálinto's decisions to leave his people behind, go away to college, and enroll in the Army as a spy charged with protecting the very US-Mexican border where he was raised is a slow, sad progression, possibly influenced by the lessons of the Great Depression. The progression comes as a shock to readers since, in the graduation-speech scene just prior to the end of the novel, Guálinto seems so intent on leaving education behind and fully embracing his fellow Mexican American people.

Because Paredes never revised the book and it was published from his first draft, there appear to be holes in the narrative. For example, readers are uninformed about the time that Guálinto spends at college. Paredes compounds this lack of description with the choice that occurs "off camera," in which Guálinto distances himself from his roots and consequently seeks success in the only way that it has been made apparent to him: to identify as white, to marry white, and to rid himself of all other cultural identity traits detrimental to reaching the American Dream. He has rarely been home to visit his family and has grown increasingly ashamed of his roots—embarrassed to the point that he has dropped his nickname and refers to himself as "George G. Gómez."

Guálinto has been assigned by the military to return to his hometown in south Texas to work on the military base there. However, he is apprehensive about returning home: "He had been trained for almost three years for an assignment in southern California. And what did they do but send him down to the one place he should have stayed away from" (285). Readers begin to realize that Guálinto's decision to leave home had meant abandoning his family and heritage and embracing all things "American"—the prescribed, surefire method for Mexican Americans to attain the success promised by the American Dream.

It may seem as if Guálinto has done what his father had intended for him to do when he demanded that his son never know the hatred between the Anglo Texans and his Mexican ancestors and to instead seek out success as a "leader of his people." In the last chapter of the novel, Guálinto believes in his form of success, even stating that his conscious decisions alone are the reasons for him "getting out of there" and doing something more important. In the final scene of the novel, Guálinto finally speaks to his Uncle Feliciano (the man who sacrificed all his life so that Guálinto could grow to be a successful "leader of his people"). Guálinto comments on his own success in comparison to the Mexican Americans he had grown up with as friends and schoolmates. After leaving a meeting with his old friends, who unsuccessfully implore him to join them in their local political efforts (which he sees as petty and pointless), he derides them for their laziness while simultaneously promoting his own work ethic—which illustrates his belief that the American Dream is only prohibited by one's level of effort and determination rather than having anything to do with one's particular racial or cultural identity.

Guálinto tells his uncle, "Mexicans will always be Mexicans. A few of them, like some of those would-be politicos, could make something of themselves *if they would just do like I did.* Get out of this filthy Delta, as far away as they can, and get rid of their Mexican Greaser attitudes" (300; emphasis added). Guálinto has assimilated and effaced himself to the point of judging his fellow Mexican Americans for their seeming lack of ambition and conviction to "do what it takes" to achieve the success that he enjoys. His betrayal of his roots, his uncle, and himself reveals his inability to see any measure of success while maintaining "Mexican Greaser attitudes."

Paredes portrays the realities of a Mexican American living during the early part of the twentieth century: Advancing beyond the manual-labor community or going to college were, for the most part, unrealistic goals. The idea that Guálinto could achieve all that he had and still remain tied to a consistently demeaned Mexican American community was unlikely during this era. In the restaurant scene earlier in the novel, he makes a choice to identify himself as "Mexican" and therefore ensure that he would not be admitted to a high school party. At the end of the novel, though, he chooses to pursue the available benefits that he had put on hold. Guálinto's decision reflects his desire to reject his home and assimilate fully into a world that he sees as "successful." José Aranda Jr. writes of Guálinto's path to success:

> The resolution of Guálinto's story fails to show him fulfilling any of the goals set at his birth. At the same time and importantly, the novel encourages a readerly disappointment in Guálinto's choice to "sell out." Paredes produces this effect . . . I believe, to counteract the available mainstream fantasies of immigrant life in the United States. (152)

By "fantasies," Aranda refers to the assimilation narratives that focus on the advancement, subscription to social norms, and hard, honest work of immigrants who desired to be part of the United States. Believers in this type of immigrant narrative may choose to praise Guálinto's perseverance in his quest to achieve entry into the dominant system despite such hardships. This, in fact, is the "fantasy." Aranda points out that Paredes's novel "counteracts" this type of narrative and suggests that Guálinto is a "sell out" rather than an immigrant hero. Aranda is surely influenced by the tenet of cultural sovereignty espoused by the Chicano movement and the Chicano studies field that emerged after Paredes's novel. He asserts that Paredes's depiction of "selling out" is meant to expose the immigrant myth that is a part of the American Dream and to replace it with discussion of the sacrifices and identity suppression that coincide with the attainment of that dream.

In Paredes's view the immigrants have been forced to "sell out" for the American Dream because the myth forced upon them has always included the "either/or" of assimilation narratives. During Paredes's youth (and by extension Guálinto's), Mexican Americans had not achieved success in a world that was "in between" Mexican and American. Essentially, Paredes's novel laments that absence, and Guálinto's ultimate choice of the prescribed assimilation path simply reflects what has continually been forced upon him; he is unable to see any other alternative. Thus, Paredes's novel can be seen as a "Chicano" novel that precedes the Chicano movement because it recognizes the detriments of assimilation prescriptions, points out the empty success in identity surrender, and indirectly waits, hopes, and calls for the potential of cultural sovereignty to provide Mexican American success in the United States.

Conclusion

Paredes's novel highlights the obstacles facing a young Mexican American during an era in which the American Dream had to be achieved within the boundaries of preconceived ethnic, racial, and class hierarchical structures. Because it follows much of Paredes's own youth experience, *George Washington Gómez* is told from a personal perspective and chronicles the overall narrative of the time period in history. Ramón Saldívar characterizes the merger of personal perspective with history when he describes the overall purpose of Chicano literature: "Contemporary Chicano writers are attempting to remedy this exclusion and marginalization by depicting their own bicultural experience in the context of the broad historical events that have formed our times" (23–24). The segregationist, racist, and classist attitudes and policies limited access to the American Dream during the first half of the twentieth century, leading to Guálinto's assimilation into mainstream culture. However, Paredes's writing laments the reality of the situation in which Guálinto's path is underdeveloped and points toward the need and possibility of restructuring the identity components of Mexican Americans as well as the community in which they exist. This is made more complex and significant when one considers that Paredes wrote the manuscript for this novel roughly thirty years prior to the Chicano movement, a time of radically progressive ideas about social activism and literature.

Because *George Washington Gómez* was not published until some thirty years after the onset of the Chicano movement, Paredes's critique of Mexican Americans' situations during his time matches up nicely with what scholars in 1990 had learned from the efforts and approaches developed during the movement. In other words, Paredes's analysis was ahead of its time and both supersedes the Chicano movement's critical perspective and also (retroactively) helps construct the foundation for it. He sought to shed light on the underreported experiences of Mexican Americans who desired to elevate their position in the United States but who also had to measure their futures and their pasts by an American Dream narrative that promised opportunity but often at a great cost for those that were not already racially, culturally, or ethnically screened.

Whereas the dominant Mexican American era voices around Paredes saw general opportunities in patriotism, education, and civic involvement, Paredes questioned this path toward fulfilling the American Dream. Because of his foresight, Paredes is often referred to as the "father" or "grandfather" of Chicano studies. His writing possesses many similarities to the Chicano literature at the time of his novel's publication in 1990.

Chicano literature continues to move largely along the line of thought instituted by the Chicano movement: Chicanos experience life from a perspective that is unique to their witnessed accounts. They encounter immersions, conflicts, and ongoing assimilations between the two dominant cultural forces in their lives, Mexican American and Anglo American, and recognize that the early, prescribed versions of the American Dream were not open to cultural hybridity and were based on either forced assimilation and loss of culture or exclusion. Chicano literature owes a great deal to Paredes, not only for recognizing the inherent fallacies in early twentieth-century conceptions of the American Dream but also for opening an avenue of critique that has continued into the twenty-first century.

Notes

1. There are different stories as to the origins of the term "Chicano." Most of them note that the term specifically applies to Mexicans born in the United States but also note that the term was historically used as one of derision until it was adopted by the civil rights movement in the 1960s as a term of ethnic pride. It has come to enjoy wide, though not universally accepted, usage.

2. Cesar Chavez (1927–1993) was a farmworker in California and a labor-rights organizer. He was the cofounder of the National Farm Workers Association (which later became the United Farm Workers) and supported union growth and concerns of Mexican American migrant workers through aggressive but nonviolent tactics such as boycotts and strikes. Reies Lopez Tijerina (b. 1926) was a pastor and later a civil rights activist who, among other activities, led a concerted effort to restore New Mexican land grants in the Southwest to Mexican descendants. Rodolfo "Corky" Gonzales (1928–2005) was a boxer turned Chicano political activist from Denver. In 1969, he organized the first Chicano Youth Liberation Conference, where the integral *El Plan Espiritual de Aztlán* (a plan calling for specific self-determination for Chicanos) was proclaimed and where his poem "I Am Joaquin" was disseminated as an ongoing litany of Chicano identity.

3. After the Depression subsided and the United States lost many white agricultural workers to the military during World War II, Mexican workers were allowed and encouraged to come back provisionally to work the jobs that were left behind in an agreement commonly known as the Bracero Program. See Guerin-Gonzales.

Works Cited

Aldama, Arturo. "Visions in the Four Directions: Five Hundred Years of Resistance and Beyond." *As We Are Now: Mixblood Essays on Race and Identity.* Ed. William S. Penn. Berkeley: U of California P, 1997. 140–67. Print.

Aranda, José Jr. *When We Arrive: A New Literary History of Mexican America.* Tucson: U of Arizona P, 2003. Print.

Balderrama, Francisco E., and Raymond Rodriguez. *Decade of Betrayal: Mexican Repatriation in the 1930s.* Albuquerque: U of New Mexico P, 1995. Print.

Berg, Charles Ramírez. "*Bordertown,* the Assimilation Narrative, and the Chicano Social Problem Film." *Chicanos and Film: Representation and Resistance.* Ed. Chon A. Noriega. Minneapolis: U of Minnesota P, 1992. 29–46. Print.

García, Mario T., ed. *Bridging Cultures: An Introduction to Chicano/Latino Studies.* Dubuque, IA: Kendall, 2000. Print.

Guerin-Gonzales, Camille. *Mexican Workers and American Dreams: Immigration, Repatriation, and California Farm Labor, 1900–1939.* New Brunswick, NJ: Rutgers UP, 1994.

Hume, Kathryn. *American Dream, American Nightmare: Fiction since 1960.* Urbana: U of Illinois P, 2000. Print.

Mazon, Maurizio. *The Zoot-Suit Riots: The Psychology of Symbolic Annihilation.* U of Texas P, 2002. Print.

Pagán, Eduardo Obregón. *Murder at the Sleepy Lagoon: Zoot Suits, Race, and Riots in Wartime LA* Chapel Hill: U of North Carolina P, 2003. Print.

Paredes, Américo. *George Washington Gómez.* Houston: Arte Público, 1990. Print.

Pérez, Luis. *El Coyote: The Rebel.* New York: Holt, 1947. Print.

Rosales, F. Arturo. *Chicano! The History of the Mexican American Civil Rights Movement.* Houston: Arte Público, 1997. Print.

Rivas-Rodriguez, Maggie. *Mexican Americans and World War II.* Austin: U of Texas P, 2005. Print.

Saldívar, Ramón. *Chicano Narrative: The Dialectics of Difference.* Madison: U of Wisconsin P, 1990. Print.

Villarreal, José Antonio. *Pocho.* New York: Anchor, 1959. Print.

RESOURCES

Additional Works on the American Dream_____

Fiction
The Blithedale Romance by Nathaniel Hawthorne, 1845
The Rise of Silas Lapham by William Dean Howells, 1885
The Jungle by Upton Sinclair, 1906
Martin Eden by Jack London, 1909
The Rise of David Levinsky by Abraham Cahan, 1917
My Antonia by Willa Cather, 1918
Babbitt by Sinclair Lewis, 1922
Salome of the Tenements by Anzia Yezierska, 1923
Giants in the Earth by Ole Edvart Rølvaag, 1927
Daughter of Earth by Agnes Smedley, 1929
Of Mice and Men by John Steinbeck, 1937
The Grapes of Wrath by John Steinbeck, 1939
The Day of the Locust by Nathanael West, 1939
Native Son by Richard Wright, 1940
Invisible Man by Ralph Ellison, 1952
The Adventures of Augie March by Saul Bellow, 1953
Rabbit, Run by John Updike, 1960
An American Dream by Norman Mailer, 1964
The Bluest Eye by Toni Morrison, 1970
I Know Why the Caged Bird Sings by Maya Angelou, 1970
*Fear and Loathing in Las Vegas: A Savage Journey to the Heart of the American
    Dream* by Hunter S. Thompson, 1972
Requiem for a Dream by Hubert Selby Jr., 1978
China Men by Maxine Hong Kingston, 1980
Love Medicine by Louise Erdrich, 1984
The Joy Luck Club by Amy Tan, 1989
The Mambo Kings Play Songs of Love by Oscar Hijuelos, 1989
Drown by Junot Diaz, 1997
American Pastoral by Philip Roth, 1997
A Free Life by Ha Jin, 2007

Autobiography
Narrative of the Life of Frederick Douglass by Frederick Douglass, 1845
Up from Slavery by Booker T. Washington, 1901
Promised Land by Mary Antin, 1912
A Son of the Middle Border by Hamlin Garland 1917

Black Boy by Richard Wright, 1945
The Woman Warrior by Maxine Hong Kingston, 1975

Drama

The Iceman Cometh by Eugene O'Neill, 1940
The Glass Menagerie by Tennessee Williams, 1945
The American Dream by Edward Albee, 1961
Dutchman by LeRoi Jones, 1964
The Chickencoop Chinaman by John Choo, 1972
Curse of the Starving Class by Sam Shepard, 1977
Fences by August Wilson, 1987

Bibliography

Adams, James Truslow. *The Epic of America*. Boston: Little, 1931.

Allen, Walter. *The Urgent West: The American Dream and Modern Man*. New York: Dutton, 1969.

Athearn, Robert G. *The Mythic West in Twentieth-Century America*. Cambridge, MA: Reed Business Information, 1986.

Balkun, Mary McAleer. *The American Counterfeit: Authenticity and Identity in American Literature and Culture*. Tuscaloosa: UP of Alabama, 2006.

Carpenter, Frederick. *American Literature and the Dream*. New York: Philosophical Library, 1955.

Cullen, Jim. *The American Dream: A Short History of an Idea That Shaped a Nation*. New York: Oxford UP, 2003.

Delbanco, Andrew. *The Real American Dream: A Meditation on Hope*. Cambridge: Harvard UP, 1999.

Flowers, Betty Sue. *The American Dream and the Economic Myth*. Kalamazoo, MI: Fetzer Institute, 2007.

Garfinkle, Norton. *The American Dream vs. The Gospel of Wealth: The Fight for a Productive Middle-Class Economy*. New Haven, CT: Yale UP, 2006.

Hume, Kathryn. *American Dream, American Nightmare: Fiction since 1960*. Urbana and Chicago: U of Illinois P, 2000.

Jiang, Tsui-fen. *The American Dream in African American, Asian American, and Hispanic American Drama: August Wilson, Frank Chin, and Luis Valdez*. Lewiston, NY: Mellen, 2009.

Long, Elizabeth. *The American Dream and the Popular Novel*. Boston: Routledge & Kegan Paul, 1985.

Lynn, Kenneth S. *The Dream of Success: A Study of the Modern American Imagination*. Boston: Little, Brown, 1955.

Madden, David, ed. *American Dreams, American Nightmares*. Carbondale: Southern Illinois UP, 1970.

Mogen, David, Mark Busby, and Paul Bryant, eds. *The Frontier Experience and the American Dream: Essays on American Literature*. College Station: Texas A&M UP, 1989.

Parrington, Vernon. L. *American Dreams: A Study of American Utopias*. Providence, RI: Brown UP, 1947.

Ringer, Robert J. *Restoring the American Dream: The Defining Voice in the Movement for Liberty*. New York: Wiley, 2010.

Smith, Henry Nash. *Virgin Land: The American West as Symbol and Myth*. Cambridge: Harvard UP, 1950.

Tocqueville, Alexis de. *Democracy in America*. 2 vols. Trans. Henry Reeve. Rev. ed. New York: Colonial, 1900.

Tyson, Lois. *Psychological Politics of the American Dream: The Commodification of Subjectivity in Twentieth-Century American Literature*. Columbus: Ohio State UP, 1994.

Umphlett, Wiley Lee. *Mythmakers of the American Dream: The Nostalgic Vision in Popular Culture*. Lewisburg, PA: Bucknell UP, 1983.

Weiss, Richard. *The American Myth of Success: From Horatio Alger to Norman Vincent Peale*. Champaign: U of Illinois P, 1988.

About the Editor

Keith Newlin is professor of English at the University of North Carolina Wilmington, where he teaches courses in American literary realism and naturalism, American modernism, and American drama. He is the author of *Hamlin Garland, A Life* (2008), the coeditor of *The Collected Plays of Theodore Dreiser* (2000) and *Selected Letters of Hamlin Garland* (1998), and the editor of *Garland in His Own Time* (2013), *The Oxford Handbook of American Literary Naturalism* (2011), *A Summer to Be, a Memoir by the Daughter of Hamlin Garland* (2010), *A Theodore Dreiser Encyclopedia* (2003), *American Plays of the New Woman* (2000), and two reprints of books by Hamlin Garland. The past president of the International Theodore Dreiser Society and the Hamlin Garland Society, at present he is the coeditor of *Studies in American Naturalism*, distributed by the University of Nebraska Press.

Contributors _____

Cara Elana Erdheim is a visiting assistant professor of English at Sacred Heart University whose scholarship focuses on American literary naturalism, ecocriticism, and cultural food studies. She has contributed essays to *Studies in American Naturalism*, *ALN: The American Literary Naturalism Newsletter*, and *Food, Culture, and Society*.

Steven Frye is professor of English at California State University, Bakersfield, and president of the Cormac McCarthy Society. He is the author of *Understanding Cormac McCarthy* and *Historiography and Narrative Design in the American Romance*. He is editor of *The Cambridge Companion to Cormac McCarthy*, *Critical Insights: The Tales of Edgar Allan Poe*, and *Critical Insights: The Poetry of Edgar Allan Poe*, as well as associate editor of *ALN: The American Literary Naturalism Newsletter*. He is also the author of the essay "Naturalism and Religion" published in *The Oxford Handbook of American Literary Naturalism*, as well as numerous articles on Herman Melville, Cormac McCarthy, and other novelists of the American romance tradition and the literature of the American West.

Tiffany Gilbert is an assistant professor of English at the University of North Carolina Wilmington. Her research interests include twentieth-century American literature and culture, nineteenth-century opera, and celebrity studies. She has previously published articles on Dorothy Dandridge's performance in Otto Preminger's *Carmen Jones*, the Byronic influences in Giuseppe Verdi's opera *Otello*, and on the relationship between desire and nostalgia in James Baldwin's short story "Going to Meet the Man." An essay on Meryl Streep's star persona in the film version of David Hare's play *Plenty* is forthcoming.

James R. Giles is distinguished professor emeritus at Northern Illinois University, where he taught in the Department of English from 1970 to 2007. He is the author of nine books and the coeditor of eight others, including *The Spaces of Violence* (2006), *Violence in the Contemporary American Novel* (2000), *The Naturalistic Inner-City Novel in America* (1995), and six volumes of the *Dictionary of Literary Biography* (all coedited with Wanda H. Giles). In addition, he has published over thirty articles or short stories in various journals. Most recently, he published essays in *The Oxford Handbook of American Literary Naturalism* (2011) and *A Companion to Twentieth-Century United States Fiction* (2010).

Ramón Guerra is an assistant professor of English at the University of Nebraska Omaha. His research focuses on the placement of Chicano and Latino literature within the larger American literature, particularly in the late twentieth and twenty-first centuries. He specifically examines the significances of nonfiction witness accounts, oral histories, and memoirs, all under the category of *testimonio*, as a means to expand historiography through literature.

Linda Kornasky is a professor of English at Angelo State University in Texas. She has published articles on feminist naturalism in *ALN: The American Literary Naturalism Newsletter*, *American Literary Realism*, *Mississippi Quarterly*, and *The Ellen Glasgow Journal of Southern Women Writers*.

Carol S. Loranger is associate professor and chair of the Department of English Language and Literatures at Wright State University in Dayton, Ohio, where she has taught American literature and literary theory since 1993. She is book review editor for the award-winning journal *Studies in American Naturalism* and has focused her scholarship on such groundbreaking and controversial American writers as William S. Burroughs, Thomas Pynchon, Stephen Crane, and Theodore Dreiser. Dr. Loranger is a member of the governing committee for the Dayton Literary Peace Prize and serves on its Ambassador Richard C. Holbrooke Distinguished Achievement Award subcommittee.

Quentin Martin received his BA and MA from Western Michigan University and his PhD from Ohio State University and has since taught at Loyola University in Chicago, Institut Catholique in Brussels, and (since 2004) the University of Colorado at Colorado Springs, where he teaches classes on research techniques and American literature. He has published essays on many American writers, including Hamlin Garland, Stephen Crane, Ernest Hemingway, F. Scott Fitzgerald, Sinclair Lewis, John Cheever, and Ellen Gilchrist.

Roark Mulligan is an associate professor at Christopher Newport University in Newport News, Virginia, where he teaches literature and writing. He has authored essays on Theodore Dreiser that have appeared in *American Literary Realism*, *Dreiser Studies*, and *Studies in American Naturalism*. In 2010, his edition of *The Financier* was published by the University of Illinois Press. He serves as secretary/treasurer of the International Theodore Dreiser Society.

James Nagel is the Eidson Distinguished Professor of American Literature at the University of Georgia and the president of the Society for the Study of the American Short Story. Early in his career he founded the scholarly journal *Studies in American Fiction* and the widely influential series *Critical Essays on American Literature*, which published 156 volumes of scholarship. Among his twenty-three books are *Stephen Crane and Literary Impressionism*, *Hemingway in Love and War* (which was made into a Hollywood film starring Sandra Bullock), *Hemingway: The Oak Park Legacy*, *The Contemporary American Short-Story Cycle*, *Anthology of the American Short Story*, *The Blackwell Companion to the American Short Story*, edited with Alfred Bendixen,

---

and the forthcoming *Race and Culture in Stories of New Orleans*. He has been a Fulbright Professor as well as a Rockefeller Fellow. He has published some eighty articles in the field and lectured on American literature in fifteen countries.

Keith Newlin is professor of English at the University of North Carolina Wilmington. He is the author or editor of fourteen books; recent titles include *Hamlin Garland, A Life* (2008) and, as editor, *Garland in His Own Time* (2013), *A Summer to Be, a Memoir by the Daughter of Hamlin Garland* (2008), *A Theodore Dreiser Encyclopedia* (2003), and two reprints of books by Hamlin Garland. A present he is the coeditor of *Studies in American Naturalism*, distributed by the University of Nebraska Press.

Donna Packer-Kinlaw received her PhD in English from the University of Maryland, and she currently teaches at Anne Arundel Community College. Her dissertation, "Anxious Journeys: Past, Present, and Construction of Identity in American Travel Writing" examines how American travelers respond to the displacement that occurs during their "leisurely movement" across physical spaces. Raising questions about the genre, gender, and class, as well as perceptions of travel and what constitutes a "site," she calls for a reconsideration of travel writing by authors such as Willa Cather, Theodore Dreiser, and Henry James. Her publications examine Dreiser's short fiction and masculinity in Joseph Conrad.

Lee Schweninger is a professor of English at the University of North Carolina Wilmington, where he teaches early American and American Indian literatures. Recent publications include *Listening to the Land: American Indian Literary Responses to the Landscape* (2008) and *The First We Can Remember: Colorado Pioneer Women Tell Their Stories* (2011). His current project is a book on American Indian film, *Imagic Moments: Indigenous North American Film* (under contract).

Andrew Vogel is an assistant professor of American modernism at Kutztown University of Pennsylvania. He has published scholarship on spatial form in Gertrude Stein, Columbianism in Walt Whitman's last poem, and inflections of the Good Roads Movement in Hamlin Garland's *Main-Travelled Roads*. His manuscript *Storied Road: Narrating the Geography of American Modernism, 1893–1921* is currently under review. He also publishes poetry.

Index